The SIMS 3 SUPERNATURAL

PRIMA OFFICIAL GAME GUIDE

Written by Catherine Browne

Prima Games
An Imprint of Random House, Inc.
3000 Lava Ridge Court, Suite 100
Roseville, CA 95661
www.primagames.com

Table of Contents

Introduction 4

How to Use This Guide 4

Cheats 7
Popular Cheats 7
Miscellaneous Cheats 8
Supernatural Cheats 8

New Simology 10

Create a Sim 10
Supernatural Type 11
Carried Over Cosmetic Changes 12
Expanded Closet 13
New Traits 14
New Lifetime Wishes 17

New Moodlets & Wishes 19
New Moodlets 19
New Wishes 27
Lifetime Rewards 28
Opportunities 30

New Socials 32

Achievements 36

New Careers & Skills 38

New Careers 38

Fortune Teller 39
Career Development 39
Charisma 40
Logic 43
Career Opportunities 44

New Skills 46

Alchemy Skill 46
Development 46

Brewing Elixirs 48

Meet the Supernaturals 60

Werewolves 61
Create a Sim 61
Behavior & Benefits 62
New Socials & Interactions 66
Complicating Matters 67
Werewolf Families 68

Fairies 68
Create a Sim 68
Behavior and Benefits 70
New Socials/Interactions 76

Witches 77
Create a Sim 77
Benefits and Behaviors 78
New Socials & Interactions 79
Spellcasting and Magic Wands 79
Witch Families 83

Vampires 85
Create a Sim 85
Behavior & Benefits 85
Complicating Matters 88
Survival Instincts 89
Vampire Families 91

Ghosts 91
New Haunts 93

New Venues 96

Supernatural Real Estate 96
Gypsy Wagon 96
Aleister's Elixirs and Sundries 97
Varg's Tavern 98
Arboretum 100

Vault of Antiquity 101

Red Velvet Lounge 104

The Toadstool 105

Tour of Moonlight Falls   106

Career Venues 106

Bloom Institute of Wellness 107

Everglow Academy and Coliseum 108

Commonwealth Court 108

Deja View Theater 109

Van Gould Merchant House & Cafe 110

Shopping and Commerce 112

Aleister's Elixirs and Sundries/Zoomsweeper
    Broom Arena 112

Sam's Market and Diner 113

Mind-Body Connection Bookstore and Spa . . 114

Community Spots 116

Hallowed Grounds Cemetery 116

Moonlight Falls Historical Society & Museum . . 117

Fae Ray Arboretum 118

H Two the O Indoor Pool 119

Library of Lore & Vault of Antiquity 119

Bell's Barbell House 120

Parks and Fishing Spots 121

Eerie Park 121

Playful Playground 121

La Shove Beach 122

Stone Troll Fishing Hole 122

That Old Fishing Hole 123

Houses, Households, and Lots . . . 125

Occupied Homes 125

Empty Homes 136

Empty Lots 137

Collectibles 138

Fish 138

Plants and Seeds 142

Insects 146

Metals 150

Gems 151

Meteorites 153

New Object Catalog   156

New Objects & Interactions 157

Moondial 157

Mrs. Stingley's Beekeeping Box 158

Magic Wand 159

Smack-a-Gnome! 159

The Claaaaw 160

Aleister's Alchemy Station 161

Gem-U-Cut Machine 161

Zoomsweeper Broom Arena 162

Lightning Leap Atomic Molecular Arranger
    (LLAMA) 163

Spectrum Mood Lamp 163

Orb of Answers 164

Fairy Bungalow/Castle 165

Magic Jelly Bean Bush 165

Magic Mirror 166

Bonehilda Living Quarters 166

Scary Bearys 167

Very Small Train Set 167

Sliding Bookcase Door 168

Relax-o-Rocker 169

Aurora Wardrobe/Ancestral Wardrobe . . . 170

Magic Brooms 170

Giddy-Up Rocker 171

Brittany's Tiny Garden Planter Bowls 171

Bug Lovers Display Case 171

Aleister's Antique Alchemy Cabinet 171

Object Catalog 172

3

Introduction

• • •

Who hasn't entertained thoughts of the supernatural? A curiosity about life outside the fringe—where creatures of the night lurk— is only normal for those firmly tethered to the natural world. *The Sims 3 Supernatural* offers a heady dose of electric escapism, turning over the keys to a kingdom full of the strange. But while there may be a touch of sinister going on here, *Supernatural* revels in all the fun that must flank a life where things that go bump in the night... are bumping to a great beat.

The all-new Moonlight Falls is supernatural central, home to werewolves, vampires, fairies, ghosts, and more. With this expansion, you can walk on the (literal) wild side as the full moon hangs high in the night sky. What kind of weirdness will you indulge in? Will you board the nearest magic broom and try out a day in the life of a un-wicked witch? Fuzz out as a werewolf? Flitter about as a winged fairy? Your destiny in Moonlight Falls is your own, but this guide will help you get the absolute most out of these new alt-lives.

> ## NOTE
>
> While this guide is firmly centered on *Supernatural*, this expansion offers multiple hooks into previous expansions, such as *Showtime*, *Late Night*, and *Pets*. Though you do not need those expansions to play *Supernatural*, we do show you how having those extras installed can affect your adventures in Moonlight Falls.

How to Use This Guide

Welcome to the official game guide for *The Sims 3 Supernatural*. This book serves as your guide through the mysterious realm of the occult. Best practices for werewolves? Fairy dos and don'ts. Moondial horoscopes revealed. Alchemist recipes for excellent elixirs. What's behind that secret bookcase below the Vault of Antiquity. All of this and more are revealed within the following pages. So, to help you get the strategy you need—when you need it—here's a brief summary of what you'll find inside this guide:

New Simology

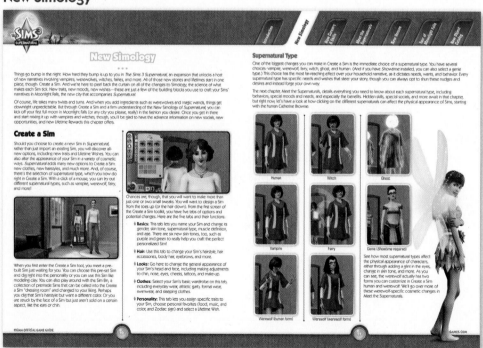

With the introduction of *Supernatural*, players now have access to all-new traits, wishes, Opportunities, and more. This chapter details all of these new features, including a breakdown of new socials, moodlets, and Lifetime Rewards. All of these tie into the arrival of vampires, werewolves, fairies, and more!

New Careers and Skills

When you check into Moonlight Falls, you have access to an all-new career: Fortune Teller. This chapter explains how to excel at both branches of the Fortune Teller career. This chapter also details the Alchemy skill, including how to make all the new elixirs. In addition to Alchemy, *Supernatural* introduces a wealth of new "hidden" skills like Broom Riding. Get behind-the-scenes strategy for these behind-the-scenes skills!

Meet the Supernaturals

Ever wanted to live the (un) life of a vampire? Howl at the moon as a werewolf? Indulge in the mischievous powers a witch? With the new supernatural elements of this expansion, you can explore these occult options (and more). This chapter includes full strategies for each new supernatural form, with tips and tricks for getting the most out of each lifestyle, such as all the perks of being a fairy. (Hint: fairies can cheat at the new arcade game...)

Introduction

New Venues

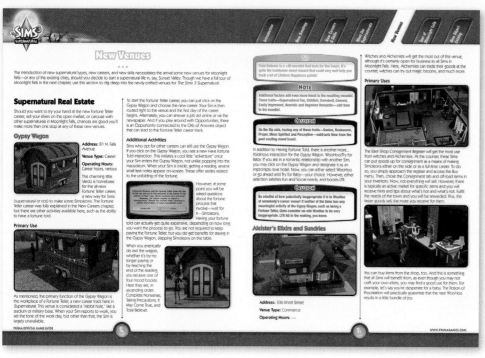

With the arrival of new careers, skills, and forms, there are new venues. Use this chapter to learn more about the Gypsy Wagon and Varg's Tavern, as well as other key locations in the lives of supernaturals running wild in Moonlight Falls.

Tour of Moonlight Falls

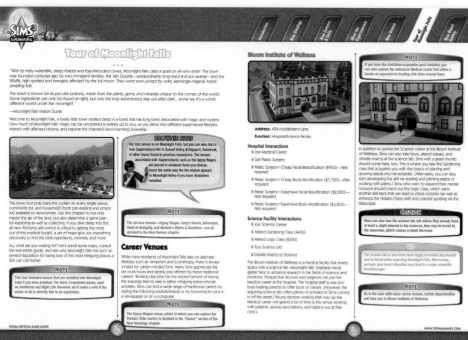

A new expansion means a new town, and *Supernatural* is no exception. Moonlight Falls is a brand-new city for you to call home. There's a touch of mystery in this new burg, and in this chapter, you'll uncover all sorts of secrets. Here, you'll find a comprehensive breakdown of every venue, business, community lot, and fishing hole. If you're on the hunt for collectibles (and you should be if you plan on becoming an expert Alchemist), maps and charts reveals the best places for gathering up goodies.

Introduction

New Simology

New Careers & Skills

Meet the Supernaturals

New Venues

Tour of Moonlight Falls

New Object Catalog

New Object Catalog

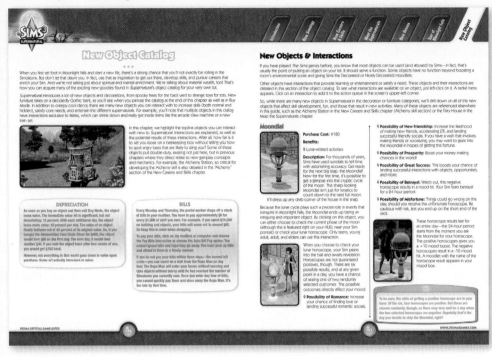

Supernatural expands the object catalog with a wealth of new practical items, decorations, and other such lovelies. Use these new objects to further develop skills, careers, and lifestyles. Or, dig deep into your pockets and splash some Simoleons for home beautification. (Or both!) This chapter includes a breakdown on new interactive objects, plus an Object Catalog that lists every new object, including prices, benefits, and more.

Cheats

Below, we've provided some information about the available cheats. But don't think of these cheats as… well… cheating. Think of these as tools that let you tell your story your way. Don't cheat yourself out of the opportunity to use these commands to spice up and personalize your game.

To access the command console, press Shift+Ctrl+C and input the text of the desired command (it appears in the blue bar on the top of the screen). For some cheats to work, you may have to type TestingCheatsEnabled true first. Type Help for a list of all the currently available commands. To exit the command console, press Enter or Esc.

> ### TIP
> Access the Cheats menu with Shift+Ctrl+C.

Popular Cheats

Help

◆ help

◆ help <cheatname>

Various cheats are available, depending on your game update and which expansion packs you have installed. To find out what cheats are available in your game, enter the cheat menu and type help. This lists all the currently available cheats. To find out more information about a specific cheat, type help <cheatname>.

Money Cheats

◆ kaching

◆ motherlode

The money cheats (kaching and motherlode) are a great way to skip some of the initial struggle. Sure, some young families have to work hard and scrimp to get by, but that's not the only option. I could pretend to be poor… ahem… but perhaps I'd rather pretend to be rich! Filthy stinking rich! Maybe I want a mansion with a moat, and a fast sports car, and a fat roll of cash to flash. Or maybe I just want to make some really neat houses, or focus on a skill, and I don't want to have to wait for my Sim to amass enough money the old-fashioned way.

Introduction

There are lots of "valid" reasons for extra cash to come someone's way. I like to think that many of my Sims have trust funds or made a killing in tech stocks. A big cash infusion could be an inheritance or lottery winnings. Smaller cash infusions are similarly explainable. Perhaps your Sim took an advance on a credit card, won a door prize, or did a job under the table. Criminal Sims have obvious explanations for unearned cash, but anyone could have done a little extra side work or taken on an extra project.

Obviously, if you choose a Lifetime Wish that involves cash, such as Swimming In Cash or Life of Luxury, then use money cheats to reach that goal, you're just pushing the "I Win" button. You can cheat at solitaire too but… why? But if you have a story to tell, there's no reason to let money, or the lack thereof, stand in your way.

Real Estate Cheats

❖ freeRealEstate

The freeRealEstate cheat is especially useful if you're editing your town and don't want to be constrained to only a few small houses when placing your pre-made Sim neighbors. You may not even plan to actively play those Sims; they're just window dressing. So why not put them wherever you like?

> **TiP**
>
> Check the readme file from your latest expansion pack to see if it includes more information about cheats.

Reset

❖ resetSim <firstname> <lastname>

❖ resetSim *

In any computer game, glitches can happen. If your Sim ever gets stuck somewhere, don't panic. You might not have to lose your progress since your last save. Try ResetSim <firstname> <lastname> to reset your Sim back to their home lot. If you don't know who is stuck, use resetSim * to reset all Sims.

> **TiP**
>
> There's another way to reset your household if you're having glitches. Go into the Edit Town menu, click on your house, and evict your household. Then use the Save Copy to Library button to copy the house. Bulldoze the house, put the copy back on the lot, and move your household back in from the clipboard. This might solve the glitch.

Frame Rate

❖ framerate on/off

If you wonder how well your computer is rendering the game, you can turn on the frame rate counter with framerate on. When the little numbers on the right become annoying, you can turn it back off with framerate off.

Miscellaneous Cheats

Joke Please

❖ jokePlease

Prints a random joke to the console.

Move Objects

❖ moveObjects [on | off]

Removes footprint limitation for all object placement in Buy Mode and Build Mode. Removes limitations placed on hand tool for when objects are in use or for objects that normally are not movable. Is known to cause issues with game elements, routing, hidden object generation and manipulation, etc. Note that using this cheat allows you to move and delete objects that normally cannot be manipulated such as Sims. If you delete these objects, there is no way to get them back, so be careful!

Constrain Floor Elevation

❖ constrainFloorElevation [true | false]

Allows all terrain adjustments regardless of objects, Sims, and other structures on them. Walls, floors, and objects will move with the terrain, allowing you to create sloped walls and floored hills. However, placing new walls/floors will still flatten terrain, and placing objects will still require the terrain to be flat initially if the objects normally require it.

Disable Snapping to Slots

❖ disableSnappingToSlotsOnAlt [on | off]

When on, objects will not snap to slots while holding ALT. Useful for placing objects such as chairs near tables without them snapping, or placing counters near other counters, etc.

Headline Effects

❖ hideHeadlineEffects [on | off]

Hides all Sim overhead effects such as thought balloons and speech balloons.

Introduction

New Simology

New Careers & Skills

Meet the Supernaturals

New Venues

Tour of Moonlight Falls

New Object Catalog

Fade Objects

◈ fadeObjects [on|off]

Toggles whether objects fade when the camera gets close to them. Does not apply to Sims.

Slow Motion

◈ slowMotionViz <level>

Puts the visuals of the game in slow motion. Entering a "level" value is optional. Valid values range from 0 = normal speed to 8 = slowest.

Unlock Outfits

◈ unlockOutfits [on|off]

Includes career outfits and service Sim outfits as options in Create a Sim. The cheat must be entered before going into CAS.

Enable Llamas

◈ EnableLlamas [on|off]

Supernatural Cheats

Supernatural Population Control

Want to control your supernatural population by adding or removing supernaturals? If you want fewer zombies, or more fairies, this is one way to do it. First open cheat mode as explained previously. Then go to the mailbox on your lot and shift click to bring up some cheat options for your game. Select "Supernatural Population Control" to bring up the option to either add or remove supernatural Sims into your game.

◈ Supernatural Population Control—Add Supernatural—Name of Supernatural

This cheat turns two Sims in the world to this supernatural type, except for the player household.

◈ Supernatural Population Control— Remove Supernatural—Name of Supernatural

This removes this supernatural status from ALL Sims in the world, except for the player household.

New Simology

• • •

Things go bump in the night. How hard they bump is up to you in *The Sims 3 Supernatural,* an expansion that unlocks a host of new narratives involving vampires, werewolves, witches, fairies, and more. All of those new stories and lifetimes start in one place, though: Create a Sim. And we're here to peel back the curtain on all of the changes to Simology, the science of what makes each Sim tick. New traits, new moods, new wishes—these are just a few of the building blocks you use to craft your Sims' narratives in Moonlight Falls, the new city that accompanies *Supernatural.*

Of course, life takes many twists and turns. And when you add ingredients such as werewolves and magic wands, things get downright unpredictable. But through Create a Sim and a firm understanding of the New Simology of *Supernatural,* you can kick off your first full moon in Moonlight Falls (or any city you please, really) in the fashion you desire. Once you get in there and start mixing it up with vampires and witches, though, you'll be glad to have the advance information on new socials, new opportunities, and new Lifetime Rewards this chapter offers.

Create a Sim

Should you choose to create a new Sim in *Supernatural,* rather than just import an existing Sim, you will discover all-new options, including new traits and Lifetime Wishes. You can also alter the appearance of your Sim in a variety of cosmetic ways. *Supernatural* adds many new options to Create a Sim: new clothes, new hairstyles, and much more. And, of course, there's the selection of supernatural type, which you now do right in Create a Sim. With a click of a mouse, you can try out different supernatural types, such as vampire, werewolf, fairy, and more!

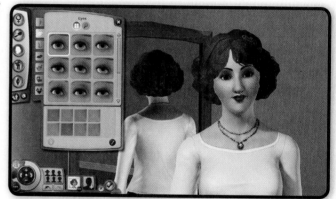

Chances are, though, that you will want to make more than just one or two small tweaks. You will want to design a Sim from the toes up (or the hair down). From the first screen of the Create a Sim toolkit, you have five tabs of options and potential changes. Here are the five tabs and their functions:

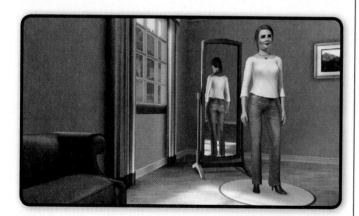

When you first enter the Create a Sim tool, you meet a pre-built Sim just waiting for you. You can choose this pre-set Sim and dig right into the personality or you can use this Sim like modeling clay. You can also play around with the Sim Bin, a collection of premade Sims that can be called into the Create a Sim "dressing room" and changed to your liking. Perhaps you dig that Sim's hairstyle but want a different color. Or you are struck by the face of a Sim but just aren't sold on a certain aspect, like the ears or chin.

- ⬥ **Basics:** This tab lets you name your Sim and change its gender, skin tone, supernatural type, muscle definition, and age. There are six new skin tones, too, such as purple and green to really help you craft the perfect personalized Sim!

- ⬥ **Hair:** Use this tab to change your Sim's hairstyle, hair accessories, body hair, eyebrows, and more.

- ⬥ **Looks:** Go here to change the general appearance of your Sim's head and face, including making adjustments to chin, nose, eyes, cheeks, tattoos, and make-up.

- ⬥ **Clothes:** Select your Sim's basic wardrobe on this tab, including everyday wear, athletic garb, formal wear, swimwear, and sleeping clothes.

- ⬥ **Personality:** This tab lets you assign specific traits to your Sim, choose personal favorites (food, music, and color, and Zodiac sign) and select a Lifetime Wish.

Introduction | New Simology | New Careers & Skills | Meet the Supernaturals | New Venues | Tour of Moonlight Falls | New Object Catalog

Supernatural Type

One of the biggest changes you can make in Create a Sim is the immediate choice of a supernatural type. You have several choices: vampire, werewolf, fairy, witch, ghost, and human. (And if you have *Showtime* installed, you can also select a genie type.) This choice has the most far-reaching effect over your household narrative, as it dictates needs, wants, and behavior. Every supernatural type has specific needs and wishes that steer your story, though you can always opt to shun these nudges and desires and instead forge your own way.

The next chapter, Meet the Supernaturals, details everything you need to know about each supernatural type, including behaviors, special moods and needs, and especially the benefits. Hidden skills, special socials, and more await in that chapter, but right now, let's have a look at how clicking on the different supernaturals can affect the physical appearance of Sims, starting with the human Catherine Browne:

Human

Witch

Ghost

Vampire

Fairy

Genie (*Showtime* required)

Werewolf (human form)

Werewolf (werewolf form)

See how most supernatural types affect the physical appearance of characters, either through adding a glint in the eyes, change in skin tone, and more. As you can see, the werewolf actually has two forms you can customize in Create a Sim: human and werewolf. We'll go over more of these werewolf-specific cosmetic changes in Meet the Supernaturals.

GAMES.COM

Carried Over Cosmetic Changes

Create a Sim features such as body hair, breast size, make-up opacity, tattoos, and astrological signs are also carried over from previous expansion packs like *Ambitions*, *Generations*, and *Late Night*. Even if you don't have these earlier expansion packs installed, the Create a Sim features introduced by these expansions are still available in *Supernatural*, offering a powerful set of Sim-altering tools for your prospective supernatural Sim.

> ### NOTE
>
> Ultimately, the appearance of your Sims is up to you. Cosmetic alterations are just that—they do not affect success in relationships, careers, or other interactions.

Tattoos

To add a tattoo to your Sim, choose the Looks tab. There is a new Tattoo button at the bottom of the menu, directly under Make-Up. When you select Tattoo, your Sim appears in front of the mirror. This gives you a near-full view of their body so you can apply the tattoo exactly where you want without any obstructions.

You may apply a tattoo to four places on your Sim: back, arm, chest, and ankle. In each body location, you can choose from a few different spots. For example, on the back, you can pick the shoulders, small of the back, or right in the dead-center.

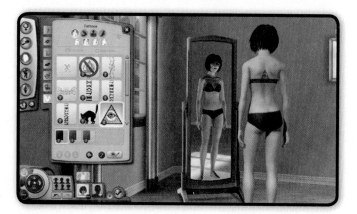

Select a tattoo from the multitude of available options.

Once you've chosen the tattoo, use the color picker to adjust the tones and hues. Some tattoos have just one color, while others are composed of multiple fields that you can alter.

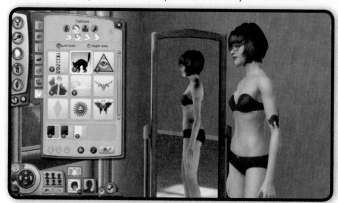

Mix and match tattoos. Place multiple tattoos on a Sim. Adjust size and opacity. The world is your oyster!

Astrological Signs

When crafting your Sim's personality, you now can give them an astrological sign. You can select from the 12 familiar signs of the zodiac. This is as close as you can get to setting an actual birthday for your Sim, because these signs are associated with time periods on this side of the screen, although Sims operate on a far different calendar than we do. The 12 zodiac signs are:

⬧ Aries	⬧ Leo	⬧ Sagittarius
⬧ Taurus	⬧ Virgo	⬧ Capricorn
⬧ Gemini	⬧ Libra	⬧ Aquarius
⬧ Cancer	⬧ Scorpio	⬧ Pisces

The zodiac signs are a part of your Sim's personality. Sims can use a flirty What's Your Sign social to hopefully learn a potential paramour's astrological sign.

If the other Sim deigns to share, this information is stored on that Sim's relationship entry in the Relationship tab of the Status panel. If the other Sim has a compatible sign, you both receive a small relationship boost. These are the compatible signs:

- **Aries:** Leo, Sagittarius, Gemini, and Aquarius
- **Taurus:** Virgo, Capricorn, Cancer, and Pisces
- **Gemini:** Libra, Aquarius, Aries, and Leo
- **Cancer:** Scorpio, Pisces, Taurus, and Virgo
- **Leo:** Aries, Sagittarius, Gemini, and Libra
- **Virgo:** Taurus, Capricorn, Cancer, and Scorpio
- **Libra:** Gemini, Aquarius, Leo, and Sagittarius
- **Scorpio:** Cancer, Pisces, Virgo, and Capricorn
- **Sagittarius:** Leo, Aries, Libra, and Aquarius
- **Capricorn:** Virgo, Taurus, Scorpio, and Pisces
- **Aquarius:** Libra, Gemini, Sagittarius, and Aries
- **Pisces:** Scorpio, Cancer, Capricorn, and Taurus

Body Hair

Male Sims are no longer hairless wonders. Now you can add body hair via a tab in the Hair section. When you click on the tab, you select which part of the body you want to graft hair to: chest, back, arms, legs. Then, choose the style of the hair. Do you want a grizzly bear or just a cropdusting of fuzz?

Bear alert!

> **NOTE**
>
> Body hair naturally lends itself to the new werewolf form, so experiment with fuzz on the werewolf form to really assemble the perfect midnight howler!

Expanded Closet

As with every *The Sims 3* expansion, *Supernatural* comes complete with a wealth of new clothes for your Sims. Many of the new duds in this expansion are designed to further support supernatural narratives, like fairy-ready pixie wear, shredded werewolf garb, Gothic vampire duds, and pointy hats befitting only the most discerning witch. Do browse through Create a Sim to peek at all of the options, including those on display here:

New Simology

New Traits

One of the final choices in Create a Sim is to assign your Sim up to five different traits. These are the most important choices in Create a Sim because they can greatly affect your Sim's Lifetime Wish (the culminating dream of their life), can sway performance at work or at skill development, and can influence how a Sim interacts with others.

There are 63 possible traits to choose from in *The Sims 3* base game. Traits include personality triggers such as Brave, Frugal, Loner, and Unlucky. They range from positive to negative, with a handful of relatively neutral traits somewhere in the middle. Because these five traits not only make up the core of your Sim's personality but also affect what Lifetime Wishes are suggested to them, consider how they might factor into the kind of life you'd like to live.

CAUTION

Focusing on a set of traits to support a career or new skill is great for that particular goal, but it comes at a cost. Your Sims are defined more by what they do rather than who they are.

Supernatural introduces several new traits to the equation: Brooding, Gatherer, Night Owl, Proper, Supernatural Fan, and Supernatural Skeptic. All of these traits are directly dialed into the new supernatural theme and will serve you well in crafting a personalized narrative for each Sim you sculpt in Create a Sim.

Brooding

Description: Brooding Sims often can't help themselves from contemplating the riddles, mystery, and meaning of life. Sometimes the weight of these incredibly deep thoughts can become a distraction, and can actually slow down the creative process slightly.

Earliest Age Available: Teen

Disallowed Trait: Excitable

Benefits: Writers can pen poetry books right away when starting the Writing skill. Offers exclusive self-socials Contemplate the Meaning of Meaning and Consider Hollowness of Life, plus new Talk about Feelings social.

Shortcomings: Cooking, Writing, and Painting skills development increases 10 percent slower for Brooding Sims. If a Brooding Sim loses a friend while having a low Social need, they are dinged with the Misunderstood warning moodlet. If this moodlet times out, they get the Need to Brood moodlet. This moodlet can be removed with the Contemplate Meaning of Meaning or Consider Hollowness of Life self-socials.

Unique Features: Brooding Sims can take Brooding Showers, which last longer but offer a mood bump. When in mourning, Brooding Sims do not cry—instead, they pensively stare off into space. Both Brooding self-socials satisfy both Fun and Social needs.

Gatherer

Description: If you can pick it, plant it, or catch it, then a Gatherer is the right Sim for the job. Gatherers are especially talented at finding ingredients out in the world, and they produce the finest crops. They even achieve better results when working with rare materials like ore and gemstones!

Earliest Age Available: Teen

Benefits: Gatherer Sims excel at finding collectibles. The chance of successfully catching insects jumps 10 percent. The value of the insect rises by 5 percent. When harvesting a plant, there is a 30 percent chance of receiving an extra two units of the plant/harvestable. Seeds found by Gatherers produce higher quality harvestables. Smelted ore ingots come back with an extra 5 percent value. Cut gems are worth 5 percent more. Analyzed meteorites are worth 10 percent more.

Shortcomings: None!

Unique Features: When Gatherers use the Gem-U-Cut Machine, they receive extra gem powder. Objects found during the Werewolf Hunt interaction (usable only by werewolves) are worth five percent more.

Introduction | New Simology | New Careers & Skills | Meet the Supernaturals | New Venues | Tour of Moonlight Falls | New Object Catalog

Night Owl

Description: Some Sims love the night life and occasionally feel the need to boogie. They are called Night Owls. While Night Owls might come alive at night, do not even bother getting them out of bed before 10 AM.

Earliest Age Available: Child

Benefits: Night Owls get the Past My Bedtime moodlet if awake past 10 PM. Night Owls have more fun when engaging in activities like playing computer games, watching TV, writing, painting, reading, doing homework, using the telescope, and roasting marshmallows.

Shortcomings: Night Owls are hit with the It's Too Early negative moodlet if they are out of bed before 10 AM.

Unique Features: Night Owls get three new socials—Enthuse about Sleeping In, Ask How Late Stayed Up, and Complain about Sleep Deprivation. Night Owls are also more likely to do the previously mentioned more fun activities while idle after 10 PM.

Proper

Description: Proper etiquette has quite become a thing of the past. Luckily, Proper Sims still remember the old ways and conduct themselves by a code of honor. Or at least a code of nice manners...

Earliest Age Available: Teen

Disallowed Traits: Slob, Inappropriate

Benefits: Decorated, Beautifully Decorated and Nicely Decorated moodlets provide a more positive effect on overall mood.

Shortcomings: Disgusted, Dirty Surroundings, Filthy Surroundings, and Vile Surroundings moodlets have a larger negative effect on overall mood.

Unique Features: Proper Sims use a new Formalize animation when switching into formal wear. Proper Sims bow and curtsey when about to dance or pillow fight with another Sim.

Supernatural Fan

Description: Supernatural Fans love everything having to do with supernatural Sims, be they vampires or werewolves or witches or whatever! They like to hang out where supernatural Sims hang out, and they always have something special to say when meeting a supernatural Sim face-to-face.

Earliest Age Available: Child

Disallowed Traits: Supernatural Skeptic, Coward

Benefits: Supernatural Fans develop the Alchemy skill a smidge faster than other Sims. Can write horror genre books at the beginning level of the Writing skill. Sim gets the positive Wow, a Supernatural moodlet when speaking to any supernatural Sim, such as a vampire or fairy, as well as all other supernatural introduced in other expansions, such as the Imaginary Friend of *Generations* or the Mummy of *World Adventures*..

Shortcomings: None

Unique Features: Supernatural Fans have many new socials, such as Talk about the Supernatural, Ask about Unfinished Business (social to ghosts), Complain about Ordinary Dust (social to fairies), Enthuse about Hunting (social to werewolves), Enthuse about Brooms (social to witches), and Compliment Dental Hygiene (social to vampires). These new social help build LTR with supernatural Sims. Supernatural Fans also get the Lunacy mood booster when a full moon hangs high in the sky. If you have other expansions installed, any Sim with Supernatural Fan also has socials for those occult beings.

- Enthuse About Toys—social to Imaginary Friends (requires *Generations*)
- Enthuse About Rainbows—social to Unicorns (requires *Pets*)
- Enthuse About Appliances—social to SimBot (requires *Ambitions*)
- Talk About Freedom—social to Genie (requires *Showtime*)
- Enthuse About Bandages—social to Mummy (requires *World Adventures*)

Supernatural Skeptic

Description: There's a world of magic and unexplainable wonders out there, and Supernatural Skeptics don't care for any of it. That stuff might be exciting for some, but Supernatural Skeptics prefer the security and comfort of normality.

Earliest Age Available: Teen

Disallowed Traits: Supernatural Fan

Benefits: This trait increases job performance at the Business, Politics, Law Enforcement, and Journalism careers. Supernatural Skeptics get the Magical Rubbish moodlet when another Sim attempts to use an elixir or wand on them, as well as when the moon is full.

Shortcomings: Supernatural Skeptics will naturally avoid supernatural venues, like the Vault of Antiquity. Cannot write horror or monster books. Supernatural Skeptics develop the Alchemy skill approximately 10 percent slower than other Sims. Sims with this trait are more likely to fail when using magic wands or brewing elixirs.

Unique Features: When a Supernatural Skeptic gets their fortune told, they receive the Complete Nonsense moodlet. Supernatural Skeptics have a special Appreciate the Ordinary social. They have a slew of new socials that are all impolite to supernatural Sims:

- Complain about the Supernatural—offensive to all occults

- Express Disbelief in Fairies—offensive to fairies

- Enthuse about Witch Hunts—offensive to witches

- Enthuse about Garlic—offensive to vampires

- Ask about Fleas—offensive to werewolves

- Suggest Moving On—offensive to ghosts

- Enthuse about Real Friends—offensive to Imaginary Friends (requires *Generations*)

- Brag about Freedom—offensive to Genies (requires *Showtime*)

- Enthuse About Stealing Mummy's Treasure—offensive to Mummies (requires *World Adventures*)

- Enthuse about Appliances Breaking—offensive to SimBots (requires *Ambitions*)

There are a handful of hidden traits that are assigned to some of the supernatural types and Lifetime Rewards. For example, the Alpha Wolf trait is the Lifetime Reward for werewolves, which in turn grants the special Terrifying Howl and some fearsome moves like Cursed Bite. These hidden traits will be discussed in the Meet the Supernatural chapter, with each of the supernatural types.

BROWNIE BITES

Wait a second—why would you want this trait in a game that celebrates vampires, werewolves, and fairies (oh my)? Creating counter-narratives and setting up conflict is a great way to tell a unique, personalized story. Maybe you create a household with a witch and a skeptic, setting the scene for some odd, awkward situations. Plus, this trait also gives access to some great, powerful socials that annoy supernaturals. Those alone are excellent building blocks for creating the town skeptic, an intriguing character that can keep things more than interesting in Moonlight Falls.

New Lifetime Wishes

In Create a Sim, you select a Lifetime Wish. Each Sim has six possibilities. Five are determined by the traits you give them. The sixth option allows you to select any Lifetime Wish you want, regardless of assigned traits. Satisfying a Lifetime Wish takes a lot of work, but is worth a lot of Lifetime Happiness points, the currency used to purchase Lifetime Rewards.

In addition to maintaining the Lifetime Wishes of *The Sims 3*, *Supernatural* introduces several new Lifetime Wishes. The easiest way to access a specific Lifetime Wish is to select one or two traits that are directly related to it. For example, if you select the new Gatherer trait, it's likely that the Alchemy Artisan Lifetime Wish will appear in your five possible Lifetime Wishes.

Alchemy Artisan

⬧ Reach level 10 in Alchemy skill

⬧ Use 50 Alchemy Elixirs

When chefs combine ingredients, they make something tasty. When an Alchemy Artisan mixes ingredients, they rewrite the rules of human existence. Mastery of the Alchemy skill is not easy, but incredible powers await the dedicated. Only through constant practice, careful study, and the application of a wide variety of powerful elixirs will a Sim earn the title of Alchemy Artisan.

Celebrity Psychic

⬧ Reach level 10 of the Fortune Teller career (Scam Artist branch)

Telling people what they want to hear can be an extremely lucrative business, provided you can find the right people and anticipate what they desire. The ultimate destination for any pseudo seer is the position of Celebrity Psychic, where you are actually celebrated for your vague promises and double-speak. It's like being a politician, except people give you their money voluntarily!

Bone up on the Logic skill to make a strong run at the Scam Artist track of this career.

Leader of the Pack

⬧ Convert five Sims to Werewolves

⬧ Find 40,000 Simoleons worth of objects while hunting in a pack

Anyone can be in a pack, but few Sims are capable of being Leader of the Pack. Being the alpha dog takes hard work, discipline, and a nose for fine treasure. But it can't be done alone—a loyal following of fellow werewolves is required to show everyone who the big dogs in town are. It is not for the faint of heart to take the journey to become Leader of the Pack. Find 40,000 Simoleons worth of objects while hunting with the pack

TIP

The Alpha Wolf Lifetime Reward is a huge booster for completing this Lifetime Wish. The Cursed Bite, which any werewolf can use to turn Sims into werewolves, is never rejected.

Magic Makeover

⬧ Grant 12 different Sims Inner Beauty

⬧ Reach level 10 in Charisma skill

The fairest fairies know that everyone could use a little inner beauty. But it also takes a charismatic fairy to really know what inner beauty is. Teaching Sims about inner beauty won't be easy but it's a lesson well worth teaching. Spread the beauty and everyone will have a better day!

WWW.PRIMAGAMES.COM

Mystic Healer

◆ Cure 12 different transformed Sims using a witch's Sunlight Charm or Potent Cure Elixir

These days, Sims can be transformed into all sorts of odd things like toads, zombies, and tragic clowns. Even Sims who are feeling blue or have inner beauty can't catch a break! It takes a selfless Sim who cares deeply for others to cure these poor souls of their afflictions. Not many are up to the task of being a Mystic Healer, but for those who are they can feel good inside for doing so.

Turn the Town

◆ Drink from 20 Sims

◆ Turn five Sims into vampires

Some vampires believe that the measure of a vampire's greatness can be seen in their number of conquests. Rest during the day so the long nights can be spent quenching the thirst for plasma and converting those you find worthy. There will be many challenges to face in order to Turn the Town, but the reward will be worth it when you leave a bite in town lore.

> ### TIP
> Build up Charisma to help convince Sims around town to let you get all fangy with them.

Zombie Master

◆ Turn 10 different Sims into a zombie using the Reanimation Ritual or Potent Zombification Elixir

For a Zombie Master, there's no better friend than a staggering brain-craving zombie. They're just sooooooo cute!

But for other Sims, there's nothing more terrifying than seeing a relentless zombie off in the distance. To be a Zombie Master is to accept responsibility in the event of a zombie apocalypse.

> ### TIP
> Build up the Alchemy skill or become a powerful witch to tackle this Lifetime Wish.

Master of Mysticism

◆ Reach level 10 of the Fortune Teller career (Mystic branch)

Why are we here? What does the future hold? Will it hurt? These questions are so large as to be exclusively rhetorical, yet we keep asking. What if you had the talent to discover the answers? What if you could nurture a unique ability to find understanding in the chaos of the universe? You could be the ultimate Master of Mysticism?

Greener Gardens

◆ Reach level 10 in Gardening skill

◆ Make 100 plants grow using Bloom

Fairies have a natural green thumb that'll make others jealous with their pristine lawns and green gardens. But even for fairies it's not easy to tame the lawn and make it their own. It requires a lot of practice to reap the reward of having a yard that's the envy of the neighborhood.

New Moodlets & Wishes

There are many avenues to happiness and fulfillment (and a few back roads to misery, too). You'll get the most out of *Supernatural* by discovering the best ways to get your Sims feeling good about themselves. To do this, let's zero in on the smartest (and easiest) ways to deliver unto your Sims their dreams, such as helping them build careers, develop skills, or seek out exciting opportunities.

New Moodlets

The quick-glance measurement of a Sim's current happiness—or lack thereof—is mood. Mood is displayed in the Mood meter that occupies the bottom-center of the screen, right next to the portrait of the active Sim. The Mood meter is shaped like an upside-down exclamation point. Good mood is represented by green. As the Sim dips toward neutral or tense feelings, the meter turns yellow. When the meter displays red, your Sim is seriously bummed or agitated about something going on in their life or the world around them. You must pay immediate attention to the Sim and rectify whatever situation or interaction is upsetting them or else mood will tank out you not only won't bank Lifetime Happiness points, but you also risk spoiling opportunities and relationships.

Because moodlets contribute to your Sim's overall mood, you need to pay close and constant attention to the Moodlet panel. Moodlets are the fleeting bits of emotion that come and go with the flow of time as well as the presence of external influences. Some negative moodlets require direct attention. Others, especially the positive moodlets, should be enjoyed and whenever possible maintained so you can extend or at least maximize their benefits. Neutral moodlets often act as indicators, such as hints as to hunger level. A neutral moodlet left unattended will sometimes devolve into a negative moodlet, which in turn spoils the day. Keeping an eye on neutral moodlets is an enormous time-saver, because having to redirect activity to negate a negative moodlet can absorb multiple hours... and often some Simoleons!

Icon	Name	Effect	Duration	Description
	A Twinkle in the Eye	0	480	Sim is feeling rather saucy right now…with an eye twinkling like that, there might be twins or triplets in his/her future!
	All Glowy on the Outside	20	180	You know how people say that someone with a positive spirit is glowing? This isn't that. This is actual glowing skin.
	Animal Familiar	10		Witches can have unique connections to animals. These pets become "familiars" and, some say, can help their masters cast more powerful spells.
	Aura of Body and Mind			A fairy is projecting an Aura and Sim feels stronger and his/her mind is totally clear! Sim won't have any problem improving his/her logic, charisma, and athletic abilities.
	Aura of Body and Mind			Sim's mind never felt so clear and his/her body so strong! Sim won't have any problem improving his/her logic, charisma, and athletic abilities.
	Aura of Creativity			A nearby fairy is projecting an Aura and Sim can feel it! Anything to do with music, painting, and writing feels quite natural to him/her.
	Aura of Creativity			That Fairy Aura is making Sim extra creative! Anything to do with music, painting, and writing feels quite natural to him/her.
	Aura of Soothing			Sim feels relaxed from an Aura emanating from a nearby fairy. There's nothing in the world that'll worry him/her now.

New Simology

Icon	Name	Effect	Duration	Description
	Aura of Soothing			Sim is feeling quite relaxed thanks to that Aura. There's nothing in the world that'll worry him/her now.
	Awkward!	0	30	Well that was awkward... Sim is feeling a bit embarrassed and doesn't really feel like socializing right now.
	Bathed In Sunlight	15	120	It feels like the sun is reaching down and giving Sim a great, big hug!
	Bee Attack!	-200	15	Bees! BEES! They're huge and sting-crazy! Weapons are useless against them!! (Does not affect SimBot or Mummy.)
	Bee Sting	-15	1440	Ouch. Stupid bee. It was able to defend itself somehow. (Does not affect SimBot or Mummy, only affects humans.)
	Berry Blue	-10	180	Like they say, you are what you eat. In this case, Sim is some kind of artificially-sweetened blueberry jelly bean.
	Brain Freeze	5	60	What a tasty snack! Now Sim knows why zombies are raving about how delicious brains are.
	Chlorofizzled			Sim is ready for a nap. A very long nap.
	Chloroformed			So sleepy... must... find... zzzzzzzz....
	Clothes Encounter	40	120	Don't worry. No one will see those hanger marks on your back!
	Complete Nonsense	-10	60	Please. Sim has seen better predictions fall out of a cookie.
	Conflicted	-10	480	Will Sim give up his/her powers and become a human Sim?
	Dark Slumber	-50	120	What part of "poisoned apple" was difficult to understand? Sim is going to take a little nap now...
	Dazed!	0	60	Whoa. What? What happened? Sim is in a daze, and having trouble remembering what to do next.
	Drank from a Fairy	20	240	Drinking from a fairy gave Sim a buzz and a half!
	Energized by Moonlight	0		The moon isn't just for werewolves! Even fairies can have Full Moon Fever!
	Enjoying the Late Night	10		Look at the clock! It's past 11 PM and the night is just getting started... and that's exactly the way Sim likes it!

Icon	Name	Effect	Duration	Description
	Enlightened	0		The neurons are really firing in your brain now! The next time Sim sleeps, who knows what epiphany might occur?
	Fairest of Them All	20	360	The Mirror knows all! Sim really must be the fairest of them all!
	Fairy Magic Critical	-5		Using too many fairy powers is really exhausting Sim. He/she won't be able to grant Auras if he/she doesn't take a break or uses an Essence of Magic elixir. A ride on a Train Set will also help.
	Fairy Magic Depleted	-15	360	Sim used too many fairy powers and won't be able to use Fairy Auras for a while. Best to take a break and do some other things to regenerate Fairy Magic or use an Essence of Magic elixir.
	Fairy Magic Waning	0		Using fairy powers is starting to take a toll on Sim. It can be exhausting using those magical fairy powers! Hanging out in the Fairy House or riding the Train Set will help him/her, but to replenish magic power more quickly, drink an Essence of Magic elixir.
	Feeling Blue	-5		Sim feels as blue as the deep blue, empty, meaningless sea.
	Feeling Cured	25	120	Something's very different. Is this strange new feeling… normalcy?! Sim is cured!!
	Feeling Green	5		Who says it's not easy being green?
	Feeling Pink	5		What's that soft, pink light? And is it just Sim, or did things just get a little more "rrrawr" in here?
	Feeling Purple	5		Somewhere between joy and sadness, above healthy but around the corner from queasy, there is a place where one just feels kinda purple. Sim feels purple.
	Feeling Red	5		Sim is feeling red…and it ain't no sunburn!
	Feeling Yellow	5		It's hard to say exactly why, but right now everything seems to tickle the funny bone. It's time to get silly!
	Feral Change	0	360	Rrrawrrrr!! Sometimes it just can't be helped - the wolf has to come out!
	Flight of Felicity	20	1200	Wheeee!! That tickly sensation in the stomach is almost enough to lift Sim right off the ground!
	Frozen Solid	0	90	Sim has been frozen solid, and not by something metaphorical like indecision. Quite literally. (Does not affect SimBot or Mummy.)
	Gold and Toad	-10	360	Sim isn't feeling so well… It's as if something is trying to escape his/her stomach. Will it be gold or a toad? (Does not affect SimBot or Mummy.)
	Golden!	15	360	Sim feels an incredible energy surging through both hands, like almost anything he/she touches could turn to gold!

New Simology

Icon	Name	Effect	Duration	Description
	Haunted	-20	2880	Sim looks like he/she just saw a ghost! Who you gonna call?
	Heart of Gold	0	360	Some Sims have a heart of gold. Sim is gold from head to toe.
	Historian	10	60	Those who ignore history are doomed to repeat it, but not so for Sim. He's/she's quite the history buff!
	Hungry Like The Wolf	0		There's hungry, and then there's hungry like the wolf. "Like the wolf" in this case means "with little disregard to the food's age or quality."
	Imminent Nemesis	0	1440	That's it! Next person that approaches Sim is going down, and he/she doesn't care WHO it is!
	Imminent Romance	0	1440	Sim has a heart that's about to explode with passion! Cupid's got his bow trained on whoever he/she talks to next!
	Immunity	0	2880	Suffering the effects of a Pestilence Plague has left Sim immune to being Sick and Tired! He/she feels invincible!
	In Bliss			A shot of liquid that makes you forget all your troubles? Who knew?
	Inner Beauty	-20	1440	Unbeknownst to your Sim, he/she won't win many beauty pageants. Time for the inner beauty to shine through!
	Invigorated			Life is much too short to spend it sleeping. Good thing Sim won't be needing to sleep for a while.
	It May Come True	20	180	Sim doesn't really buy into that prediction, but then again... You never know, right?
	It's Just So Tragic!	-20		The only thing sadder than a clown crying on the inside is one crying inside AND outside. It's unbearable!!
	It's Too Early	-10		Ugh. It is WAY too early for a Night Owl to be up and around. Back to bed!
	Jobtastic!	0	1440	Oh yeah! There's nothing that can stop Sim from doing the best darn job possible at work today. As long as Sim HAS work today...
	Kissed under a Full Moon	20	1440	There's nothing more romantically heart-fluttering than smooching underneath the full moon!
	Life is Sweet	0	360	What is it about the sweet, sweet taste of honey that just makes life seem a little more bearable?
	Lost a Spellcasting Duel	-10	180	Sim lost this one, but it could be worse. Much worse...

Icon	Name	Effect	Duration	Description
	Lunacy	40	660	You don't have to be a werewolf to feel the effects of the full moon. Even a "normal" Sim can start feeling a little loony!
	Magic in the Air	5	480	Sim is in the mood for something – it begins with L and ends with OVE. Woo-hoo!
	Magic Power Critical	-5		Sim has cast too many spells and is almost out of magic power! His/her spells are likely to fail unless he/she waits for magic power to regenerate or uses an Essence of Magic elixir. A lap or two around the Broom Arena will help as well.
	Magic Power Depleted	-25	360	All that spell casting has worn Sim out! Spells cast while magic power is depleted will fizzle and fail, sometimes with disastrous or even fatal results! He/she must wait for magic power to regenerate or use an Essence of Magic elixir.
	Magic Power Waning	0		Sim has expended a lot of magical power. Continuing to cast spells will make him/her dangerously low on magic. A ride around the Broom Arena will help him/her, but to replenish magic power more quickly, drink an Essence of Magic elixir.
	Magical Rubbish	-10	120	Bah! All this magic, supernatural hoojoo is just a bunch of simple tricks and nonsense!
	Melancholy			Some days, nothing matters. Nothing.
	Misunderstood	0	120	Why, oh why can't other Sims understand you? If it gets much worse, Sim will Need To Brood.
	Monsters Under the Bed	-15	120	NOOO!! Monsters are totally real and they're under the bed and they totally want to eat up Sim! PANIC!!
	Need To Brood	-15	240	Sim has some pretty heavy stuff to work through. It's going to be hard to get anything accomplished until he/she can start to figure out this thing called life.
	No Monsters	15	240	Whew! It was all in your imagination. There are no monsters under the bed... this time!
	Not so Fair	-20	360	That mirror has to be defective! Sim can't believe he/she isn't the fairest Sim of all!
	Once Bitten, Twice Shy	-5	2880	Ever since that bite, things have been... strange. Deep in your subconscious is a primal urgency growing in strength by the minute. It's distracting, and a little nauseating!
	Pestilence Plague	-30	2880	Sim isn't feeling very well right now and needs plenty of food and rest. It'll take being Bathed in Sunlight, sweet honey, or a spicy chili pepper to rid him/her of the effects of the Pestilence Plague.
	Played Fairy Games	10	180	Who needs video games when fairy games are way more fun!
	Possibility of Betrayal	-10	1440	That horoscope didn't bode well... It's possible that Sim will experience betrayal.
	Possibility of Great Success	10	1440	Sim is really hoping that horoscope turns out to be true. He/she sure wouldn't turn down a successful future!

New Simology

Icon	Name	Effect	Duration	Description
	Possibility of Misfortune	-10	1440	According to the horoscope, Sim may not have Lady Luck at his/her side today.
	Possibility of New Friendship	10	1440	Sim should take special notice of chance encounters today. The Sim he/she bumped into might turn into his/her new best friend! …Or they might not.
	Possibility of Prosperity	10	1440	What a horoscope reading! Sim is excited at the prospect of experiencing prosperity.
	Possibility of Romance	10	1440	Cupid has his bow ready and aimed. The question is – is it aimed at Sim?
	Promise to Protect	0	2880	Being a guardian is a promise Sim takes very seriously.
	Pure Enlightenment	0		Sim has a perfectly clear mind. It will never be more receptive to learning than it is right now! If Sim were to sleep, there's no telling what discoveries the unconscious mind could unlock.
	Quenched the Thirst for Knowledge			While not as tasty as plasma, knowledge can be surprisingly thirst-quenching.
	Rocked Asleep	10	320	Whoa, did Sim nod off in the rocking chair again? There's just something about that gentle swaying that zzZZZzzzZZzz…
	Rocking Out	10		Sometimes it means letting your emotions burst out of you through the language of music, and sometimes it means gently swaying back and forth. Both feel good.
	Sanguine Snack	50	480	Sated beyond the needs of mere nourishment, vampires sometimes consume a real delicacy to truly satisfy their thirst.
	Sated	15	480	The Thirst has been kept at bay…for now. It always returns!
	Sick and Tired	0	1440	Oof. Sim is fighting something! Better go find a Cure elixir before it turns into something serious!
	So Cold	-10	120	So cold. So very, very cold. It feels like Sim may never know the comfort of warmth again!
	Someone to Watch Over Me	10	2880	Scary things just don't seem so scary for Sim now that he/she has someone to watch over him/her.
	Sparkly!	5	720	As if just being sparkly wasn't enough, Sim can now go out in the sun!
	Spellcasting Duel Draw	5	180	Well, you win some and you lose some. Except when you don't do either. Oh well.
	Spicy!	10	180	HOT!! It's like there's a 3-alarm fire in your mouth, and no one called the fire department!

Icon	Name	Effect	Duration	Description
	Starving for Moonlight	-5		The moon? Where is it? Will it ever return? Or did Sim make it angry? Sim just can't seem to focus without the moon gazing down on him/her.
	Taking Precautions	10	120	Okay, there was probably nothing to that psychic prediction. Still, Sim can't quite seem to put it completely out of mind…
	Terrified!	-20	60	Sim is starting to freak out with terror! He/she can only hope his/her greatest fears don't come true. (Does not affect SimBot or Mummy.)
	The Gift of Giving	20	120	Sharing is caring! Sim feels great about giving to another Sim! (Does not affect SimBot or Mummy.)
	Thirsty	0		Vampires must quench their thirst by Drinking from other Sims, growing fresh Plasma Fruit, or settling for a Plasma Juice.
	Toadified!	-5		Turns out being a toad is actually far easier than popular opinion. Receiving a special kiss or a Sunlight Charm will remove this curse.
	Too Much Sun	-50	2880	Vampires cannot long endure the pulsing beams of the sun. Alas, the warnings of legend and time were ignored! Now, scarred and vastly weakened, the vampire must struggle forth.
	Too Spicy!	-20	120	There's "spicy" and then there's the complete Mouthpocalypse happening to your taste buds right now. Sim DID sign the waiver before eating that spicy food, right?
	Top Dog!	15	240	AW-WOOOOO!!! Looks like Sim was the Alpha in that fight!
	Total Believer	40	300	Wow, that fortune teller knew everything! What a relief. Nothing to do now but sit back and surrender to the inescapable hands of fate!
	Tragic Clown	-40	2880	Sim has been cursed with the tears of laughter, the grimace of glee. He/she will force others to laugh 'til it hurts, which will be immediately. Sim is the Tragic Clown.
	Tricked by a Fairy	-5	60	A sneaky fairy sure got the best of Sim! He/she can't believe he/she fell for that!
	Vampiric Vigor	15		The night fills you with energy as you're invigorated by the moon beams and starlit night. Such power!
	Very Thirsty	-40		Very few things can topple a vampire's near immortal reign. One of them is leaving one's Thirst unquenched.
	Werewolf!	30		Where wolf? There wolf! Sim has unleashed the beast within!! (Does not affect SimBot or Mummy.)
	What Just Happened?	0	180	What — what happened? Recent memory is all a blur, but Sim can't shake this feeling that he/she was just doing something incredibly awesome…
	Wish Master			Now is the time for Sim to get things done! Satisfying wishes is far more satisfying than normal while the effects of the elixir last.

New Simology

Icon	Name	Effect	Duration	Description
	Won a Spellcasting Duel	10	180	Boom! Sim magically served someone else! Nothing beats the swell of pride and accomplishment after winning a spellcasting duel.
	Wow! A Fairy!	5	120	Oh, man! That was a real fairy! Sim can't believe it. How cool was that?
	Wow! A Genie!	5	180	Oh, man! That was a real Genie! Sim wonders what the most common wish is, or what the Genie would wish for! So many questions!
	Wow! A Ghost!	5	120	Wow! Communication with an actual spirit! Sim has gotten a glimpse into the afterlife!
	Wow! A Mummy!	5	120	Sim is so lucky! Very few people get to sit down and "rap" with a mummy.
	Wow! A SimBot!	5	120	Sim just had an encounter with an entirely artificial Sim. How fascinating! The temptation to teach it how to love is almost overwhelming! (They probably get that all the time...)
	Wow! A Supernatural Sim!	5	120	This is incredible! An encounter with a real supernatural Sim! And it turns out they're just like normal everyday Sims, except that they have incredible powers and they are totally unique and amazing!!
	Wow! A Vampire!	5	120	Incredible! A real, living, breathing vampire!! Well, maybe not "living" and "breathing" but definitely real!
	Wow! A Werewolf!	5	120	So that was a real werewolf. Cool! It was everything Sim expected, except with bigger teeth!
	Wow! A Witch!	5	120	Sim just had an encounter with a real, live witch! Sim could feel the magic from the witch!
	Wow! An Imaginary Friend!	5	120	Well it's certainly not every day that one can have an actual, real conversation with an Imaginary Friend. Wait... Sim isn't going insane, right?
	Yummy Pollen Punch	50	120	Turns out, when fairies whip up some punch they are really not messing around!
	Zombified!	-30	2880	Braains... Braaaaaiiiiiinnnnnsssss!!!!!

New Wishes

As soon as your Sims arrive in town, they start expressing wishes to you via the Wish panel at the bottom of the screen. In addition to their Lifetime Wish, which you selected in Create a Sim, Sims can have up to four active wishes at a time. When a Sim has a new wish appears in the arched bubble on top of the Wish Panel. Multiple wishes can stack up in that arched area, so use the arrows on either side to scroll through them and see what the active Sim desires at that given moment.

To promise a wish and add it to your Sim's active wishes, left-click on the wish. To deny a wish, right-click on it. There is no punishment for denying a wish. A Sim will just forget about it—there are no grudges for canning a Gardening class wish or whatever. However, dismissing a wish doesn't necessari mean a new wish will immediately take its place. You may have to wait a while before your Sim conceives of a new wish. Exploring town or mingling with other Sims often encourages your Sim to develop new wishes, so if you need to nudge your Sim, get out there!

CAUTION

You cannot undo a wish denial, so think before you right-click on that little dream.

Wishes are not universal across age groups. Sims of differing ages will want different things. A child will never desire to join a specific career track, but instead want to be talked to, played with, or receive a new object like a toy. Teen Sims start to mingle wishes with young adult and adult Sims, although you will see slight variations on wishes—many are socially oriented, too. Because Sims can undergo personality changes as they age, some wishes do not survive the move between age groups. For example, the desire to have a baby will disappear when your adult Sim moves into the elder age bracket.

To learn more about a wish, just move the cursor on top of it. The full details of the wish appear in a box. The box explains what the wish is, what needs to happen to fulfill the wish (you can sometimes get hints here), and how many Lifetime Happiness points the wish is worth once fulfilled. Wishes with loftier or more time-consuming goals are commonly worth more Lifetime Happiness points.

Wishes are spread across multiple categories, such as career wishes or supernatural wishes. Supernatural wishes are typically exclusive to specific supernatural types. For example, a vampire will not get werewolf-oriented wishes and vice versa.

Object Wishes

- Ask Orb of Answers a question
- Be attacked by bees
- Check Lunar Horoscope
- Eat a Ghost Chili
- Eat a Magic Jelly Bean
- Eat X Magic Jelly Beans
- Feed bees in beekeeping box
- Fight a [Supernatural type]
- Kiss a toadified Sim
- Nap in a rocking chair
- Perform a Stunt Show for tips
- Perfrom a stunt on a Broom
- Play Smack-a-Gnome
- Play with the Giddy-Up
- Read in a rocking chair
- Ride a Magic Broom
- Rock with a baby in a rocking chair
- Score X points playing Smack-a-Gnome
- Socialize with a [Supernatural type]
- Take broom for Joy Ride
- Transmute something into Gold
- Use a LLAMA
- Use a rocking chair
- Use The Claaaw (Arcade Claw Machine)
- View Moondial
- Win a fight against [Supernatural type]
- Win a prize from The Claaaw (Arcade Claw Machine)

Simology Wishes

- Become a [Supernatural type]
- Brood for X hours
- Catch flies (as Toadified Sim)
- Clean Sink
- Clean Toilet
- Do the Smustle
- Get Toadified!
- Get Zombified!
- Give a Sim What For
- Host a party during a full moon
- Reach level X of [specific skill]
- Send a gift to X friend(s)
- Send an elixir to a friend
- Stay up past bed time

Werewolf Wishes

- Ask for Werewolf Curse
- Eat something raw
- Give the Werewolf Curse to a Sim
- Howl at moon
- Hunt As Pack
- Hunt solo
- Scratch up furniture in wolf form
- Transform due to low mood
- Transform into werewolf X times
- Transform into wolf form!
- Transform under a full moon
- WooHoo In Wardrobe

Fairy Wishes

- Bestow a Fairy Gift to [Sim name]
- Bloom X Plants
- Collect Fairy Dust
- Dance at a Fairy House party
- Drink Fairy Nectar
- Get tricked by a Fairy
- Give a Fairy Gift
- Prank a Sim
- Project any Fairy Aura
- Project Body and Mind Fairy Aura
- Project Creative Fairy Aura
- Project Soothing Fairy Aura
- Receive a Fairy Gift
- Request a Fairy Gift from [Sim name]
- Set a Booby Trap
- Throw Fairy House Party
- Trick [Sim name]
- WooHoo in the Fairy House

Social Wishes

- Befriend [Supernatural type]
- Kiss Under the Full Moon
- Meet a [Supernatural type]
- Receive a Potion from a Friend
- Receive a Surprise Gift from a Friend
- See a [Supernatural type]
- WooHoo with [Sim name] During a Full Moon

Fortune Teller Wishes

- Have Fortune Told
- Hold a Psychic Convention
- Perform Private Reading for a Sim
- Perform X Private Readings
- WooHoo in the Gypsy Wagon

Venue Wishes

- Dance under a Full Moon
- Enter a Gardening Competition
- Enter a Trivia Contest
- Go out during a full moon
- Go Swimming During a Full Moon
- List a [specific elixir] for Consignment
- Research the Supernatural
- Search for Fairies at the Arboretum
- Visit Graveyard under a Full Moon
- Visit the Arboretum
- Visit the Vault of Antiquity
- Win a Gardening Competition
- Win a Trivia Contest

Vampire Wishes

- Drink from X Sims and Turn X of Them to Vampires
- Hunt Under a Full Moon

Collectible Wishes

- Analyze X Space Rocks
- Catch a [specific fish] During Full Moon
- Catch X Beetles
- Catch X Beetles Under a Full Moon
- Catch X Butterflies
- Catch X Butterflies Under a Full Moon
- Collect a [harvestable] During a Full Moon
- Collect Mushrooms
- Collect X Gems

- Collect X Gems Under Full Moon
- Get X [specific cut] Gems
- Get X Metals Smelted
- Grow [specific harvestable] During a Full Moon
- Harvest [specific quality] Honey
- Pick Up X Seeds
- Pick Up X Seeds Under a Full Moon
- Sweeten up a Dessert

Witch & Alchemy Wishes

- Throw an Elixir at Another Sim
- Toadify a Sim
- Turn a Sim into a Toad
- Turn another Sim into [Supernatural type] Using an Elixir
- Upgrade a Wardrobe into a Magic Wardrobe
- Use [specific elixir]
- Use X [specific elixirs]
- Win a Spellcasting Duel

Lifetime Rewards

When you max your mood into the bubble at the top of the Mood meter, you begin accumulating Lifetime Happiness points. Lifetime Happiness points are also earned by fulfilling wishes. Lifetime Happiness points are a precious commodity indeed, as they are then traded in for Lifetime Rewards, which are a series of special skills, traits, and objects with unique properties. Gather as many Lifetime Happiness points as possible—this is a great way to measure to the progress of your Sim and see how well they are doing in life.

> ### NOTE
> Lifetime Rewards exclusive to specific supernaturals only appear in the picker when you are playing as the matching supernatural. For example, only vampires see Immortal in the picker.

Flying Vacuum

- **Cost:** 10,000
- **Supernatural Exclusive:** None
- **Description:** It's a bird! It's a broom! No, it's a flying vacuum! Step up and ride in the luxury and style that only a vacuum can provide.

The Flying Vacuum operates exactly like a magic broom, but much, much faster. If you want to get places around town in a jiff, the Flying Vacuum does the trick!

> ### NOTE
> The Flying Vacuum can be used only by Sims teen and older.

Philosopher's Stone

- **Cost:** 40,000
- **Supernatural Exclusive:** None
- **Description:** Creating gold from ordinary objects isn't for the casual alchemy hobbyist—this is the big league! Grant yourself power never before imagined, but remember that with great power comes great responsibility.

This reward performs two amazing functions: it can bind a ghost to your household, and it will transmute objects into gold. If you want to Bind a Ghost to Family, click on the Philosopher's Stone and choose that interaction. Browse a listing of all of the ghosts in town. Pick which ghost you want to join your household. The ghost is then added and the headstone is placed in the personal inventory.

Want to try turning objects into gold? Drag an object on to the pedestal, then click on the Philosopher's Stone and choose Transmute Gold. There's a strong chance the interaction will succeed, and the object will turn into a valuable gold ingot. It's not impossible for the interaction to fail, which ends up destroying the object. Plus, there is a very slight risk that the interaction will not only fail, but also totally backfire. The Sim casting the transmutation spell is instead turned into gold. This, as you might imagine, results in insta-death.

Immortal

- **Cost:** 30,000
- **Supernatural Exclusive:** Vampire
- **Description:** Become the greatest of vampires by tolerating sunlight and never die of old age.

When a vampire is Immortal, they can withstand the otherwise withering heat and light of the sun. While daywalking, their skin sparkles. In addition, this reward halts aging and noticeably reduces the Thirst need, which often results in better moods.

NOTE

Immortal is only available to young adult and older vampires.

Alpha Dog

- **Cost:** 20,000
- **Supernatural Exclusive:** Werewolf
- **Description:** Sims will tremble at your new Terrifying Howl while Cursed Bites and growls are guaranteed to be fearsome.

Only werewolves may purchase this reward. When you are the Alpha Dog, your Cursed Bite is never rejected, meaning you always sink your teeth into a target Sim and turn them into a werewolf. Growling is never

rejected by another Sim either. Alpha Dogs also have access to a new, powerful Terrifying Howl interaction that results in all Sims on the lot getting the Terrified moodlet. Like Immortal, this reward is only purchasable by young adult Sims or older.

Magic Hands

- **Cost:** 20,000
- **Supernatural Exclusive:** Witch
- **Description:** Wands are for amateurs! Real witches can do magic with only their hands, and their spells never fail.

When a witch with Magic Hands attempts to cast a spell, they no longer require a magic wand. Their own two hands are more than capable of dispensing magic. In fact, spell unleashed from Magic Hands never fail and they often result in the same perks/bonuses that come from spells that previously required specific wands. As a cool visual, Magic Hands pop and glow when casting a spell.

NOTE

Only young adult or older witches may acquire this reward.

King/Queen of the Fae

- **Cost:** 30,000
- **Supernatural Exclusive:** Fairy
- **Description:** Summon other fairies, change your wing color/shape at will, and make fairy magic less taxing.

This reward allows fairies to instantly (and as many times as they like) change the shape or color of their wings. It's a cool cosmetic perk, but many fairies will get more mileage out of the reduced fairy magic costs that come with this reward. Now, your magic goes farther! Also neat: fairy Sims can now use the self interaction Summon Fairies. This opens a menu that shows nearby fairies that the Sim currently has a relationship with. Select multiple fairies from the list and they'll show up at your location. Talk about an instant social gathering.

New Simology

Opportunities

Opportunities are occasional events related to your skills and/or career. The rewards for completing opportunities include Simoleons, promotions, skill gains, and more. *Supernatural* offers many new opportunities connected to the new supernatural lifestyles.

NOTE

Many opportunities are time sensitive. If you are presented with an opportunity with a time limit, such as participating in a cook-off, you are given the deadline right up front. Keep these deadlines in mind because many opportunities actually require a little work. You cannot expect to complete an opportunity with just 10 minutes left on the clock. To track your active opportunities, use the Opportunity tab in the Status panel.

Name	Description	How to Complete
Horror scopes? Oh, horoscopes!	The basics of fortunetelling is all in the horoscopes. Master reading the horoscope and your Sim will be well on their way to becoming a world renowned fortune teller.	Read "The Horrors of Horoscopes" and return to work to increase your job performance and relationship with your boss.
The Fortunes of Fortune Telling	Instead of blindly picking an event so far into the future that your client will just forget about, how about adding some finesse to your Sim's fortune telling?	Read "Unfortunate Fortune Telling" and return to work to increase your job performance and relationship with your boss.
Divine Beings	Understanding the divinity of divine beings is key to anyone in a mystical profession. What makes one so divine? What is divinity for that matter? All will be revealed soon enough.	Read "Divine Divinity" and return to work to increase your job performance and relationship with your boss.
Importance of Palms	Palms. Is there a more crucial piece to telling a good fortune? Of course not! But this obvious piece to fortune telling isn't always obvious to a burgeoning fortune teller. At least not anymore.	Read "Passing Palms" and return to work to increase your job performance and relationship with your boss.
A Lesson in Psychics	Fortune tellers may not have much need for normal physics, but the meta style of physics are of utmost importance. A deep understanding of metaphysics lays the path to your client's fortune.	Read "Fabrication of Metaphysics" and return to work to increase your job performance and relationship with your boss.
Tricks of the Tarot	Knowing how to read tarot cards is an important part of any professional fortune teller. The perfect blend of showmanship and deciphering is a mystery to many…	Read "Tricky Tarots" and return to work to increase your job performance and relationship with your boss.
Mastering Motifs	It's not easy painting the right motif to draw upon the fortune of your client. Use too much and your client will laugh it off and too little makes the fortune unbelievable. It needs to be just right.	Read "Minnie Mystic's Mystical Motifs" and return to work to increase your job performance and relationship with your boss.
Guiding the Elements	The other tips and tricks to amazing fortune telling? They're all fake. The elements are the true key to otherworldly fortune telling. Master the elements and your Sim will master fortune telling.	Read "Psychic's Guide to the Elements" and return to work to increase your job performance and relationship with your boss.
Fictional Fortunes	Your Sim is becoming a master of accurate fortune telling. Just one problem – not all fortunes are good! Nobody likes to hear a bad fortune and the key to repeat business is ending on a happy note.	Read "Turning Bad Fortunes Good" and return to work to increase your job performance and relationship with your boss.
Help Investigation	The case of the missing Golden Llama is getting ice cold and the local police could sure use your Sim's help! Only a psychic can dissect the scene of the crime to reveal the criminal mastermind.	Go to the Police Station and offer your psychic services.
Give Private Reading	Your client is very important, so your Sim better deliver a favorable fortune!	Give a Private Reading.
Stay Late	Murphy's Law has no boundaries. Of course nobody needed their fortune told until the end of your Sim's shift. And fortunes aren't going to tell themselves.	Stay late to help read fortunes.
Forsake My Fairy Charms	Some will do anything for love, even if it means giving up being a fairy for your loved one.	Go to the Arboretum to Forsake the Fae and lose your Fairy Powers.

Name	Description	How to Complete
Forsake My Vampire Guile	If true love was meant to be, then losing your Sim's vampiric powers is in their destiny. It also means no more need for Vampiric Sunscreen!	Enter the Vault of Antiquity to forsake your Sim's vampiric powers and become a human Sim.
Forsake My Witchitude	Your Sim has a decision to make: lose the fur and become a human or keep the beast within. The choice won't be easy but true love's destiny will show the way.	Go to the Day Spa to Forsake Werewolf Powers and become a normal, not so hairy human Sim.
Forsake My Werewolf Powers	Name of love, your Sim can lose their witchy ways and fancy spells to become a normal everyday human Sim.	Go to the Science Lab to Forsake Witchitude and lose all those magical spells to become a human Sim.
Becoming a Fairy (step 1)	Not everyone has the opportunity to become a fairy, but for a lucky few it's the chance of a lifetime!	Find a Bloodstone, Moonstone, Sunstone, and Yellow Sapphire and bring them to the Arboretum.
Becoming a Fairy (step 2)	Just a small taste of being a fairy was quite thrilling for your Sim. The first step was a small one, but the next step in becoming a fairy won't be so easy!	Return the following four Nice Quality or better harvestables to the Arboretum: Beeswax, Spotlight Mushroom, Glow Orb Mushroom, and Ghost Chili.
Becoming a Fairy (step 3)	If Pollen Punch is any indication, it's totally gonna be worth it to take the next step in becoming a fairy!	Find the following four metals and return them to the Arboretum: Iron, Palladium, Silver, and Gold.
Becoming a Fairy (step 4)	This is it! Your Sim is so close to becoming a fairy they can feel the pixie dust on their fingers!	Bring the following four butterflies back to the Arboretum: Moth, Monarch, Gold, and Red.
Alchemic Mastery (step 1)	Any Sim can become a great alchemist, but achieving Alchemic Mastery is something few individuals can achieve. It won't be easy but for those who dare its quite an accomplishment!	Find four insects of any kind and return them to the Science Lab.
Alchemic Mastery (step 2)	Buckle up because now things are getting serious! Your Sim handled the first challenge with aplomb, but will they be able to continue in their quest for Alchemic Mastery?	Return the following three Nice Quality or better harvestables to the Arboretum: Wolfsbane, Mandrake, and Red Valerian.
Alchemic Mastery (step 3)	Precious gems and metals hold the key to unlocking Alchemic Mastery. Nothing can stop your Sim now in separating themself from a common run of the mill alchemist.	Return any two of each fem or metal to the Vault of Antiquity.

New Socials

New socials in *Supernatural* greatly increase the number of conversation options available to your Sims. All the original socials from *The Sims 3* are still available, but this new set of socials is added to the mix so your Sims have even more to gab about—and more avenues for building relationships. Some socials are related to encounters with different supernaturals. Others are available depending on career/skill choices and more.

> **NOTE**
>
> Most socials affect LTR (Long Term Relationship). That's the measurement of your overall relationship with another Sim. The STC (Short Term Commodity) of a social influences LTR. For example, if you use multiple Friendly STC socials and they are well received, that improves the LTR with the other Sim in the conversation, which we call the Target Sim in the following chart of new socials.

Use this table of socials added to *Supernatural* to help guide conversations. Here's how the table breaks down:

- **Social:** Name of social as seen in the conversation menu
- **Commodity:** Commodity associated with the social
- **Actor/Target Age:** Ages in which the social is applicable
  - C = Child
  - T = Teen
  - Y = Young Adult
  - A = Adult
  - E = Elder
- **Social Available When?:** What prompts the use of the social
- **Supernatural Actor?:** Social is exclusive to Actors with this supernatural type
- **Supernatural Target?:** Social is exclusive to Targets with this supernatural type
- **Special Success Result?:** If social is successful, the following special condition or reward happens

Social	Commodity	Actor Age	Target Age	Available When?	Supernatural Actor?	Supernatural Target?	Special Success Result?
Accuse of Being a Vampire	Insulting	CTYAE	CTYAE			Vampire	
Accuse of Impropriety	Insulting	TYAE	TYAE	Actor is Proper			
Apologize for Becoming a Werewolf	Friendly	CTYAE	CTYAE		Werewolf		
Appreciate the Ordinary	Friendly	TYAE	TYAE	Actor is Supernatural Skeptic			
Argggh!	Friendly	TYAE	TYAE	Actor is Zombified			
Argue About Who is the Better Protector	Insulting	TYAE	TYAE	Actor has Promise to Protect moodlet			
Ask about Ancestry	Friendly	CTYAE	CTYAE	Actor has Historian Buff moodlet			
Ask about Fleas	Insulting	CTYAE	CTYAE	Actor is Supernatural Skeptic		Werewolf	
Ask about Unfinished Business	Friendly	CTYAE	CTYAE	Actor is Supernatural Fan		Ghost	
Ask for a Kiss	Friendly	TYAE	TYAE	Actor is Toadified			Actor is cured of Toadification curse

Social	Commodity	Actor Age	Target Age	Available When?	Supernatural Actor?	Supernatural Target?	Special Success Result?
Ask for Fairy Dust	Friendly	CTYAE	CTYAE			Fairy	Actor receives Fairy Dust
Ask for Fairy Magic	Friendly	TYAE	YAE			Fairy	Actor receives Flight of Felicity, Gold and Toads, or Inner Beauty
Ask for Werewolf Curse	Friendly	CTYAE	CTYAE			Werewolf	Actor receives Once Bitten, Twice Shy moodlet
Ask How Late Sim Stayed Up	Friendly	TYAE	TYAE	Actor & Target are Night Owls			Actor receives Promise to Protect, Target recevies Someone to Watch Over Me
Ask to Be Protected	Friendly	CTYAE	TYAE			Fairy	
Ask to Forsake Fairy Charms	Neutral	YAE	YAE	LTR between Actor & Target must be spouse, partner, fiancee, or romantic interest			Actor receives Forsake My Fairy's Charm Opportunity chain
Ask to Forsake Vampire Guile	Neutral	YAE	YAE	LTR between Actor & Target must be spouse, partner, fiancee, or romantic interest		Vampire	Actor receives Forsake My Vampire's Guile Opportunity chain
Ask to Forsake Werewolf Powers	Neutral	YAE	YAE	LTR between Actor & Target must be spouse, partner, fiancee, or romantic interest		Werewolf	Actor receives Forsake My Werewolf's Power Opportunity chain
Ask to Forsake Witchitude	Neutral	YAE	YAE	LTR between Actor & Target must be spouse, partner, fiancee, or romantic interest		Witch	Actor receives Forsake My Witchitude Opportunity chain
Braaaiiins!	Friendly	TYAE	TYAE	Actor is Zombified			
Brag About Broom Riding	Friendly	TYAE	TYAE		Witch		
Brag about Playing Pranks	Friendly	CTYAE	CTYAE		Fairy		
Brag About Wing Color	Friendly	TYAE	TYAE		Fairy	Fairy	
Bestow Fairy Gift	Friendly	YAE	TYAE		Fairy		Target receives Flight of Felicity, Gold and Toads, or Inner Beauty
Challenge to Spellcasting Duel	Neutral	TYAE	TYAE		Witch	Witch	Actor and Target start duel
Compare Ghastliness	Friendly	TYAE	TYAE		Ghost	Ghost	
Complain About Fairies	Friendly	CTYAE	CTYAE				
Complain About Ordinary Dust	Friendly	CTYAE	CTYAE			Fairy	
Complain About Sleep Deprivation	Friendly	CTYAE	CTYAE	Actor is Night Owl			
Complain About Supernatural	Friendly	TYAE	TYAE	Actor is Supernatural Skeptic			
Complain About Werewolves Curse	Friendly	CTYAE	CTYAE	Target must be in human form	Werewolf	Werewolf	
Complain About Vampires	Friendly	CTYAE	CTYAE				
Complain About Werewolves	Friendly	CTYAE	CTYAE				
Complain About Witches	Friendly	CTYAE	CTYAE				
Compliment Dental Hygiene	Friendly	CTYAE	CTYAE	Actor is Supernatural Fan		Vampire	
Compliment Fur	Friendly	CTYAE	CTYAE	Target is in wolf form		Werewolf	
Compliment Ghastliness	Friendly	TYAE	TYAE			Ghost	
Compliment Propriety	Flirty	TYAE	TYAE	Actor is Proper			

Social	Commodity	Actor Age	Target Age	Available When?	Supernatural Actor?	Supernatural Target?	Special Success Result?
Confess to Being Vampire	Friendly	TYAE	TYAE		Vampire		
Confess to Watching You Sleep	Flirty	TYAE	TYAE				Actor receives Promise to Protect, Target receives Someone to Watch Over Me
Demonstrate Bite Strength	Insulting	TYAE	TYAE		Fairy	Vampire	
Deny Being a Vampire	Friendly	TYAE	TYAE		Vampire		
Discuss Matters of Etiquette	Friendly	TYAE	TYAE	Actor is Proper			
Enthuse About Appliances	Friendly	CTYAE	CTYAE	Actor is Supernatural Fan		SimBot	
Enthuse About Bandages	Friendly	CTYAE	CTYAE	Actor is Supernatural Fan		Mummy	
Enthuse About Brooms	Friendly	CTYAE	CTYAE	Actor is Supernatural Fan		Witch	
Enthuse About Garlic	Friendly	TYAE	TYAE	Actor is Supernatural Skeptic			
Enthuse About Hunting	Friendly	CTYAE	CTYAE		Werewolf		
Enthuse About Magic	Friendly	TYAE	TYAE	Actor is Supernatural Fan	Witch		
Enthuse About Sleeping In	Friendly	CTYAE	CTYAE	Actor is Night Owl			
Enthuse About Toys	Friendly	CTYAE	CTYAE	Actor is Supernatural Fan		Imaginary Friend	
Enthuse About Witch Hunts	Friendly	TYAE	TYAE	Actor is Supernatural Skeptic			
Express Disbelief in Fairies	Friendly	TYAE	TYAE	Actor is Supernatural Skeptic			
Fairy Frolic	Friendly	CTYAE	CTYAE		Fairy	Fairy	Satisifies Fun
Give What For	Insulting	TYAE	TYAE	Actor is Proper			
Growl At	Steamed	TYAE	TYAE		Werewolf		Actor receives Amused moodlet
How'd You Kick the Bucket?	Friendly	TYAE	TYAE			Ghost	
Hypnotic Gaze	Friendly	TYAE	TYAE		Vampire		Target gets Dazed moodlet
Imply Mother was a Chupacabra	Insulting	TYAE	TYAE			Vampire	
Imply Mother was a Glowbug	Insulting	TYAE	TYAE			Fairy	
Imply Mother was a Poodle	Insulting	TYAE	TYAE			Werewolf	
Intimidate	Steamed	TYAE	TYAE		Vampire		Target becomes Scared
Joke About Shedding	Friendly	CTYAE	CTYAE		Werewolf		
Kiss the Toad	Friendly	TYAE	TYAE	Target must be Toadified			Target is cured of Toadification curse
Lament the Moonless Night	Friendly	TYAE	TYAE	New Moon	Fairy		
Make Promise to Protect	Friendly	TYAE	CTYAE	Target must be Acquaintance or above			Actor receives Promise to Protect, Target receives Someone to Watch Over Me
Nuzzle	Flirty	YAE	TYAE		Werewolf		
Play Catch the Fairy	Friendly	CTYAE	CTYAE		Fairy	Werewolf	
Play Catch	Friendly	TYAE	TYAE	When there is enough room to play, will not work in tight spaces		Werewolf	
Play Fetch with Wand	Friendly	TYAE	TYAE	When there is enough room to play, will not work in tight spaces	Witch	Werewolf	

Social	Commodity	Actor Age	Target Age	Available When?	Supernatural Actor?	Supernatural Target?	Special Success Result?
Roshambo	Friendly	CTYAE	CTYAE				Fun little game, bumps LTR
Play Trick	Friendly	CTYAE	CTYAE	Target cannot have Tricked By Fairy moodlet	Fairy		Target receives trick and associated moodlet
Practice Fighting	Friendly	TYAE	TYAE	Both Sims must transform into wolf form	Werewolf	Werewolf	Awkward!, Embarassed, and Upset moodlets removed from Target
Promise to Protect	Friendly	TYAE	TYAE				
Proper Introduction	Friendly	TYAE	TYAE	Actor is Proper			
Quip a Witticism	Funny	TYAE	TYAE	Actor is Proper			
Rub Belly	Friendly	TYAE	TYAE			Werewolf	
Show Off Teeth	Friendly	TYAE	TYAE		Werewolf/ Vampire	Werewolf/ Vampire	
Slap with Glove	Insulting	TYAE	TYAE	Actor is Proper			
Sniff Inappropriately	Friendly	CTYAE	CTYAE	Actor must be in wolf form	Werewolf		
Suggest Moving On	Insulting	TYAE	TYAE	Actor is Supernatural Skeptic		Ghost	
Talk About Feelings	Flirty	TYAE	TYAE	Actor is Brooding			
Talk About Flight Experience	Friendly	TYAE	TYAE		Fairy	Fairy	
Talk About Flowers	Friendly	CTYAE	CTYAE		Fairy	Fairy	
Talk About Freedom	Friendly	CTYAE	CTYAE	Actor is Supernatural Fan		Genie	
Talk About the Joys of Plasma	Friendly	TYAE	TYAE		Vampre	Vampire	
Talk About the Supernatural	Friendly	CTYAE	CTYAE	Actor is Supernatural Fan			
Tell a Fairy Tale	Friendly	CTYAE	CTYAE		Fairy		
Tell Origin Story	Friendly	CTYAE	CTYAE	Actor has Historian Buff moodlet			
Threaten to Exploit Weakness	Insulting	TYAE	TYAE			Vampire	
Throw Elixir At	Neutral	CTYAE	CTYAE	Actor has elixir in inventory			
Warn Away	Friendly	TYAE	TYAE		Vampire		
Whack on Nose	Insulting	TYAE	TYAE			Werewolf	

Achievements

If you're logged into your *The Sims 3* account, you can earn new Achievements and Badges associated with *The Sims 3* and *Supernatural* expansion. Here's a complete list of all Achievements and their associated Badges. How many can you collect?

Achievement	Requirement
Spellslinger	Participate in 50 Spellcasting Duels
An Amazing Alchemic Achievement	Have your Sims create 300 elixirs
Trickathalon	Trick 50 Sims
Mischievious Tokens of Divinity	Have Sim become a Master of Mysticism then give 25 fairy enchantments to other Sims
Swan Dive	As a non-supernatural female, Make Out with your vampire partner, then break up and make out with a new werewolf partner, then break up and marry a vampire
Gratified Grifter	Send 30 gifts to online friends
Fairly Fine Enchanter	Perform the Gold and Toads, Inner Beauty, and Flight of Felicity fairy enchantments 8 times each, and then sleep until well rested
Psychic Sycophant	Have Sim becomes a Celebrity Psychic and then hold 5 Psychic Conventions
I Smelt A lot	Get 30 metals smelted
Cutter McCuttington	Cut one of each type of gem
Celebratory Psychic	Earn the Celebrity Psychic Lifetime Wish
Clawsome!	Have a Sim win 10 prizes from the Claaaaw machine
Brood Sire	Turn 8 Sims into vampires
1 Girl, 15 Fairy Companions	As a female Sim, get a fairy partner 15 times -- and break up with 14 of them

Achievement	Requirement
Covenant	As a witch, have 8 witch friends
Master of Seduction	As a vampire, make 15 Sims think of you
The Fairy House Party Party	As a fairy, have 8 fairy friends
I Don't Believe in Fairies	As a witch, have 8 fairy enemies
Mystic Mastery	Earn the Master of Mysticism Lifetime Wish
Curiouser and Curiouser	Research the Supernatural at the Vault of Antiquity 5 times
It's All in the Wrist	Throw 30 elixirs at other Sims
Thaumaturgist	Successfully cast 25 charms
Total Toadification	Toadify 10 Sims
Van Helping	Have your Sims help 15 supernatural-type Sims
1 Boy, 15 Magical Consorts	A a male Sim, get a witch partner 15 times and break up with 14 of them
Meatarian	As a werewolf, eat 30 raw fish or raw meat
Talk to the Palm	As a Fortune Teller, conduct two Private Readings
Participatory Package	Send a gift to an online friend

Introduction

New Simology

New Careers & Skills

Meet the Supernaturals

New Venues

Tour of Moonlight Falls

New Object Catalog

Achievement	Requirement
Take a Break from Those Monsters	Have a witch Sim and vampire Sim marry, then have ghost, fairy, and werewolf children -- and then all ride brooms to a community lot
The Odd Bunch	Get a Supernatural Fan Sim to have 3 werewolf, vampire, fairy, ghost, and witch friends
Where Opposites Attract	As a werewolf, marry a vampire
Waxing Poetic	Write a poetry novel
And Your Little Gnome Too	As a witch, kick a gnome 10 times
You've Been Told	Get your fortune told at the Gyspy Wagon
Seedling	Collect 5 seeds
Potent Possibilites	Visit Aleister's Elixirs and Sundries
Makin' Magic	WooHoo in the Gypsy Wagon as a witch
Rocker	Collect 5 rocks
Spacious Curiosity	Analyze a meteorite (any size)
Metalhead	Collect 5 metal
Bugger	Collect 5 insects
All Things Great and Smal	Make out with a werwolf, fairy, ghost, vampire, witch and human Sim
My Precious!	Cut 20 gems with the Gem-U-Cut Machine
Unnatural Enemies	As a fairy, have 8 witch enemies

Achievement	Requirement
Glitter Groupies	As a vampire, have 5 vampire friends
Self-Saving	Throw 5 elixirs at yourself
Where Wolves Hangout?	Visit a supernatural hangout (Varg's Tavern, Toadstool, or Red Velvet)
All-Knowing Orb	Check the Orb of Answers 5 times
Seeker of Signs	Have Fortune Teller reach the Horoscope Reader promotion, then ask 5 Sims what their sign is

New Careers & Skills

• • •

As with most expansions for *The Sims 3, Supernatural* introduces new careers and skills. These serve to further change and enhance the lives (and livelihoods) of your Sims. To fit with *Supernatural's*, well, supernatural theme, the new career and skills are decidedly mystical. Sims may now embark on an exciting Fortune Teller career as well as research and develop the new Alchemy skill. In addition to Alchemy, there are all-new hidden skills like Broom Riding.

> ## NOTE
>
> Hidden skills directly related to supernatural types such as the Lycanthropy skill (which is tied to werewolves) are detailed in the specific supernatural sections of the Meet the Supernaturals chapter.

New Careers

Sadly, it's not always ice cream and hugs that make the world go round—sometimes some hard-earned Simoleons are needed to grease the wheels of industry and get things done... and purchased. Though Moonlight Falls is a small town, it's not without industry. All of the original careers from *The Sims 3* are present in Moonlight Falls, but *Supernatural* introduces an all-new job for those with mystic minds: Fortune Teller.

To sign up for a career, simply report to the building that headquarters the job, such as the military base or police station. Applying is as easy as left-clicking on the location and then choosing the offered career. When your Sim reports to the job location, the career is immediately offered and the starting position/salary flashed onscreen. If you accept, you are given a schedule and expected to show up at the designated times.

There are multiple ways to advance a career. Promotions are the most common benchmark of success and always come with a one-time Simoleon bonus, but there are social aspects to each career that involve getting to know co-workers, which has the potential to widen your circle of friends. While

at work, you can set the "tone" for your performance (more on this in a moment), which affects how you interact with co-workers or approach the job itself. As you advance, your schedule changes and your salary rises. Typically, there are perks or benefits for hitting certain promotions.

> ## TIP
>
> Going to work in a good mood boosts your chances of promotion. Go see a movie the night before work to get the powerful Enjoyed a Great Movie moodlet—it lasts almost the entire next day!

You can be fired from a career. If you stop showing up for work, your employer will call you and let you know that your services are no longer needed. You can also perform so poorly on the job that you're handed a pink slip. So, keep a good eye on the Performance meter in the Career tab of the Status panel. It's also a good cheat sheet for the metrics that the next promotion is based on.

Tones

Although you do not actually see what your Sim does on the original jobs, you can dictate general behavior for that work day through tones. Tones include behaviors such as working hard, getting to know co-workers, and sucking up to the boss. Many of these tones play into earning promotions at work, so look at the provided promotion metrics for each career to see what tones are best for the next step in that career.

Not all tones are available from the first day. In some careers, additional tones are earned when you reach specific promotions or choose a specific career path.

> ## RETIRING
>
> Later in life, Sims can retire from a career and make a daily pension. This pension is smaller than the wages normally made at that promotion level, but it is a great way to pull in daily income for necessary food and objects while pursuing skills.

BROWNIE BITES

Supernatural's new careers do not come at the expense of any of the original careers. Every single career you can embark on in *The Sims 3* base game can be signed up for in *Supernatural*, including all careers introduced in any installed expansion. The venues for the careers might be different in Moonlight Falls, but otherwise the scope and structure of those careers remains the same.

Fortune Teller

Do Fortune Tellers truly have the ability to peer into the future and forsee what is yet to come? Or are they nothing more than charlatans that make a buck by humoring the gullible or superstitious? Well, in *Supernatural*, you may explore both sides of the coin. In this new career, you can either choose to be a real-deal soothsayer and translate the future for eager (and paying clients), or branch off into the Scam Artist track and fleece the unsuspecting. Either way, Simoleons are going into your pocket.

- ◆ **Work Location:** Gypsy Wagon
- ◆ **How Hired:** Newspaper, Computer, Gypsy Wagon
- ◆ **Work Week:** M, W, F, Sa, Su
- ◆ **Salary Progression:** The Fortune Teller career path starts at a low salary level, but the pay increases as the Sim approaches the higher levels of the career, eventually earning a better than average amount.

Level	Title	Weekly Base Pay	Work Days	Hours in a Day	Metrics	Special Benefit?
1	Horoscope Reader	§390	M, W, F, Sa, Su	4	Mood	
2	Fortune Guesser	§600	M, W, F, Sa, Su	5	Mood, Clientele	
3	Vague Visionary	§890	M, W, F, Sa, Su	6	Mood, Clientele	
4	Palm Reader	§1130	M, W, F, Sa, Su	6	Mood, Clientele, Charisma	Private Reading interaction unlocked
5	Metaphysical Fabricator	§1,435	M, W, F, Sa, Su	6	Mood, Clientele, Charisma	

Tone	Benefit
Really Sell It	Work hard (adds stress)
Fake It	Slack off at work (lower stress)
Meet Clientele	Meet co-workers
Group Readings	Increase relationship with co-workers
Study Body Language	Increases Logic skill
Peer into the Unknown	Increases Alchemy skill
Learn from Mentor	Increase relationship with boss

Career Development

There are multiple ways to begin this new career. The easiest is to look in the morning paper or respond to a computer ad. However, you can also report to the Gypsy Wagon on the edge of town (provided you didn't move it during town customization) to sign on to the Fortune Teller career. Finally, there is an Opportunity attached to the Orb of Answers object (which you may purchase in Buy Mode) that leads you to an entry-level Fortune Teller position.

To develop this career, you must pay attention to a host of metrics. The easiest to manage, of course, is mood. Reporting to work at the Gypsy Wagon in a good mood is a building block of success, so make sure to indulge in mood-boosting activities like going out, eating yummy (and high quality) food, or being social prior to punching the clock. If you can hit the wagon with your mood in the little bubble, you will be in great shape for a productive day and possibly in line for a promotion.

Mood, however, is only the beginning. Having a good relationship with your clientele is also essential for advancement. To meet clientele, use the Meet Clientele tone and you'll start some new relationships. To improve your relationships, use the Group Readings tone. Also, monitor LTR of clientele and—after hours—engage them in positive manners. Talk to them, use friendly socials, and don't let relationships decay. Repeat, happy customers are critical for advancement early in this career, so take the time to mingle and schmooze. Of course, the Charisma skill will help with that and, in fact, Charisma becomes a metric for development when you reach level 3 of the career: Vague Visionary. If you want to become a Palm Reader, better start developing that skill. You can opt to take a class, practice in a mirror (even better, one of the new Magic Mirrors), and more to build up that skill.

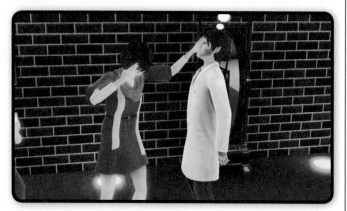

Upon reaching level 4, you unlock a new interaction: Offer Private Reading. Now you can earn even more Simoleons (and

boost relationships) by offering personal readings with Sims in town. Yes, these take time outside the workplace, but they pay off in the long run, especially as they help launch you toward level 6, which is where the Fortune Teller career splits. Now you have a big choice to make. Will you stay on the straight and narrow by choosing the Mystic branch? Or will you go for the Scam Artist branch and prove the old adage: a fool and his money are soon parted.

Charisma

Everybody knows someone who can breeze into a room, seamlessly enter any conversation, and suddenly become the focus point of attention. The key to such feats is charisma. This skill is essential for Sims who want to effectively socialize. Tuning this skill unlocks new social interactions that simplify befriending other Sims and developing meaningful relationships.

NOTE

If you enjoy socializing with other Sims, make sure to develop this skill.

Acquire by: Take Charisma Class, Read Charisma Manual, Practice Speech in a Mirror

Development tools: Books, Socials, Mirror, Parties

Available ages: Teen, Young Adult, Adult, Elder

Development Benefits

Enhancing the Charisma skill opens exciting new avenues of conversation as well as a special social that guarantees a smooth recovery from any conversational snafus. However, developing the skill requires more than just taking a class and then practicing your charismatic moves with a book or by talking into the mirror. It requires making friends and maintaining relationship during the course of the skill development. Each level of the skill requires a specific number of friends and relationships. Without these connections, you cannot advance up the skill tree, no matter how long you practice that wolfish grin in the mirror.

NOTE

Those relationships must be non-familial. Your mother's *supposed* to love you.

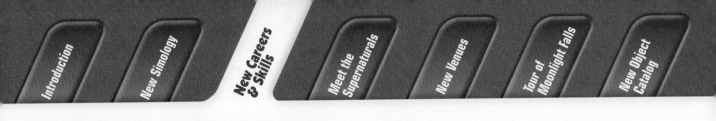

TIP

Sims who develop the Charisma skill increase the effectiveness of social interactions at work, such as Meet Co-Workers or Suck Up to Boss.

TIP

Whenever you use a positive social, the Charisma skill gets a little boost.

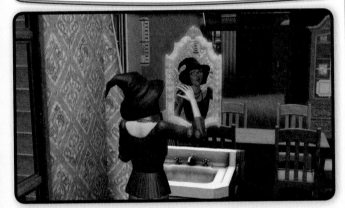

Practice your Charisma skill by working on your speech in the mirror.

Charismatic Sims get additional greetings that start a conversation right, such as Amusing Introduction and Friendly Introduction. These greets are more potent than regular greets. As the skill develops, more greet modifiers appear that increase the social weight of the greeting and can steer the conversation.

The following chart shows the number of friends and relationships required for each level advance, and the greetings that the level bestows.

Level	Required Friends	Required Relationships
1	0	0
2	0	2
3	1	3
4	2	4
5	3	6
6	4	8
7	5	10
8	6	15
9	8	20
10	10	25

TIP

If you ever want to truly manipulate a conversation, boost the Charisma skill. Greeting modifiers get you much closer to the desired outcome of any social interaction.

Three special socials unlock as you develop the Charisma skill. Once you reach a specific level, you learn these new socials:

Charming Introduction (Level 1): Sometimes, introductions are the toughest part of the conversation. Sims with high Charisma levels become more adept at introductions, as seen by the modified greets. Once charismatic Sims reach level 10, their Charming Introduction rockets them into Friend status right away.

Get to Know (Level 3): This social helps with discovering the traits and interests of other Sims. Once learned, this social becomes more powerful as the Sim approaches level 10 of the skill. Eventually, there is no possibility of rejection when inquiring about traits and interests.

Smooth Recovery (Level 5): Oops. You said the wrong thing. If you have the Smooth Recovery social, you can try to revive the conversation. It may not always work, but as the skill nears level 10, the chance of success increases.

Mystic Branch

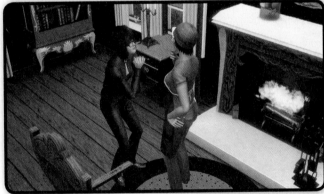

So you decided to become a Mystic? Well, now you have a new metric: Alchemy. You must develop this skill to continue climbing the sorta-corporate ladder of the Fortune Teller career. Fortunately (pun intended), the Peer into the Unknown work tone helps build the Alchemy skill while you are at work, but you must be mindful of doing too much to the exclusion of other important tones/metrics such as Group Readings.

In this branch, you must also keep doing Private Readings as a career metric. Fortunately, this replaces the need to meet and sustain relationships with clientele. For Mystics, Private Readings pay out more than they do for Scam Artists. And, even better, work hours decrease so that you have more time to perform these profitable readings.

Mystics score sweet discounts!

There are definite benefits to taking this branch. At level 7, you start getting a small discount on elixirs at Aleister's Elixirs & Sundries. And when you hit the highest level in the Mystic branch, Master of Mysticism, you are awarded the Mystic Aura, a positive mood booster for you and those around you.

Level	Title	Weekly Base Pay	Work Days	Hours in a Day	Metrics	Special Benefit?
6	Conjurer of Cheap Tricks	§1,560	M, W, F, Sa, Su	5	Mood, Alchemy, Private Readings	
7	Spiritual Guide	§1,584	W, F, Sa, Su	5	Mood, Alchemy, Private Readings	Discounts at elixir shop
8	Traveller of Time and Space	§2,348	W, F, Sa, Su	5	Mood, Alchemy, Private Readings	
9	Dealer of Destinies	§2,478	F, Sa, Su	4	Mood, Alchemy, Private Readings	
10	Master of Mysticism	§3,352	Sa, Su	4	Mood, Alchemy, Private Readings	Mystic Aura

Scam Artist Branch

Nobody here is going to judge you for going on the Scam Artist track, especially because it has some cool perks like the limo rides that start when you hit level 8: Pseudo-Psychic. But to reach that level, you need to start working on the Logic skill, because it's now a metric for success. This skill can be started via a class, the computer, a chess set, and more—you have options. There's even a work tone—Study Body language—that improves the Logic skill.

Sims following the Scam Artist branch maintain the clientele metric, so Private Readings are not nearly as important. (Nor are they as profitable for Scam Artists as they are for Mystics.) However, there is a payday on the horizon for Sims who go scam: Hold Psychic Convention. This interaction on the Theater venue is the reward for hitting level 10 of the Scam Artist branch. Psychic Conventions pay out handsomely for Fortune Tellers, and thankfully, decreased hours give your Sim plenty of time to hold these events.

Level	Title	Weekly Base Pay	Work Days	Hours in a Day	Metrics	Special Benefit?
6	Tarot Card Shark	§1,875	T, W, Th, F, Sa	5	Mood, Clientele, Charisma, Logic	
7	Keen Observer of Human Behavior	§2,600	W, Th, F, Sa	5	Mood, Clientele, Charisma, Logic	
8	Pseudo-psychic	§2,982	Th, F, Sa	4	Mood, Charisma, Logic	Limo!
9	Metaphysician	§4,569	Th, F, Sa	3	Mood, Charisma, Logic	
10	Celebrity Psychic	§6,912	Th, F, Sa	3	Mood, Charisma, Logic	Hold Psychic Convention at theater venue

Logic

Intelligence is always a treasured asset, so pursue the Logic skill to improve your Sim's brainpower. The Logic skill involves the use of the telescope and chess set objects, but also gives Sims additional computer interactions.

Acquire by: Take Logic Class, Read Logic Book, Play Chess, Use Telescope

Development tools: Chess Set, Telescope, Logic Books, Computer

Development Benefits

Develop the Logic skill by attending the Logic class, playing chess at a chess board (at home or in a public location), or reading a logic-related book. This skill has many benefits beyond the ability to win chess matches. For example, this skill unlocks the Solve the Unsolvable interaction with the computer, which gives the logic-minded Sim a chance to earn some Simoleons at home. (This interaction is not a guaranteed success.)

As this skill is developed, it shortens the time it takes to develop other skills, with the exception of Athletic and Charisma. Teen and child Sims also get a homework speed boost as this skill is developed. The higher the level, the faster homework is completed. (This is a tremendous benefit with grades.) This skill also increases the chance of winning all varieties of games. Winning games gives Sims a mood boost.

A good measuring stick for the chance a logic Sim will beat another Sim is to compare Logic skill ranks. A Sim with level 5 will likely beat one at level 4—but upsets can occur.

TIP

Playing chess against other Sims not only increases the Logic skill, but it also gives LTR a little boost.

At level 3 of the Logic skill, Sims have a new interaction with the telescope. They can now do more than just Stargaze, they can Search Galaxy. This is another money-making opportunity for Sims, because every new celestial body found earns them a little extra cash from the science facility. New finds are logged in the Skill Journal, too. When a Sim finds a new object in the heavens, they can name it.

TIP

Want to really impress somebody? Name a star after them.

At level 5, Sims unlock the ability to Tutor other young Sims: children and teens. Tutoring not only develops the Logic skill, but it helps the student and can provide a mood bump. Tutored Sims always do better in school, so if a child suffers from lagging grades, interacting with a logical Sim is a great remedy. If the mentored student has the Logic skill, too, they develop the skill while being tutored, but at a slower pace.

TiP

There is a "hidden" Chess skill. Like other skills, the more you play chess, the better you get at it. You will soon start winning more and more games.

At level 5 Logic skill, Sims can start talking about the things they find while using the telescope. Talking about a celestial object is a friendly social that improves the building relationship between two Sims. However, for a real social bump, tell a Sim that you named a celestial object after them. This instant relationship builder helps with making new friends or developing a romantic relationship.

At level 10 Logic skill, the Sim can tutor any other Sim from teen to elder in any of the skills with the exception of Athletic and Charisma. The catch is that the logic Sim must also have the skill they are teaching and they cannot teach past their current level. For example, if Catherine has level 5 Writing skill, she cannot tutor Chris past level 5. This development process is much faster than reading a skill-related book but not as fast as actually practicing the skill.

Career Opportunities

The Fortune Teller career has a series of unique Opportunities. Use this chart of Opportunities to see how to complete the Opportunities randomly offered to Fortune Teller Sims and what rewards await:

Name	Description	How to Complete
Horror scopes? Oh, horoscopes!	The basics of fortunetelling is all in the horoscopes. Master reading the horoscope and your Sim will be well on their way to becoming a world renowned fortune teller.	Read "The Horrors of Horoscopes" and return to work to increase your job performance and relationship with your boss.
The Fortunes of Fortune Telling	Instead of blindly picking an event so far into the future that your client will just forget about, how about adding some finesse to your Sim's fortune telling?	Read "Unfortunate Fortune Telling" and return to work to increase your job performance and relationship with your boss.
Divine Beings	Understanding the divinity of divine beings is key to anyone in a mystical profession. What makes one so divine? What is divinity for that matter? All will be revealed soon enough.	Read "Divine Divinity" and return to work to increase your job performance and relationship with your boss.
Importance of Palms	Palms. Is there a more crucial piece to telling a good fortune? Of course not! But this obvious piece to fortune telling isn't always obvious to a burgeoning fortune teller. At least not anymore.	Read "Passing Palms" and return to work to increase your job performance and relationship with your boss.
A Lesson in Psychics	Fortune tellers may not have much need for normal physics, but the meta style of physics are of utmost importance. A deep understanding of metaphysics lays the path to your client's fortune.	Read "Fabrication of Metaphysics" and return to work to increase your job performance and relationship with your boss.
Tricks of the Tarot	Knowing how to read tarot cards is an important part of any professional fortune teller. The perfect blend of showmanship and deciphering is a mystery to many…	Read "Tricky Tarots" and return to work to increase your job performance and relationship with your boss.
Mastering Motifs	It's not easy painting the right motif to draw upon the fortune of your client. Use too much and your client will laugh it off and too little makes the fortune unbelievable. It needs to be just right.	Read "Minnie Mystic's Mystical Motifs" and return to work to increase your job performance and relationship with your boss.
Guiding the Elements	The other tips and tricks to amazing fortune telling? They're all fake. The elements are the true key to otherworldly fortune telling. Master the elements and your Sim will master fortune telling.	Read "Psychic's Guide to the Elements" and return to work to increase your job performance and relationship with your boss.
Fictional Fortunes	Your Sim is becoming a master of accurate fortune telling. Just one problem – not all fortunes are good! Nobody likes to hear a bad fortune and the key to repeat business is ending on a happy note.	Read "Turning Bad Fortunes Good" and return to work to increase your job performance and relationship with your boss.

Name	Description	How to Complete
Help Investigation	The case of the missing Golden Llama is getting ice cold and the local police could sure use your Sim's help! Only a psychic can dissect the scene of the crime to reveal the criminal mastermind.	Go to the Police Station and offer your psychic services.
Give Private Reading	Your client is very important, so your Sim better deliver a favorable fortune!	Give a Private Reading.
Stay Late	Murphy's Law has no boundaries. Of course nobody needed their fortune told until the end of your Sim's shift. And fortunes aren't going to tell themselves.	Stay late to help read fortunes.

Lifetime Wishes & Achievements

◊ **Master of Mysticism:** Reach Level 10 of the Fortune Teller career (Mystic Branch)

◊ **Celebrity Psychic:** Reach Level 10 of the Fortune Teller career (Scam Artist Branch)

◊ **Achievement 1:** Hold a Psychic Convention

◊ **Achievement 2:** Conduct a Private Reading

New Skills

Supernatural introduces a new skill for your Sims to develop and master: Alchemy.

As well as giving your Sims something to do when not pursuing traditional careers like Law Enforcement or Military, the Alchemy skill unlocks a wealth of elixirs to brew, consume, and throw. This skill comes in handy with the Fortune Teller career. And if you're a Witch, you'll find even more nefarious uses for this skill... but more on that in the "Witch" section of the Meet the Supernaturals chapter.

The Skill panel is an easy place to track your Sims' skill levels. Any skill the Sim has learned appears in the Skill panel. A meter next to the skill shows the Sim's level. Hover the cursor over the meter to see how close the Sim is to the next level. Click on the page to the right of each skill measurement to read the Skill Journal. The Skill Journal offers a detailed look at that specific skill, such as how long the Sim has been working at the skill and how many of a certain object/item related to that skill the Sim has made.

The Skill Journal also displays skill-specific challenges associated with that skill. Challenges are requirements that, when met, result in improved results or financial rewards for activities related to that skill. Each skill challenge is associated with a title.

Use these tips to speed skill development:

- Sims in a good mood develop a skill slightly faster.

- Use community equipment when just starting out to save a little cash. You can use the Alchemy Station at Aleister's or the Vault of Antiquity gratis.

- Unless you feel pressed for time to start developing a new skill, save books on the subject for skill levels higher than 2. Reading a book reduces the amount of time needed to attain the next level—within reason.

Alchemy Skill

What can be more supernatural than magic? This new skill allows Sims to dabble in the art of elixir-making, of turning ingredients into powerful elixirs that can change others Sims into different forms, cure conditions, boost mood, and much more. Crafted elixirs are also a good way to make Simoleons on the side, and some Sims will opt to support themselves as self-employed Alchemists rather than enroll in a more traditional career—even one as untraditional as Fortune Teller.

- **Acquire By:** Use Alchemy Station, take Alchemy class, read Alchemy books

- **Development Tools:** Alchemy Station, Creating elixirs

- **Age Availability:** Teen, Young Adult, Adult, Elder

Development

The Alchemy skill is a natural fit with the supernatural setting in this expansion, especially if you are playing as the Witch supernatural type. However, any Sim who is teen or older may learn this new skill. Sims who master the Alchemy skill become incredible elixir mixologists, whipping up vials of fanciful concoctions with powerful effects. As you'll see in the recipe list below, there are indeed some potent elixirs that have the ability to change lives for the better... and perhaps for the worse.

However, it takes time to become a top Alchemist. It requires study, Simoleons, and a good eye for finding collectibles to use in elixirs. (Fortunately, we have full maps of Moonlight Falls that show you exactly where to find ingredients.) The easiest way to launch the development of the Alchemy skill is to take the Alchemy class (§100) at the Vault of Antiquity. However, there are other means for starting this skill. You can also pick up Alchemy skill books at the bookstore. Using these tools in early levels will speed the development of the skill.

Take the Alchemy class at the Vault of Antiquity!

TIP

There are three Alchemy books. The first book, Alchemy Basics, can be read right away. Alchemy Vol. 2: Secret Motions and Super Potions requires level 3. Alchemy Vol. 3: Omnimustericon: The Ultimate Book of Shadows requires level 6. Use books to jump-start the drive to the next level of the skill.

The Alchemy Station is a critical object for the development of this skill. It's not cheap, but if you are going to make Alchemy a central facet of your Sim's character or lifestyle, it's a good idea to invest in one and install it on your lot. It will just save time, rather than visiting a community-based Alchemy Station, such as the station at Aleister's Elixirs & Sundries. Fortunately, there is only one Alchemy Station, so you don't have to juggle upgrades—one and done, you know. Any time spent at the Alchemy Station then starts developing and eventually upgrading the skill.

Level Progression

⬧ When you achieve the first level of the Alchemy skill, you unlock the Mix Elixirs interaction, which allows you to start creating elixirs at the Alchemy Station. At first, you only have access to one recipe: Bliss. (You're also given some free ingredients—check your inventory to see Mandrake, Valerian Root, and more.) However, as you level up the Alchemy skill and uncover new recipe books, you learn new elixirs.

⬧ **Level 1:** Sims can use the Mix Elixirs interaction.

⬧ **Level 6:** Sims have a tunable chance to make 2 elixirs per successful creation attempt.

⬧ **Level 10:** Sims have a tunable chance to create 3 elixirs per successful creation attempt.

PHILOSOPHER'S STONE

The Philosopher's Stone is the pinnacle of the Alchemist skill. When you reach level 10, you can start an Opportunity chain that leads to the creation of the Philosopher's Stone. It can also be purchased as a Lifetime Reward. This object performs two amazing functions: it can bind a ghost to your household, and it will transmute objects into gold.

If you want to Bind a Ghost to Family, click on the Philosopher's Stone and choose that interaction. You get a listing of all of the ghosts in town. You can then pick which ghost you want to have join your household. The ghost is then added and the headstone is placed in the personal inventory. However, if you have a full household (or if a Sim is pregnant with a baby that will fill the household), the interaction is not available.

PHILOSOPHER'S STONE (CONTINUED)

Want to try turning objects into gold? Drag an object on to the pedestal, then click on the Philosopher's Stone and choose Transmute Gold. There's a strong chance the interaction will succeed, and the object will turn into a valuable gold ingot. Sometimes the interaction fails, which ends up destroying the object.

However... there is a very slight risk that the interaction will not only fail, but also totally backfire. The Sim casting the transmutation spell is instead turned into gold. The risk of this occurring significantly rises if you attempt to transmute a very inexpensive object or item into gold.

This, as you might imagine, results in insta-death. The Grim Reaper comes to collect and leaves with his bounty, a glittering ghost. The surviving Sims in the household, though, at least get a gold statue of the recently deceased. To add insult to injury, the statue can be sold for huge Simoleons.

Brewing Elixirs

Now, once you reach level 1 of the Alchemy skill, you unlock the Mix Elixir interaction and can start brewing up a storm on the Alchemy Station. Good to go, right? Hold your horses. You need to keep upgrading the skill to unlock new recipes for different, more powerful elixirs. Plus, certain recipe books at the bookstore are only available to Alchemists at specific levels.

Collecting is the most common method of gathering ingredients.

TIP

The Gatherer trait is exceedingly useful if you are going to pursue the Alchemy skill!

Every recipe requires specific ingredients. These ingredients are found in the wild through collecting, fishing, or purchasing at stores. We have a full recipe list below that reveals what ingredients are required for every recipe. To create an elixir, you must click on the Alchemy Station and choose the Mix interaction. Without the proper ingredients for a specific elixir in your inventory, you cannot select it from the menu. When you create an elixir, the required ingredients are permanently removed from your inventory. However, if you have learned every recipe and satisfied the Master Alchemist challenge, there is a chance you won't use all of the required ingredients.

Introduction

New Simology

New Careers & Skills

Meet the Supernaturals

New Venues

Tour of Moonlight Falls

New Object Catalog

NEW COLLECTION JOURNAL

There's a new method for keeping track of what collectibles are available in your town—the Collection Journal. This journal has a master tab that displays the current statistics for all of your collectibles, including the number of each collectible found and the percentage of unique collectibles in each category (gems, butterflies, etc.) found. Separate tabs itemize each collectible type. These tabs show all of the possible collectibles, the expansion in which the collectible is introduced, rarity, number collected, and the highest value found.

NOTE

The recipes for your elixirs are also stored in your Collection Journal.

Recipe Book	Elixir Learned	Sale Value	Alchemy Skill Level Required
Procreation Elixir Recipe Book	Procreation Elixir	§75	5
Liquid Job Booster Recipe Book	Liquid Job Booster	§132	6
Potent Enlightenment Recipe Book	Vial of Potent Enlightenment	§187	7
Potent Personality Adjuster Recipe Book	Potent Personality Adjuster	§225	8
Fountain of Youth Elixir Recipe Book	Fountain of Youth Elixir	§471	9
Potent Zombification Recipe Book	Potent Zombification	§607	9
Origin of the Tragic Clown Recipe Book	Origin of the Tragic Clown	§800	10

Alchemy Skill Level	Name	Description	Effect When Consumed	Effect When Thrown	Cannot Be Used On	AgeSpeciesAvailability	ServicesAllowed	Active Roles Allowed	Inactive Roles Allowed	Ingredient1	Ingredient2	Ingredient3	BenefitValue
1	Flask of Sleep	Early to bed, early to... zzzzzzzzzzz	Thanks to the Flask of Sleep, Sim can feel the energy draining away as his/her eyelids get very, very heavy.....	This seemed like a good way to get Sim to calm down a little. Sim threw a Flask of Sleep at him/her!		C,T,Y,A,E	Babysitter, Butler, Maid, Repairman	Paparazzi, Tourist, Explorer	Paparazzi, Tourist, Explorer, Generic Merchant, Elixir Shop Merchant, Location Merchant, Special Merchant, Pet Store Merchant, Pianist	Mushroom: Any			-3
1	Ad Nauseum	A nauseating elixir for a nauseating experience.	Sim just consumed an elixir whose sole purpose is to make Sims feel nauseous. Sour milk may have been a cheaper alternative...	After Ad Nauseum exploded all over Sim, he/she started feeling very queasy – partly from the effects of the elixir and partly just from being covered in goop!		C,T,Y,A,E	Babysitter, Butler, Maid, Repairman	Paparazzi, Tourist, Explorer	Paparazzi, Tourist, Explorer, Generic Merchant, Elixir Shop Merchant, Location Merchant, Special Merchant, Pet Store Merchant, Pianist	Insect: Any			-3
1	Vial of Bliss	Sims who drink this won't be bored or lonely anytime soon.	As the old saying goes, you can't bottle happiness. WRONG! Sim drank that bottled happiness and won't be feeling bored or lonely for a while!	Sim is perfectly content at the moment. No need to socialize or have fun. In fact, doing anything at all, no matter how mundane, will be absolutely wonderful.		C,T,Y,A,E	Babysitter, Butler, Maid, Repairman	Paparazzi, Tourist, Explorer	Paparazzi, Tourist, Explorer, Generic Merchant, Elixir Shop Merchant, Location Merchant, Special Merchant, Pet Store Merchant, Pianist	Ingredient: Any			3
1	Invigorating Elixir	Take a sip and stay awake for a long time!	That Invigorating Elixir was great! Sim feels like he/she can do anything without using too much energy.	The Invigorating Elixir gave quite the pick-me-up to Sim. He'll/she'll be feeling that energy boost for hours!		C,T,Y,A,E	Babysitter, Butler, Maid, Repairman	Paparazzi, Tourist, Explorer	Paparazzi, Tourist, Explorer, Generic Merchant, Elixir Shop Merchant, Location Merchant, Special Merchant, Pet Store Merchant, Pianist	Ingredient: Wolfsbane Flower			3
1	Jar of Discord	Provides a small amount of destruction to the relationship with another Sim.	Provides a small amount of destruction to the relationship with another Sim.	Sim just threw discord elixir all over Sim. Yes, some harsh words might have been just as effective, but bonus points for the theatrics.		C,T,Y,A,E	Babysitter, Butler, Maid, Repairman	Paparazzi, Tourist, Explorer	Paparazzi, Tourist, Explorer, Generic Merchant, Elixir Shop Merchant, Location Merchant, Special Merchant, Pet Store Merchant, Pianist	Ingredient: Mandrake Root			-20
2	Cure Elixir***	Magical afflictions vanish without affecting supernatural powers.	Now that's better. Sim used the Cure Elixir and is now free of his/her magical afflictions. Sim is ready to go out and face the world again!	Magical afflictions are no fun for anyone, and Sim understands that. From the kindness of his/her heart, Sim cured Sim!	Mummy, SimBot, Imaginary Friend	C,T,Y,A,E	Babysitter, Butler, Maid, Repairman	Paparazzi, Tourist, Explorer	Paparazzi, Tourist, Explorer, Generic Merchant, Elixir Shop Merchant, Location Merchant, Special Merchant, Pet Store Merchant, Pianist	Ingredient: Red Valerian Root	Ingredient: Mandrake Root		3

Name	Jar of Friendship	Flask of Angry Bees	Zombification*	Melancholy Serum	Vampiric Sunscreen	Vial of Enlightenment
Alchemy Skill Level	2	2	3	3	3	3
Description	Break the ice and become a slightly better friend with someone.	A swarm of angry bees in a bottle ready to attack!	Get a brief craving for brains by temporarily turning into a zombie.	This will make anyone feel the need to have fun and socialize but, struggle with both.	Vampires can enjoy time in the sun without any nasty side effects.	Take a sip and settle down for a rest to gain a quick skill boost!
Effect When Consumed	Sim liked himself/herself just fine before. But now he/she is BFFs...with himself/herself.	Sim is a glutton for punishment and made a very interesting decision by deliberately throwing an elixir to cause a swarm of bees to attack.	Realizing how easy zombies have it, Sim decided to chug a Zombification elixir, stagger around for a little while, and turn off his/her braaaaiiiiiinnn....	No matter how much fun something is, Sim will get bored of it right away. Even worse, Sim is feeling socially awkward and can't seem to socialize right now...	Sim is feeling extra sparkly! He/she won't have to worry anytime soon about the badness that happens when vampires go out into the sun!	Sim has an exciting tingle in the brain as if some incredible discovery is almost within reach! Take a nap and see what epiphanies await!
Effect When Thrown	Many relationships have started with potent liquids. In this case, Sim used a Friendship elixir to become friends with Sim.	These bees aren't beehaving! A swarm of angry bees was unleashed upon Sim, courtesy of Sim.	Not realizing how easy it is to kick off the zombie apocalypse, Sim tossed a bottle of Zombification directly at Sim. Deliberately.	After being doused with Melancholy Serum, Sim thinks that socializing or doing anything fun is about as enjoyable as getting doused with Melancholy Serum.	Vampires don't get enough sun, but now Sim doesn't have any excuses! He/she can get a tan without having to worry about catching on fire thanks to the Vampiric Sunscreen.	There are many ways to share enlightenment. Sim just chose the way where you throw a bottle of liquid at Sim.
Cannot Be Used On		Mummy, SimBot	Mummy, SimBot, Imaginary Friend			
AgeSpeciesAvailability	C,T,Y,A,E	C,T,Y,A,E	Y,A,E	C,T,Y,A,E	C,T,Y,A,E	C,T,Y,A,E
ServicesAllowed	Babysitter, Butler, Maid, Repairman	Babysitter, Butler, Maid, Repairman	Babysitter, Butler, Maid, Repairman	Babysitter, Butler, Maid, Repairman	Babysitter, Butler, Maid, Repairman	Babysitter, Butler, Maid, Repairman
Active Roles Allowed	Paparazzi, Tourist, Explorer	Paparazzi, Tourist, Explorer	Paparazzi, Tourist, Explorer	Paparazzi, Tourist, Explorer	Paparazzi, Tourist, Explorer	Paparazzi, Tourist, Explorer
Inactive Roles Allowed	Paparazzi, Tourist, Explorer, Generic Merchant, Elixir Shop Merchant, Location Merchant, Special Merchant, Pet Store Merchant, Pianist	Paparazzi, Tourist, Explorer, Generic Merchant, Elixir Shop Merchant, Location Merchant, Special Merchant, Pet Store Merchant, Pianist	Paparazzi, Tourist, Explorer, Generic Merchant, Elixir Shop Merchant, Location Merchant, Special Merchant, Pet Store Merchant, Pianist	Paparazzi, Tourist, Explorer, Generic Merchant, Elixir Shop Merchant, Location Merchant, Special Merchant, Pet Store Merchant, Pianist	Paparazzi, Tourist, Explorer, Generic Merchant, Elixir Shop Merchant, Location Merchant, Special Merchant, Pet Store Merchant, Pianist	Paparazzi, Tourist, Explorer, Generic Merchant, Elixir Shop Merchant, Location Merchant, Special Merchant, Pet Store Merchant, Pianist
Ingredient1	Ingredient: Red Valerian Root	Ingredient: Beeswax	Ingredient: Mandrake Root	Ingredient: Mandrake Root	Metal: Any	Mushroom: Any
Ingredient2		Ingredient: Honey	Mushroom: Any	Fish: Any	Insect: Any	Gem: Any
Ingredient3			Insect: Any			
BenefitValue	40	-15	-20	-3	0	8

	Essence of Magic	Lean and Mean	Large and in Charge	Vial of Potent Bliss	Skill Booster	Flask of Potent Sleep
BenefitValue	3	8	-8	8	3	-8
Ingredient3						
Ingredient2	Mushroom: Any	Ingredient: Apple	Ingredient: Links	Ingredient: Red Toadstools	Gem: Any	Ingredient: Red Toadstools
Ingredient1	Ingredient: Honey	Ingredient: Wolfsbane Flower	Ingredient: Wolfsbane Flower	Ingredient: Any	Ingredient: Red Valerian Root	Mushroom: Red Toadstools
Inactive Roles Allowed	Paparazzi, Tourist, Explorer, Generic Merchant, Elixir Shop Merchant, Location Merchant, Special Merchant, Pet Store Merchant, Pianist	Paparazzi, Tourist, Explorer, Generic Merchant, Elixir Shop Merchant, Location Merchant, Special Merchant, Pet Store Merchant, Pianist	Paparazzi, Tourist, Explorer, Generic Merchant, Elixir Shop Merchant, Location Merchant, Special Merchant, Pet Store Merchant, Pianist	Paparazzi, Tourist, Explorer, Generic Merchant, Elixir Shop Merchant, Location Merchant, Special Merchant, Pet Store Merchant, Pianist	Paparazzi, Tourist, Explorer, Generic Merchant, Elixir Shop Merchant, Location Merchant, Special Merchant, Pet Store Merchant, Pianist	Paparazzi, Tourist, Explorer, Generic Merchant, Elixir Shop Merchant, Location Merchant, Special Merchant, Pet Store Merchant, Pianist
Active Roles Allowed	Paparazzi, Tourist, Explorer	Paparazzi, Tourist, Explorer	Paparazzi, Tourist, Explorer	Paparazzi, Tourist, Explorer	Paparazzi, Tourist, Explorer	Paparazzi, Tourist, Explorer
ServicesAllowed	Babysitter, Butler, Maid, Repairman	Babysitter, Butler, Maid, Repairman	Babysitter, Butler, Maid, Repairman	Babysitter, Butler, Maid, Repairman	Babysitter, Butler, Maid, Repairman	Babysitter, Butler, Maid, Repairman
AgeSpeciesAvailability	T,Y,A,E	C,T,Y,A,E	C,T,Y,A,E	C,T,Y,A,E	C,T,Y,A,E	C,T,Y,A,E
Cannot Be Used On		SimBot	SimBot			
Effect When Thrown	Sim threw some Essence of Magic at Sim for a magical pick-me-up. It's magic time for Sim!	Diet drinks never worked for Sim before. Maybe it was all that fake sugar. But who cares? Time to go shopping for new clothes!	BOOM! Thanks to that sudden splash of Large and in Charge, Sim is large, in charge, wet, and confused.	No one likes feeling like a wet blanket. And thanks to the Vial of Potent Bliss Sim just showered in, it'll be impossible NOT to have a great time for the foreseeable future!	Sim is short on time and needs help towards self-improvement. Thanks to Sim, that's not a problem and Sim just took a small step in improving one of his/her skills.	There are many way to get someone to sleep but Sim opted to toss a Flask of Potent Sleep from afar. Now it's night-night for Sim!
Effect When Consumed	Sim was feeling magically exhausted but not anymore! He/she is ready to use his/her magical powers again!	Sim just discovered how slimming elixirs can be. Isn't that more effective than diet fads and gimmicky exercise equipment?	Who has time to not exercise and eat junk food? BOOM! Sim found a shortcut and is now large and in charge!	WHOOOOO!!! One sip and Sim feels like he's/she's having the time of his/her life! Now that Sim doesn't have to worry about socializing or having fun for a very long time, there are probably more productive things to accomplish.	And just like that, Sim got a small boost towards improving a skill to become an even more productive Sim.	Sometimes counting sheep just doesn't do the trick. Sim feels drained of energy and wants some much needed sleep thanks to the Flask of Potent Sleep.
Description	Restore a fairy's or witch's magic power!	Get fit and trim without hitting the gym.	Take a drink and gain weight the quick and easy way!	Find long-lasting happiness, no matter how miserable or boring life really is.	Get a small boost towards improving a skill.	Put a Sim on the express train to dreamland.
Name	Essence of Magic	Lean and Mean	Large and in Charge	Vial of Potent Bliss	Skill Booster	Flask of Potent Sleep
Alchemy Skill Level	4	4	4	4	4	5

Alchemy Skill Level	Name	Description	Effect When Consumed	Effect When Thrown	Cannot Be Used On	AgeSpeciesAvailability	ServicesAllowed	Active Roles Allowed	Inactive Roles Allowed	Ingredient1	Ingredient2	Ingredient3	BenefitValue
5	Potent Melancholy Serum	The perfect antidote to having fun or enjoying the company of others.	Sim has, to use the medical terminology, a serious case of the blahs. If anything or anyone seems even remotely interesting, it won't be for very long. Thanks a lot, Potent Melancholy Serum.	Being social and having fun? Has Sim ever known such a thing? Thanks to that splash of Potent Melancholy Serum, it's hard for him/her to even remember now.		C,T,Y,A,E	Babysitter, Butler, Maid, Repairman	Paparazzi, Tourist, Explorer	Paparazzi, Tourist, Explorer, Generic Merchant, Elixir Shop Merchant, Location Merchant, Special Merchant, Pet Store Merchant, Pianist	Ingredient: Mandrake Root	Fish: Any	Ingredient: Spotlight Mushrooms	-8
5	Personality Adjuster	Take the first step in becoming a new Sim with a small change to your personality.	Sim needed a change, and a new hair color just wasn't going to cut it. Thanks to the Personality Adjuster Elixir, he/she discovered a whole new facet of his/her personality!	Sim needed an attitude adjustment, and Sim was happy to facilitate that with a Personality Adjuster elixir. What new trait will Sim exhibit now?		C,T,Y,A,E	Babysitter, Butler, Maid, Repairman	Paparazzi, Tourist, Explorer	Paparazzi, Tourist, Explorer, Generic Merchant, Elixir Shop Merchant, Location Merchant, Special Merchant, Pet Store Merchant, Pianist	Ingredient: Red Valerian Root	Insect: Monarch Butterfly		0
5	Procreation Elixir*	The chance of conception is increased and twins and triplets are also very likely.	Sim wants a larger family, and now's the time! Sim might get more than he/she bargained for with twins or triplets!	Sim decided that Sim could use a larger family. Sim better get ready! his/her family is about to grow!	SimBot	Y,A,E	Babysitter, Butler, Maid, Repairman	Paparazzi, Tourist, Explorer	Paparazzi, Tourist, Explorer, Generic Merchant, Elixir Shop Merchant, Location Merchant, Special Merchant, Pet Store Merchant, Pianist	Ingredient: Wolfsbane Flower	Ingredient: Red Toadstools		15
6	Jar of Potent Discord	Instantly destroys any Sim's relationship with another.	Great. Now Sim has used an elixir to take vague feelings of doubt and insecurity and blow them up into true self-loathing.	Sim has had it with Sim! Now Sim and Sim absolutely despise each other.		C,T,Y,A,E	Babysitter, Butler, Maid, Repairman	Paparazzi, Tourist, Explorer	Paparazzi, Tourist, Explorer, Generic Merchant, Elixir Shop Merchant, Location Merchant, Special Merchant, Pet Store Merchant, Pianist	Ingredient: Mandrake Root	Ingredient: Beeswax		-200

	Liquid Job Booster	Jar of Potent Friendship	Potent Invigorating Elixir	Bottled Mummy Curse */**	Potent Cure Elixir
BenefitValue	15	200	8	0	20
Ingredient3				Fish: Black Goldfish	Gem: Ruby
Ingredient2	Ingredient: Spotlight Mushrooms	Ingredient: Beeswax	Ingredient: Spotlight Mushrooms	Insect: Scarab Beetle	Ingredient: Glow Orbs
Ingredient1	Gem: Smoky Quartz	Ingredient: Red Valerian Root	Ingredient: Wolfsbane Flower	Insect: Crypt Moth	Ingredient: Wolfsbane Flower
Inactive Roles Allowed	Paparazzi, Tourist, Explorer, Generic Merchant, Elixir Shop Merchant, Location Merchant, Special Merchant, Pet Store Merchant, Pianist	Paparazzi, Tourist, Explorer, Generic Merchant, Elixir Shop Merchant, Location Merchant, Special Merchant, Pet Store Merchant, Pianist	Paparazzi, Tourist, Explorer, Generic Merchant, Elixir Shop Merchant, Location Merchant, Special Merchant, Pet Store Merchant, Pianist	Paparazzi, Tourist, Explorer, Generic Merchant, Elixir Shop Merchant, Location Merchant, Special Merchant, Pet Store Merchant, Pianist	Paparazzi, Tourist, Explorer, Generic Merchant, Elixir Shop Merchant, Location Merchant, Special Merchant, Pet Store Merchant, Pianist
Active Roles Allowed	Paparazzi, Tourist, Explorer	Paparazzi, Tourist, Explorer	Paparazzi, Tourist, Explorer	Paparazzi, Tourist, Explorer	Paparazzi, Tourist, Explorer
ServicesAllowed	Babysitter, Butler, Maid, Repairman	Babysitter, Butler, Maid, Repairman	Babysitter, Butler, Maid, Repairman	Babysitter, Butler, Maid, Repairman	Babysitter, Butler, Maid, Repairman
AgeSpeciesAvailability	C,T,Y,A,E	C,T,Y,A,E	C,T,Y,A,E	Y,A,E	C,T,Y,A,E
Cannot Be Used On				Mummy, Imaginary Friend, Unicorn	Imaginary Friend
Effect When Thrown	It's a strange way to increase productivity, but Sim has successfully been doused with Liquid Job Booster!	Sim was wanting a new best friend to spend quality time with. Sim is the lucky Sim to become the new "besty."	Sim received a sudden burst of energy from the Potent Invigorating Elixir! Expect to see him/her running around since he/she has more important things to do than sleep.	I want my mummy! Sim is now under wraps!	Sim understands that traditional supernatural and magic affliction cures are difficult to use. That's why Sim just got a splash of the Potent Cure Elixir. Sim is now a normal, human Sim!
Effect When Consumed	A quick shot of Liquid Job Booster and Sim is making the other employees look like slackers! That next promotion can't be far off now!	The Jar of Potent Friendship confirmed what Sim already knew: he's/she's already on good terms with himself/herself. Sim is in a better mood for confirming this.	Suddenly Sim feels like running a marathon! He's/she's bursting with energy! See how much Sim can accomplish without the need to sleep!	Sim got so wrapped up in thinking about mummies that he/she used Bottled Mummy Curse and poof! Sim is now a mummy!	After using the Potent Cure Elixir, Sim feels... different. Magical afflictions appear to be gone... maybe a little weaker, but definitely more human? It worked! Sim is cured!!
Description	Impress your co-workers for a day and show them a thing or two about working!	Gain a new best friend in a jiffy with this powerful elixir.	Better than coffee, this elixir gives an invigorating boost of energy without the crash.	The curse of a mummy in a convenient, easy to carry bottle.	Tired of being cursed, inhuman or undead? Use this.
Name	Liquid Job Booster	Jar of Potent Friendship	Potent Invigorating Elixir	Bottled Mummy Curse*/**	Potent Cure Elixir
Alchemy Skill Level	6	6	6	7	7

	Vial of Potent Enlightenment	Opposite Personality	Bottled Vampire's Bite*/**	Clone Drone*	Bottled SimBot Converter*/**
BenefitValue	15	0	0	0	0
Ingredient3	Ingredient: Red Toadstools	Ingredient: Mycenas	Fish: Vampire Fish	Gem: Diamond	Metal: Palladium
Ingredient2	Gem: Emerald	Metal: Any	Gem: Bloodstone	Fish: Luminous Salamander	Metal: Gold
Ingredient1	Mushroom: Any	Fish: Toad	Ingredient: Red Valerian Root	Metal: Any	Metal: Iron
Inactive Roles Allowed	Paparazzi, Tourist, Explorer, Generic Merchant, Elixir Shop Merchant, Location Merchant, Special Merchant, Pet Store Merchant, Pianist	Paparazzi, Tourist, Explorer, Generic Merchant, Elixir Shop Merchant, Location Merchant, Special Merchant, Pet Store Merchant, Pianist	Paparazzi, Tourist, Explorer, Generic Merchant, Elixir Shop Merchant, Location Merchant, Special Merchant, Pet Store Merchant, Pianist	Paparazzi, Tourist, Explorer, Generic Merchant, Elixir Shop Merchant, Location Merchant, Special Merchant, Pet Store Merchant, Pianist	Paparazzi, Tourist, Explorer, Generic Merchant, Elixir Shop Merchant, Location Merchant, Special Merchant, Pet Store Merchant, Pianist
Active Roles Allowed	Paparazzi, Tourist, Explorer	Paparazzi, Tourist, Explorer	Paparazzi, Tourist, Explorer	Paparazzi, Tourist, Explorer	Paparazzi, Tourist, Explorer
ServicesAllowed	Babysitter, Butler, Maid, Repairman	Babysitter, Butler, Maid, Repairman	Babysitter, Butler, Maid, Repairman	Babysitter, Butler, Maid, Repairman	Babysitter, Butler, Maid, Repairman
AgeSpeciesAvailability	C,T,Y,A,E	C,T,Y,A,E	C,T,Y,A,E	C,T,Y,A,E	Y,A,E
Cannot Be Used On			Vampire, Imaginary Friend, Unicorn	Imaginary Friend	SimBot, Imaginary Friend, Unicorn
Effect When Thrown	Sim might not realize it yet, but the next time he/she falls asleep his/her brain is going to accomplish amazing things. Sim will improve some skill thanks to the Vial of Potent Enlightenment.	Sim will now behave like someone completely different. If Sim liked this Sim, this might be a bad thing, but if Sim hated this Sim, congratulations! Maybe they can be friends now!	Sim has been changed into a vampire, and without any of the usual mess (except for all the spilled liquid and broken glass).	Hopefully Sim isn't angry that Sim threw a Clone Drone his/her way, because now it's two against one.	Sim just got a metallic taste in his/her mouth. And everywhere else.
Effect When Consumed	Sim has a perfectly clear mind. While he/she is so receptive to new ideas, Sim should sleep and see what epiphanies his/her unconscious can unlock. Who knows what skills Sim will improve!	Sim just stepped through the looking glass by drinking the Opposite Personality elixir. Everything that was once frightening or repellant now seems to be calling out with a siren's song! But is this new Sim an improvement?	Sim is now a full-fledged vampire after using the Bottled vampire's Bite! No partially-fledged vampires here!	Sim has successfully created a clone using the Clone Drone. BUT WHICH IS THE ORIGINAL AND WHICH THE COPY?! Just kidding, your Sim is the original.	Bloop bleep bloop bleep! Sim better get used to speaking in ones and zeros now that he/she is a genuine SimBot!
Description	A supercharged elixir that will bring a skill boost to any Sim.	Make Opposite Day permanent for a Sim's personality with this elixir!	A vampire's bite in bottled form to turn a Sim into a vampire!	Create the perfect (or possibly evil) clone of any Sim.	Gain a shiny metal body by becoming a SimBot!
Name	Vial of Potent Enlightenment	Opposite Personality	Bottled Vampire's Bite*/**	Clone Drone*	Bottled SimBot Converter*/**
Alchemy Skill Level	7	7	7	8	8

BenefitValue	8	0	0	-20	0
Ingredient3	Ingredient: Red Valerian Root	Metal: Silver	Ingredient: Glow Orbs	Insect: Rhinocerous Beetle	Gem: Moonstone
Ingredient2	Fish: Any	Gem: Moonstone	Insect: Monarch Butterfly	Ingredient: Glow Orbs	Insect: Light Beetle
Ingredient1	Insect: Royal Purple Butterfly	Ingredient: Wolfsbane Flower	Ingredient: Red Valerian Root	Ingredient: Mandrake Root	Fish: Toad
Inactive Roles Allowed	Paparazzi, Tourist, Explorer, Generic Merchant, Elixir Shop Merchant, Location Merchant, Special Merchant, Pet Store Merchant, Pianist	Paparazzi, Tourist, Explorer, Generic Merchant, Elixir Shop Merchant, Location Merchant, Special Merchant, Pet Store Merchant, Pianist	Paparazzi, Tourist, Explorer, Generic Merchant, Elixir Shop Merchant, Location Merchant, Special Merchant, Pet Store Merchant, Pianist	Paparazzi, Tourist, Explorer, Generic Merchant, Elixir Shop Merchant, Location Merchant, Special Merchant, Pet Store Merchant, Pianist	Paparazzi, Tourist, Explorer, Generic Merchant, Elixir Shop Merchant, Location Merchant, Special Merchant, Pet Store Merchant, Pianist
Active Roles Allowed	Paparazzi, Tourist, Explorer	Paparazzi, Tourist, Explorer	Paparazzi, Tourist, Explorer	Paparazzi, Tourist, Explorer	Paparazzi, Tourist, Explorer
ServicesAllowed	Babysitter, Butler, Maid, Repairman	Babysitter, Butler, Maid, Repairman	Babysitter, Butler, Maid, Repairman	Babysitter, Butler, Maid, Repairman	Babysitter, Butler, Maid, Repairman
AgeSpeciesAvailability	C,T,Y,A,E	C,T,Y,A,E	C,T,Y,A,E	Y,A,E	C,T,Y,A,E
Cannot Be Used On	Mummy, SimBot, Imaginary Friend	Imaginary Friend, Unicorn, werewolf		Mummy, SimBot, Imaginary Friend	Imaginary Friend, Unicorn, witch
Effect When Thrown	While Sim was pondering what it must feel like to be older, Sim read his/her mind and finished the thought!	Sim has become a werewolf Bites he/she can protect himself/herself against, but he/she never expected a bottle of liquid curse!	Some people will just never change. But Sim will completely change when Sim throws a Potent Personality Adjuster at him/her and replaces all of his/her traits with new ones!	Zombie outbreaks are usually an accident, but not this time! Sim used Potent Zombification on Sim.	Sim has been looking for a way to introduce a little more magic to his/her life. Assuming he/she meant that as literally as possible, Sim soaked him/her with a batch of Witches' Brew – guaranteed to turn any Sim into a powerful witch!
Effect When Consumed	Sim was sick and tired of being too young, and decided to do something about it. It's great being older!	Sim has just become a slave to the full moon by using the Bottled Curse of the Lycan. Better start practicing that howl – things are going to be different during the next full moon!	Ready for a whole new Sim? The Potent Personality Adjuster has completely scrambled his/her personality. Hopefully the world is ready.	Wanting the never ending zombie experience, Sim used Potent Zombification and now has an indefinite craving for braaaaaiiiinnnnnsssss... braaaaaiiiinnnnnsssssss!!!!!!	Sim chuckles to think of all the kids studying for years to become witches. All Sim had to do was use Bottled Witches' Brew!
Description	It's like the Fountain of Youth, except the exact opposite!	Unleash your inner beast and become a werewolf with this elixir.	Take a spin on the Personality Roulette Wheel!	When temporarily being a zombie just isn't enough!	Grant the gift of magic by turning any Sim into a witch.
Name	Age of Instant*	Bottled Curse of the Lycan*/**	Potent Personality Adjuster	Potent Zombification*	Bottled Witches' Brew*/**
Alchemy Skill Level	8	8	8	9	9

	Fountain of Youth Elixir*	Vial of Bottled Genie*/**	Potent Skill Booster*	Midas Touch	Origin of the Tragic Clown*	Bottled Blessing of the Fae*/**
BenefitValue	0	0	15	20	-20	0
Ingredient3	Mushroom: Any	Insect: Firefly purpureus	Ingredient: Mycenas	Fish: Luminous Salamander	Fish: Tragic Clownfish	Fish: Fairy Damsel
Ingredient2	Insect: Green Swallowtail Butterfly	Insect: Firefly caeruleus	Gem: Any	Gem: Yellow Sapphire	Ingredient: Mycenas	Gem: Sunstone
Ingredient1	Gem: Tanzanite	Insect: Firefly pratinus	Ingredient: Red Valerian Root	Metal: Gold	Insect: Any	Ingredient: Red Toadstools
Inactive Roles Allowed	Paparazzi, Tourist, Explorer, Generic Merchant, Elixir Shop Merchant, Location Merchant, Special Merchant, Pet Store Merchant, Pianist	Paparazzi, Tourist, Explorer, Generic Merchant, Elixir Shop Merchant, Location Merchant, Special Merchant, Pet Store Merchant, Pianist	Paparazzi, Tourist, Explorer, Generic Merchant, Elixir Shop Merchant, Location Merchant, Special Merchant, Pet Store Merchant, Pianist	Paparazzi, Tourist, Explorer, Generic Merchant, Elixir Shop Merchant, Location Merchant, Special Merchant, Pet Store Merchant, Pianist	Paparazzi, Tourist, Explorer, Generic Merchant, Elixir Shop Merchant, Location Merchant, Special Merchant, Pet Store Merchant, Pianist	Paparazzi, Tourist, Explorer, Generic Merchant, Elixir Shop Merchant, Location Merchant, Special Merchant, Pet Store Merchant, Pianist
Active Roles Allowed	Paparazzi, Tourist, Explorer	Paparazzi, Tourist, Explorer	Paparazzi, Tourist, Explorer	Paparazzi, Tourist, Explorer	Paparazzi, Tourist, Explorer	Paparazzi, Tourist, Explorer
ServicesAllowed	Babysitter, Butler, Maid, Repairman	Babysitter, Butler, Maid, Repairman	Babysitter, Butler, Maid, Repairman	Babysitter, Butler, Maid, Repairman	Babysitter, Butler, Maid, Repairman	Babysitter, Butler, Maid, Repairman
AgeSpeciesAvailability	Y,A,E	C,T,Y,A,E	C,T,Y,A,E	Y,A,E	C,T,Y,A,E	C,T,Y,A,E
Cannot Be Used On	Mummy, SimBot, Imaginary Friend	Imaginary Friend, Unicorn, Genie			Mummy, SimBot, Imaginary Friend, werewolf, Unicorn	Imaginary Friend, Unicorn, fairy
Effect When Thrown	Whoa! What just happened? Sim was just minding their own business and all of a sudden he/she is now younger!	Hoping he/she could bum a few wishes, Sim threw a Vial of Bottled Genie at Sim and turned him/her into a genie.	Sim just had an amazing epiphany! A skill that was once so confusing and difficult is suddenly so ridiculously simple!	Sim is experiencing a sudden lust for gold after being hit with the Midas Touch. He/she should be careful about what he/she touches until the effect wears off!	Sim just gave Sim the gifts of a horrifying visage and a questionable wardrobe upgrade. Sim is the Tragic Clown. There is no escape.	Who wouldn't want a bottle of liquid wings? Sim used the potent essences in this elixir to transform Sim into a shimmery-winged fairy!
Effect When Consumed	Sim wanted to take a trip down memory lane, and there's no better way to do it than becoming a younger Sim.	The genie is literally out of the bottle after Sim used a Vial of Bottled Genie. Sim always wished for this moment and can't believe it came true!	Phew! So many skills and so little time to get better at them. Sim gained a huge boost towards mastering a skill.	ZAM! Sim can feel the Touch tingling in his/her fingertips. Try using the Midas Touch interaction on various things or even Sims to give them a golden sheen.	Tragedy has arrived... Sim is the Tragic Clown. There is no escape! It's just so tragic!!	The proof is in the wings! Sim used the Bottled Blessing of the Fae and has been transformed into a fairy!
Description	When being old is getting old, reverse the aging process with this elixir.	No, this isn't a bottled genie, but it will turn Sims into a genie!	Take a mammoth leap towards becoming more proficient in a skill.	Grants the golden finger to turn objects and other Sims into gold!	A clown costume in a bottle! Warning: May cause depression.	Become the fairy you always wanted to be!
Name	Fountain of Youth Elixir*	Vial of Bottled Genie*/**	Potent Skill Booster*	Midas Touch	Origin of the Tragic Clown*	Bottled Blessing of the Fae*/**
Alchemy Skill Level	9	9	9	10	10	10

Attribute	Wish Enhancing Serum	Pollen Punch
Alchemy Skill Level	10	10
Name	Wish Enhancing Serum	Pollen Punch
Description	Double down on lifetime happiness!	Sims go crazy for this sweet, all-natural treat!
Effect When Consumed	With the power of the Wish Enhancing Serum, Sim wants to achieve his/her goals twice as badly. And the satisfaction from achieving those goals is going to be twice as good!	Yum! Sim is feeling full and in an especially good mood thanks to the Pollen Punch!
Effect When Thrown	Sim looked like he/she could use a little more satisfaction out of life, and thanks to Sim, he/she will feel twice as happy from realizing his/her wishes thanks to a dash of the Wish Enhancing Serum.	Sim was nice and treated Sim to some Pollen Punch. Sim has a full tummy and is in a better mood now!
Cannot Be Used On		
AgeSpeciesAvailability	C,T,Y,A,E	C,T,Y,A,E
ServicesAllowed	Babysitter, Butler, Maid, Repairman	Babysitter, Butler, Maid, Repairman
Active Roles Allowed	Paparazzi, Tourist, Explorer	Paparazzi, Tourist, Explorer
Inactive Roles Allowed	Paparazzi, Tourist, Explorer, Generic Merchant, Elixir Shop Merchant, Location Merchant, Special Merchant, Pet Store Merchant, Pianist	Paparazzi, Tourist, Explorer, Generic Merchant, Elixir Shop Merchant, Location Merchant, Special Merchant, Pet Store Merchant, Pianist
Ingredient1	Insect: Red Admiral Butterfly	
Ingredient2	Gem: Any	
Ingredient3	Mushroom: Glow Orbs	
BenefitValue	20	

* = Cannot consume if pregnant

** Cannot consume as ghost

***Fail notice: Sim was already healthy before experiencing the Cure Elixir, so it had no effect. Fortunately, that also means there were no negative side-effects to worry about.

TIP

Some recipes are rewards for completing Opportunities.

THROWING ELIXIRS

While many elixirs can be used on yourself, you can also use them on other Sims. Throwing an elixir at another Sim unleashes its effect on them, but not necessarily with 100 percent accuracy or reliability. All of the effects of throwing an elixir are in the recipe table above.

Though throwing an elixir appears as a social interaction in the menu, it's really an action. But that doesn't mean it doesn't have an affect on LTR. If a throw is "accepted," the reaction is positive—the throw then has a Friendly STC and increases LTR. If the throw is received as a negative, it results in a Steamed STC and negative effect on LTR.

There are sneakier ways to get elixirs into other Sims. You can Mix Into Drink, which hides the elixir in a regular glass. The glass can be placed into your inventory, in a fridge, or left out on a surface. Leaving a drink out, though, may have unintended consequences, though, if the wrong Sim guzzles it.

Skill Challenges

Excellent Elixirs

♦ **Requirement:** Create 150 elixirs.

♦ **Reward:** All elixirs created by Sim will produce three vials every time.

Master Alchemist

♦ **Requirement:** Learn all Alchemy Recipes.

♦ **Reward:** Occasionally, brewed recipes will not use all the ingredients. Also, prices are discounted at Aleister's Elixirs & Sundries.

Alchemists Anonymous

♦ **Requirement:** Throw 50 elixirs at other Sims.

♦ **Reward:** Never lose LTR for throwing a harmful elixir at another Sim. In addition, increased positive LTR for throwing a beneficial elixir at another Sim.

Tracked Statistics

- Number of Alchemy elixirs created
- Number of Sims turned into supernaturals
- Number of supernaturals turned into humans
- Number of Alchemy Recipes discovered (out of 44)
- Elixirs thrown at other Sims
- Simoleons earned selling elixirs

Skill Memories

- Created First Alchemy Elixir (once only)
- Learned Your First Alchemy Recipe (once only)
- Created Clone Drone Elixir (once only)
- Created Midas Touch Elixir (once only)
- Created Origin of the Tragic Clown Elixir (once only)
- Created Opposite Personality Elixir (once only)
- Created Zombified Elixir (once only)
- Created a Batch of Elixirs (once only)

Skill Achievements

- Create 300 Elixirs
- Turn 15 Sims into supernatural beings (fairies, vampires, werewolves)
- Cure 15 Sims of their supernatural status
- Use X of [specified Elixir]
- Use X Elixirs
- Create [specified Elixir]
- Turn Sim into [specified supernatural type]
- Throw a [Specified Elixir] at another Sim
- Throw X Elixirs at other Sims

HIDDEN SKILLS

As you know from *The Sims 3* and previous expansions, there are hidden skills as well as those you develop at venues or outwardly on books and objects. These skills are not tracked in the Skill Journal and you never see a progress meter above your Sims' head while working on them. Previous hidden skills include Chess or Arcade Game. In *Supernatural*, there are hidden skills related to many of the supernaturals, such as Lycanthropy for werewolves. Those hidden skills are detailed in the Meet the Supernaturals chapter.

Broom Riding is a hidden skill. Whenever any Sim rides a broom or flies around the arena, they develop the behind-the-scenes Broom Riding skill. The higher this skill, the better chance they have at pulling off some insane stunts at the arena, which in turn satisfies the Fun need to a greater degree. And if the Sim is stunt-riding for tips, an improved Broom Riding skill can lead to bigger post-ride paydays!

As mentioned in the New Object Catalog chapter, the hidden Arcade skill returns. Here, you develop the skill by playing Smack-A-Gnome! and The Claaaaw. The more you play, the better you do at these games. Not only does

this result in higher scores, but also more Fun and increased Social bumps when audiences watch. If you need to bump mood, being able to get a sweet boost from a short gaming session is really beneficial.

The hidden Dance skill is also woven into *Supernatural*. Whenever you dance at an audio object, you increase your Dance skill. The longer you dance, the better your moves, which in turn means you have more Fun and you decrease the odds of embarrassing yourself.

WWW.PRIMAGAMES.COM

Meet the Supernaturals

• • • •

Supernatural doesn't always equate with horror. Beings and powers that exist just outside the reach of the natural world aren't evil by definition, and in *The Sims 3 Supernatural*, your personal storytelling will serve to prove that witches and werewolves, magic elixirs and spectral forces can be rather fun.

When you launch a new lifetime or a new narrative in *Supernatural*, one of the most important choices you make is which supernatural being to become. Or, decide to remain steadfastly human in a world that walks on the wild side. Every supernatural type you can select in Create a Sim (or convert to in the active world once your story has started to unfold), has strengths and weaknesses, exclusive benefits, and special interactions that will help you conjure up exciting narratives. Will you wolf out under the gauzy glow of a full moon? Or seductively bare your fangs as a vampire lothario? Or flit about town, sprinkling Fairy Dust upon those who could use a little magic in their lives? These are just some of the possible scenarios that await when your cursor hovers over the supernatural type choice in Create a Sim.

To best prepare you for that decision, or to aid in your mid-game exploits as any of the supernaturals, peruse this chapter for complete rundowns on every being, plus an explanation of the lunar cycle, which is directly wired to several supernatural features for beings such as the werewolf.

LUNAR CYCLE

When that silvery disc bares its all, strange things happen in Moonlight Falls—or any city you call home while playing *Supernatural*. The lunar cycle can trigger all sorts of goings-on in town, such as heralding the arrival of zombies to affecting the transformation of werewolves. The stages of the moon are:

◊ New Moon

◊ Full Moon

◊ Waxing Crescent

◊ Waning Gibbous

◊ First Quarter

◊ Third Quarter

◊ Waxing Gibbous

◊ Waning Crescent

You can always look up into the sky are behold the moon, but there's an all-new quick-glance meter right on your Sim's toolbar. Look next to your Sim's portrait. That's the Moon icon. Mouse over the Moon Icon to not only get a reading of the phase, but also the number of days until the next full moon.

 Now, you do not have to wait for the moon to complete a normal cycle. You have full control over the lunar cycle in the Options menu. Click on the Lunar tab. Here, you can adjust the frequency of the phases or even lock in a particular phase. Because there are specific actions that unfold when the moon is full, there are definite reasons/uses for setting up a constant full moon.

The default lunar cycle is 6 days/6 phases. You can shrink that to as short as 2 days or stretch it into 10 days—with multiple options between:

◊ 2 days: New Moon, Full Moon

◊ 4 days: New Moon, First Quarter, Full Moon, Third Quarter

◊ 6 days: New Moon, Waxing Crescent, Waxing Gibbous, Full Moon, Waning Gibbous, Waning Crescent

◊ 8 days: New Moon, Waxing Crescent, First Quarter, Waxing Gibbous, Full Moon, Waning Gibbous, Third Quarter, Waning Crescent

◊ 10 days: New Moon, Waxing Crescent, First Quarter, First Quarter, Waxing Gibbous, Full Moon, Waning Gibbous, Third Quarter, Third Quarter, Waning Crescent

As mentioned, the full moon is when the supernatural goes full-tilt boogie. Up to three Sims in the city turn into zombies (meaning, they have the Zombified moodlet) during a full moon. (This excludes werewolves and Sims within your own household.) Many more ghosts drift through the town during the full moon, too. NPC werewolves in town turn feral during a full moon. And if you have *Pets* installed, some of your animals may get the Skittish moodlet.

This is the core of the lunar cycle, but you'll find more about how it specifically affects different supernaturals in their individual sections. Just know this: all the suspicions that a full moon brings out the bizarre in our world are proved true inside the realm of *Supernatural*.

BROWNIE BITES

Eager to have a baby? Then look to the night sky. WooHooing beneath a full moon increases your odds of pregnancy.

Werewolves

Howl at the moon, y'all. Werewolf Sims, powerful beings of strength and sometimes unchecked emotion, are a brand-new addition to *The Sims 3* universe. Werewolves must strike a fragile balance between a normal life and their animal instincts, which manifest as a fearsome (and occasionally funny) wolf form due to the Werewolves Curse.

Werewolves, like pack dogs, are social creatures and prefer to exist in the company of other lycanthropes. Not that there aren't a few lone wolves and alpha dogs who prefer to buck the social order of a pack and assert either dominance or self-reliance. In groups, werewolves can often get a little rowdy and possess a series of social functions that reflect this mindset. Werewolves also display a natural suspicion of vampires, and will often serve to protect the citizenry of Moonlight Falls from the insatiable hunger of the fang gang.

This section details the lifestyle of a werewolf Sim, including all of the new interactions, pack behaviors, and beneficial behaviors. That's not to say that there aren't a few drawbacks to being a werewolf. Possessing such power is not without cost, and werewolves must maintain high energy to keep control over their baser instincts. Otherwise, they risk turning forms right before the very eyes of friends and family—maybe even in front of those not privy to their secret!

Create a Sim

As with all supernatural types, you may designate your Sim as a werewolf without pageantry. The choice is available right from the get-go, as a clickable options in the Basics section of Create a Sim. Once you select the werewolf option, you must then fashion the appearance of both the human form and the wolf-beast form. To switch between forms in Create a Sim, click the small werewolf button above your Sim's portrait in the toolbar.

Human Form

As a werewolf, you can create an entirely "normal" human form that gives little away about your furry secret. Your hair, face, and other features are largely unchanged, although your irises take on a golden hue, not unlike a wolf or large dog. (Gold is only the default. You may, of course, change that color to anything of your liking within the Looks tab.) That's the only real indicator in human form that something wild lurks below the surface, just waiting for an excuse to get out.

Werewolf Form

However, once you make the switch over to werewolf form, things get hairy. First, your eyes burn even more golden and your lower canines emerge from your lower mandible. Your jaw sticks out farther. Your ears draw into points. Claw-like fingernails grow from your hands. There is some serious lupine action happening here. (You may certainly use the sliders to adjust your Sims' face to your liking. You are not required to leave the default jaw, nose, and other facial changes.)

However, not everything is out of your control. You may customize multiple features, such as hair. You can create a modified version of your Sim with werewolf characteristics, including a longer mane of hair such as the locks seen here. Like normal hair, you may set different colors and add tips or highlights. (In the case of Catherine Browne's werewolf, I made sure to add red highlights to her werewolf 'do so it matches her human form hair.) You may also adjust other facial features, such as broadening the nose or other on-the-fly cosmetic surgeries to create a distinct physical persona for your werewolf.

By default, your Sim sports eyebrows that are more animal in nature. You may use the sliders to re-adjust the brows.

And if new hair and eyebrows weren't enough for you, you may also add werewolf-specific body hair to your Sim. Doesn't this lovely coat of fur look luxurious on Catherine here? Thankfully, the body hair is limited to werewolf form or Catherine would need to cover up even more in human form, lest her secret get loose.

NOTE

You may not set specific clothes or traits for werewolf form.

Werewolf-inspired Clothing

Back in human form, dress your Sim up in any available clothes. There are, though, a few frocks that look tailor-made for werewolves. And by tailor-made, I mean it looks like somebody wolfed out inside of them. (Were these shirts washed and pressed by Edward Scissorhands?) Again, feel free to put your werewolf in an evening gown, but if you desire the full werewolf narrative, you may wish to stick to the included ripped wardrobe.

Behavior & Benefits

Werewolves are powerful beings and, as such, their behaviors are often dictated by either thirst for exploring the limits of this power or attempting to temper it with self-control. Your narratives will likely deal with the careful balance between the two because, as fun as it is to give in to the beast, it can result in negative impacts on relationships or needs.

Transformation

As a werewolf, you are not required to wait for a full moon to transform into a wolf-beast. You may do so at any time with the Transform self-interaction. In a flash, your Sim explodes into their wolf form. When in wolf form, your movements are low and exaggerated, just like you would expect from a werewolf. You hunt and stalk just like a wild animal, sniffing out danger in the night.

When you transform into a wolf at your own discretion, you may also revert to human form at will—unless you happened to transform during a full moon.

Then, you must remain in wolf form until the next phase of the lunar cycle. Sometimes, transforming back into human form results in the What Just Happened moodlet, which indicates disorientation.

> **TIP**
>
> Sim enjoy many perks you enjoy while in werewolf form, such as decreased Bladder and Fun decay.

However, sometimes you have no control over werewolf transformation. If you are caught out in human form when the lunar cycle goes into its full moon phase, you are automatically transformed into wolf form. During this time, you may not revert back to human form until the end of the full moon phase. Mood also triggers auto-transformation. If your Sim's mood just tanks out, there is a chance they will switch into wolf form. Like the full moon-inspired transformation, this cannot be undone with a self-interaction. You must either reverse the terrible mood or just wait it out.

> **CAUTION**
>
> Stress can also trigger transformation. If your Sim has the Stressed Out moodlet, get them happy and relaxed soon or you risk an unintended transformation.

LYCANTHROPY SKILL

Werewolves have a hidden skill: Lycanthropy. Like visible skills, Lycanthropy has 10 levels. The more time you spend in werewolf form and performing werewolf-specific interactions, the more you raise this hidden skill. Developing Lycanthropy has several benefits, especially related to transformation. The higher the skill level, the lower the chance of auto-transforming when mood is low or when the Sim has the Stressed Out moodlet. Raising this skill also increases your chance of finding collectibles while out gathering. (Pair the Gatherer trait with a werewolf Sim and you'll sniff out the best ingredients!)

At level 3 of this skill, you unlock the Cursed Bite interaction. This is a social that werewolves can use on other Sims. It is not a friendly social—it has the Steamed STC and results in lost LTR. In fact, it plays out not unlike a fight. During the scuffle there is a chance you indeed sink your canines into your target Sim. The target then receives the Once Bitten, Twice Shy moodlet... and the target Sim becomes a werewolf on the next full moon.

If the social is rejected and your werewolf loses the fight, the target Sim actually bops your Sim on the nose with a rolled up newspaper. This also reduces LTR because the swat has the insulting STC.

So, though you cannot "see" the skill as it develops, there are rewards for specific levels:

◊ **Level 3:** Sim is beginning to understand the Werewolves Curse. His/her feral werewolf instincts fill him/her with the desire to use the Cursed Bite on other Sims and transform them into werewolf pack mates!

◊ **Level 6:** Being a werewolf has its perks. Fantastic scents dance all around your Sim! He/she can now use this ability to hunt for specific types of objects. (More on this shortly.)

◊ **Level 8:** Sim gained a lot of control over his/her transformations! While the full moon will forever bring out the wolf, your Sim can resist transforming out of anger a bit more than before.

◊ **Level 10:** Sim has reached his/her full potential as a werewolf! But that doesn't mean your Sim's feral journey has come to a close. Creating new packs, sniffing out new friends, and terrifying old enemies are in your Sim's future. The hunt continues!

Hitting level 10 is great because the decreased decay in needs your werewolf experiences while in beast form are transferred over to human form, too!

Needs, Aging, & Relationship Perks

There are a wealth of perks to being a werewolf that affect the basic functions of a Sim. These perks affect daily functionality in a busy world, allowing you to get more done, be more efficient, and have stronger relationships. As you might imagine, there are caveats to all of those things, but after reviewing this list of perks, you may determine that—on the whole—the benefits to being a werewolf far outweigh the drawbacks (which we'll get to in just a moment via the Complicating Matters section).

Werewolves age slower than human Sims—much slower. Yes, you can always adjust the lifespan of your Sims on your own via the Options menu, but if you are a purist and want to leave lifespans at default levels or at least not stretch them out into fantastical levels, the increased werewolf lifespan is a fascinating way to affect your narratives. Werewolves outliving normal or other supernatural Sims can set up some great stories—although there may be a touch of tragedy at play.

Werewolves develop the Athletic skill much faster than other Sims, even vampire Sims which also have a notably faster skill development perk. If you want your Sim to have a career, consider pairing a werewolf with the Professional Sports career or Law Enforcement. Their improved physical prowess will help them rack up promotions at a faster rate!

TIP

While in wolf-beast form, the Nice Nails moodlet from the Day Spa is worth three times as much!

TIP

While in wolf or human form, werewolves can eat raw meat and fish to satisfy hunger.

TIP

Werewolves, regardless of form, enjoy a slower Energy decay when performing physical activities.

While in wolf form, werewolves benefit from decreased decay to basic needs. Energy, Bladder, and Fun needs dip at a noticeably slower rate. As a wolf, your stress is naturally lower, too. And activities that would increase stress and perhaps ding your Sim with the Stressed Out moodlet provide stress at a much slower rate.

It's kind of a catch-22 here, because decayed needs like these can trigger terrible moods—which in turn can trigger transformation into wolf form... at which point these needs decay at a slower rate. So, while in wolf form, satisfy these needs so when you do switch back to human form, they remain at a fairly high level.

Hunt

One of the best perks of being a werewolf is the Hunt interaction, which is the reward for hitting level 3 of the hidden Lycanthropy skill. This interaction—available only in wolf-beast form—directs your Sim to begin searching a lot for collectibles. Once you reach level 6, you determine the collectibles via the picker when you choose to Hunt. You may choose to seek out insects, gems, and metals.

Once started, your Sim drops to all fours and leaps around the lot, sniffing out hidden collectibles that a human Sim simply cannot see. It's quite a lot of fun to watch a Hunt, as your Sim rears back to howl before lunging about in search of secreted goodies. Your wolf Sim will paw and scratch at the ground, hopefully digging up some great collectibles. After several moments, the Hunt ends and you receive a message telling you what collectibles were found on the Hunt. The maximum number of collectibles you may find on a Hunt is four.

NOTE

If you have *Pets* installed, you'll notice that this is similar to the Hunt interaction with dogs and cats.

TIP

As you improve the hidden Lycanthropy skill, the rarity and quality of the collectibles you uncover during a Hunt improves as well.

The Hunt satisfies more than just the need to seek out collectibles. Going on a Hunt is fun for a werewolf. However, it does expend Energy. Thankfully, because you are in wolf form, Energy drops slower than it would for a human Sim performing a similar strenuous activity.

You may also Hunt in your pack (if you've grouped up). Doing so does not necessarily result in more collectibles, but it does increase the chance of finding rare, valuable collectibles. Hunting in a pack increases the LTR with everybody, satisfies Fun and Social needs, and helps develop the Lycanthropy skill. (So does a solo Hunt, by the way.)

CAUTION

You are not guaranteed to find anything while on a Hunt. It may be unlikely to come up empty-handed, especially if the skill has been developed, but it's certainly not impossible.

Forming a Pack (Grouping)

Werewolves have a natural camaraderie with other werewolves. Every positive social or interaction results in higher LTR. When you are playing out a fiction that involves a wolf pack (more on grouping soon), enhanced LTRs is an important perk. And these LTR perks are in effect whether you are in human form or beast form.

The inherent social nature of dogs—er, werewolves—leads to an actual pack mentality. It's encouraged for werewolves to group up, or in the case of *Supernatural*, form a pack. Forming a Pack works similarly to grouping up, which was introduced in *Late Night*.

To form a pack, you need at least one other werewolf Sim with an acquaintance-level relationship. Click on that Sim and choose the Form Pack interaction. If the target of the invite accepts, they join the group. Alternately, you can use your mobile phone (found in the Inventory tab of the Status panel) to Invite Out other Sims, which also encourages them to join the pack. You can also use the phone to invite multiple Sims at the same time to form a pack. If one of the invitations is declined for whatever reason, a brief message pops up telling you which Sim could not join up. When Sims are invited (and accept) to form a pack, they report to the lot or venue with the inviter. A special plumb-bob appears over the heads of every werewolf in the pack.

When you are finished with the pack, click on your Sim and choose Disband Pack. Everybody is then sent on their way.

> **NOTE**
>
> You can have only one active group at a time. You cannot organize multiple groups.

> **TIP**
>
> If you invite Sims to a pack while you are home, any Sim joining the group is automatically allowed to enter the premises without a formal greeting.

> **CAUTION**
>
> Computer-controlled Loner Sims do not want packs larger than two Sims. If you attempt to add a third, the Loner will immediately leave the pack.

> **CAUTION**
>
> Werewolves with the Commitment Issues trait will not gain LTR as quickly with other werewolves in the pack.

New Socials & Interactions

Human Form Interactions/Socials

- **Apologize for Becoming a Werewolf:** This social is only available after the What Just Happened moodlet appears (following transformation back to a human). If accepted, it has a Friendly STC and increased LTR. If rejected by another Sim, it decreases LTR.

- **Joke about Shedding:** This is a harmless, funny social.

- **Complain about the Werewolves Curse:** The target of this social must be a werewolf Sim in human form, too. It has a Friendly STC and builds LTR if socially accepted by the target.

Werewolf Form Interactions/Socials

- **Sniff Inappropriately:** This fun little social causes you to smell the other werewolf Sim (in wolf form) in a silly, suggestive manner. It has a Friendly STC and builds LTR.

- **Scratch:** The new Scratch interaction directs your wolf-form Sim to use their claws on objects like tables, desks, sofas, rugs, and more. Doing so ruins the object but it is a lot of fun for the werewolf.

> **NOTE**
>
> Neat or Proper trait werewolves will not perform this interaction autonomously.

- **Growl At:** This aggressive social directs your werewolf to bare their teeth at another Sim (or werewolf!). If successful, the target Sim will cower and get the Terrified moodlet. The actor enjoys the Amused moodlet. However, while mood goes up, LTR with the target goes down. And if you try this on somebody who is not amused, they may bonk you on the nose with a rolled-up newspaper. That also decreases LTR, but awards the actor with an Awkward STC.

- **Cursed Bite:** As mentioned in the Lycanthropy skill section, this fight interaction can turn another Sim into a werewolf.

- **Hunt:** Use the Hunt interaction to search the current lot for collectibles.

- **Howl at the Moon:** This is such a fun self-interaction. Click on your wolf and select this interaction to arch your back and howl at the moon. Now, there is a slight chance this interaction will "fail" (though not with any consequence save for not developing the Lycanthropy skill) and result in a small coughing fit. If you Howl while in a pack, the other wolves will likely follow suit.

> **TIP**
>
> Toddler werewolves can perform this self-interaction regardless of form. Cuuuuute!

Pack Interactions/Socials

- **Hunt with Pack:** Scour the current lot with the pack to dig up collectibles.

- **Go Here with Pack:** Direct the pack to a specific location with this interaction.

- **Howl for Pack:** Bring the pack in with this amazing loud howl.

Introduction | New Simology | New Careers & Skills | Meet the Supernaturals | New Venues | Tour of Moonlight Falls | New Object Catalog

Sim to Wolf-Form Werewolf Socials

◆ **Rub Belly:** This social causes the actor to playfully rub a wolf's belly. If accepted, the werewolf howls in delight and builds LTR with the actor. This is also Fun and satisfies the Social need. However, if it fails due to not being close enough to the werewolf, it's an insulting gesture and results in lost LTR.

◆ **Compliment Fur:** This social is very similar to Compliment Appearance. It doesn't increase LTR or meet needs, but it's a rather pleasant thing to say in passing.

◆ **Play Fetch:** If you have *Pets* installed, you know how this works. The actor pulls out a stick and throws it for the werewolf. The wolf bounds after it and brings it back. Both Sims involved have Fun, satisfy Social needs, and increase LTR. If rejected, this can result in decreased LTR.

◆ **Whack on Nose:** This is a very negative social to perform on a wolf-form werewolf. With a rolled-up newspaper, the actor bops the target Sim on the nose. This results in an LTR hit.

◆ **Ask for the Werewolves Curse:** This social can trigger the Cursed Bite interaction from a werewolf. However, the actor must have at least a decent LTR with the target or else the wolf may turn its snout up at the invitation to pass along the curse.

BOTTLED CURSE

If you want to turn a Sim into a werewolf but don't want to go through the actions of finding a werewolf, raising LTR, and then asking for the Cursed Bite, you can either brew up the Bottled Curse of the Lycan (an elixir) or possibly find it for sale at the elixir shop. Like other elixirs, it can be imbibed outright by the actor, or it can be sneaked into a drink and given to an unsuspecting Sim that's about to become very interested in the lunar cycle.

VARG'S TAVERN

If you are interested in finding other werewolves in Moonlight Falls, Varg's Tavern should always be your first stop. This rough-and-tumble tavern is where the wild things are. So, if you're a werewolf looking for more of your own kind or an outsider looking for a way into the pack, push through the front door of Varg's and mingle. If you're ever unsure of a werewolf in human form, just pause the action and start checking out eyes.

Complicating Matters

So, all of this werewolf stuff sounds pretty good, right? Well, there are some things you need to be aware of about the werewolf lifestyle before plunging headfirst into the pack.

Negative Socials and Actions

Here's the thing: not everybody in town is all that wild about werewolves—especially when werewolves are in beast form. The reason is that werewolves often take on aspects of the Inappropriate trait, such as knocking over trash cans and rummaging through the trash. It's also likely that werewolves will, if left unattended, sniff other Sims inappropriately and scratch up furniture and belongings. This fails to amuse a lot of other Sims, so be warned. Idle hands are the werewolf's playthings, it seems.

> **TIP**
>
> If your werewolf has the Neat trait, they will not engage in any of these autonomous negative behaviors.

Traits

Some of the traits you assign in Create a Sim can have a negative impact on your werewolf's lifestyle:

- **Commitment Issues:** Werewolves with this trait will not benefit from the increased LTR that other werewolves share while in a pack together.

- **Grumpy, Hot-Headed, Mean Spirited, Inappropriate:** These Sims will transform into beast-form against their will more often, especially when mood tanks. Plus, they will always turn into a wolf before getting in any sort of fight.

- **Insane:** Every six hours, there is a chance an Insane werewolf will turn into a wolf against their will. They are then hit with the Feral Change moodlet.

Werewolf Families

In Create a Sim, you can assign the werewolf type to any age of Sim, starting from toddler up to elder. (More on babies in a moment.) Werewolf toddlers can only Howl, Scratch, and Practice Hunting. When they Practice Hunting, there is a tiny chance they will find an insect. The only autonomous werewolf behavior for toddlers is scratching.

Child werewolves start to embrace more of the werewolf lifestyle. They can transform at will, but the rest of their behaviors mirror the toddler werewolf. At teen, though, all werewolf socials and interactions are available.

If two werewolves mate, they always produce a werewolf baby. Werewolf babies exhibit no werewolf behaviors, but they do possess the golden eyes. If a werewolf and a human Sim WooHoo and have a baby, there is a 50 percent chance they will have a werewolf baby. And if a werewolf and other supernatural mate, the chance of the baby being either supernatural type is 50/50.

Fairies

Fairies are whimsical beings in tune with the natural world as well as the supernatural. Fluttering about Moonlight Falls with their magical wings, fairies bring peace and joy to almost all they encounter. Certainly synced to plants and harvestables, fairies have extraordinary gifts in the garden, but they are also known for their powers of inspiration. Using special auras, fairies act as muses for other Sims, coaxing their creativity to the surface so that they may create unfettered works of art.

These magical gifts come with a price, though, and that price is Fairy Magic. After performing some mystical feats, fairies must recharge their spent magical powers, typically by relaxing with other fairies in cool, tiny houses.

TIP

Fairies have a special new venue geared toward them: the Arboretum. Check out the New Venues chapter to see all of the cool things a fairy does at this new venue!

Create a Sim

Inside Create a Sim, you may select fairy from right off the Basics tab. Clicking that icon immediately attaches a set of fairy wings to the back of your Sim. These can be customized in the Fairy Wings tab. Fairy Sims can utilize any of the existing traits, although you may get additional mileage out of creative- or outdoors-related traits. The Green Thumb trait in particular will aid your fairy in many gardening exploits.

In the Head and ears tab, you can bring your ears to a fine point!

You're a fairy—why not wear flowers in your hair?

Fairy Wings

After selecting the fairy Sim, you may then pick the wings that magically sprout from his or her back. There are six wing types, including Dreamy Dragonfly and Super Swirly, all of which can be customized with a color wheel or a field of swatches. Feel free to try different colors out with different outfits until you feel you have the perfect combination for your new fairy.

Willowed Wisp

Dreamy Dragonfly

Majestic Monarch

Super Swirly

Fanciful Ferns

Busy Bumblebee

TIP

If you purchase the King/Queen of the Fae Lifetime Reward, you can change your wings at any given point rather than being stuck with only the wings selected in Create a Sim at the beginning of your narrative.

Fairy Clothes

New pixie and fairy-themed clothes appear in the collection for your Sims to don, all of which seem to perfectly match with the available fairy wings. Which of these (and many other) cool clothes will you drape your fairy in? And remember, you can choose any combo you like. If you want to dress your fairy in vampire-ish clothes, there's no stopping you. You can have the most Gothic-looking fairy in the land!

TRUE FORM

Human form is not the "true form" for fairies. Fairies only take this human form so they can interact with other Sims. When mingling with fairies in the Fairy Houses, playing the toys (like the Very Small Train), or cheating The Claaaaw arcade cabinet, fairies shrink down into itty-bitty pixie form. These small beings of light flit about like the most graceful of hummingbirds. Throughout this section (and in the New Object Catalog), you'll see references to the true form.

Meet the Supernaturals

Behavior and Benefits

Should you choose to slip into a set of fairy wings and explore the world as one of these storybook beings, you have access to a host of benefits and perks. In fact, there really are few shortcomings to being a fairy, though you explore decidedly different stories than, say, a vampire or werewolf. Let's look at the benefits to fairyhood, including a rundown of the special hidden Fairy Magic skill.

Fairies don't walk around like a human or vampire—they flit and float with their magic wings!

Because fairies are magical beings, it makes sense that they utilize actual magic in their daily activities. Many actions a fairy takes consume magic. If you look beneath the Sim portrait, you'll spy a horizontal, sparkling meter. This tracks how much fairy magic you have in reserve. Casting auras, pulling pranks... these all consume magic. So, keep an eye on that meter and when you get low, replenish it by resting. If you take refuge in a Fairy House or consume fairy beverages at a Fairy House, you can regain spent magic.

Skill Development

A major benefit to being a fairy is that you enjoy speedier development of certain skills, including: Gardening, Painting, Dancing (hidden skill), and Guitar. If you have *Ambitions* installed, the Sculpting skill is accelerated. With *Late Night* installed, all of the extra musical skills like drums and piano are also accelerated. The developmental speed bump is approximately twice as fast as for a normal Sim.

TIP

Fairies who win chess games or foosball games also get bumped points into those respective hidden skills.

Though fairies do not enjoy an accelerated Handiness skill, when they do choose to repair objects, they transform into true form and poke around the object. If they fail the repair, they are bounced back into human form.

Introduction   New Simology   New Careers & Skills   Meet the Supernaturals   New Venues   Tour of Moonlight Falls   New Object Catalog

FAIRY MAGIC HIDDEN SKILL

Fairies develop a hidden skill called Fairy Magic, which is developed as they perform fairy activities and interactions. Fairy Magic is developed at any age, from child to elder. All fairies are gifted with the skill from the moment they begin their stories—there is no ramping up period. Right off the bat, they enjoy some small benefits. As the skill is developed, fairies unlock more interactions, more auras, and more pranks. More on these in a moment, but here is how the skill develops and which interactions are unlocked at specific levels.

Level	Unlock
0	Hot Head Trick, Chattering Teeth Trick, Soothing Aura
1	Creativity Aura, Flight of Felicity
2	Booby Trap Toilet, Booby Trap Shower
3	Body and Mind Aura
4	Booby Trap Trash Can, Tummy Twister Trick
5	Bloom
6	Booby Trap Sofa, Skivvies Trick
7	Gold and Toads Trick
8	Booby Trap Mailbox
9	Booby Trap LLAMA
10	Inner Beauty Trick

Auras

The simple presence of a fairy can inspire other Sims in the immediate vicinity. Fairies can project auras—unlocked and learned as they develop the hidden Fairy Magic skill—that bolster the productivity and mood of surrounding Sims. Projecting an aura costs magic, so fairies must maintain vigilance over the Magic meter lest the aura cut out before they intended. However, the higher the Fairy Magic hidden skill, the slower the decay in the Magic meter while projecting an aura.

CAUTION

You may only have one aura active at a time. If you wish to stop projecting an aura, use the Stop Aura self-interaction. Selecting a different aura off the menu will automatically shut down the current aura.

When a fairy chooses to project an aura, their feet leave the ground and release a burst of magic energy. While the aura is active, a magical glow circles their being. Any Sim within range of the aura also displays the glow, indicating that they are enjoying the effects of the aura. As long as the magic is active, you will also see messages that indicate how much the aura is taxing the fairy. In addition to suggested monitoring of the Magic meter, watch for messages like "Your fairy cannot sustain any auras for much longer" to indicate when it might be time to cease the magic broadcast.

Soothing Aura (level 0)

This is the aura all fairies know from the beginning of life. The Soothing Aura projects positive vibes on nearby Sims, giving them the Soothing Aura moodlet. Depending on the hidden Fairy Magic skill level, the mood boost effect of the aura increases. As you can see here, the mood bump at the high levels of the skill are substantial.

These mood bumps can really helps Sims reverse horrible moods as well as rack up Lifetime Happiness points.

Levels 0–2: +20 mood   **Levels 7–8:** +35 mood

Levels 3–4: +25 mood   **Levels 9–10:** +40 mood

Levels 5–6: +30 mood

TIP

This aura also replenishes lost Fun on Sims who have completely zeroed out the essential need.

Creativity Aura (level 1)

When the fairy projects the Creativity Aura, nearby Sims pick up the Creative Aura moodlet. While this aura is active, affected Sims enjoy accelerated skill development on: Painting, Writing, Guitar, Piano, Drums, Bass, and Cooking. As with the Soothing Aura, the higher the hidden skill, the higher the developmental bump this aura provides.

Body and Mind Aura (level 3)

The third aura is Body and Mind. This aura projects the Body and Mind Aura moodlet on nearby Sims. During the periods they are close to the projecting fairy, they enjoy accelerated development for the following skills: Athletic, Logic, Charisma, Handiness, and (if you have *World Adventures*) Martial Arts. The higher the hidden Fairy Magic skill, the faster the development.

> **TIP**
>
> Don't think for a second that these auras are 100 percent selfless! Fairies enjoy all the benefits of the auras while projecting them, too!

> **BROWNIE BITES**
>
> If you have a multi-Sim household, fairy auras can be extremely useful for helping other Sims accomplish tasks. We're not suggesting you tether a fairy to your household and just use them exclusively as a productivity booster... but it certainly is useful!

Pulling Pranks and Setting Traps

If you have *Generations*, then you're familiar with pranks. Teen Sims in *Generations* love to mess with friends, family, and neighbors by playing little pranks and booby trapping objects. These are hilarious for the teen, but not so much for the person on the receiving end. Well, pranks are a part of the fairy life, too.

Supernatural sets up a handful of new booby traps, which are unlocked as you develop the Fairy Magic hidden skill. Setting these traps satisfies the Fun need for fairies.

Fairies can also trick Sims with silly little interactions, like setting their teeth chattering from a quick blast of cold. Now, these tricks are not surefire. They can sometimes fail to work or even backfire completely and end up affecting the fairy instead of the target Sim.

Sims on the receiving end of tricks may have a hard time getting too bent out of shape, especially if they have Evil, Good Sense of Humor, Insane, Party Animal, or Slob traits. However, if they have Grumpy, Loser, Mean, Neurotic, No Sense of Humor, Over-Emotional, Perfectionist, or Snob traits, there is a good chance they will get angry with the fairy

> **NOTE**
>
> Childish, Daredevil, Evil, Inappropriate, Insane, Loner, or Mean fairies are more likely to set traps or play tricks autonomously.

Play Trick—Hot Head/Chattering Teeth (level 0): The target starts shivering from their icy breath with the Chattering Teeth trick. The Hot Head trick results in the target emitting steam and getting either the Too Spicy! or Singed moodlet.

Booby Trap Shower (level 2): This trap turns the showerhead into a makeshift salon. After the trap is set, the Sim who uses the shower is then surprised with a crazy new hair color. The Sim reacts with shock and then goes back into the shower to wash it out. However, if setting the trap backfires on the fairy, they are hit with the Soaked moodlet.

Booby Trap Toilet (level 2): The Sim sets up a trap in the toilet so the next time another Sim uses it, the water in the bowl shoots straight up and splashes the target. Water pools around the toilet and the Sim who triggered the trap gets the Soaked moodlet.

Play Trick—Tummy Twister (level 4): Oops, this causes the target Sim to release a rather loud belch. The target gets the Awkward moodlet and there's a small chance they also receive the Nauseous moodlet.

Booby Trap Sofa (level 6): Fairies hide a small amount of Fairy Dust in the sofa so when another Sim sits down, they are enveloped in a cloud. The Fairy Dust makes the Sim temporarily pass out and get the Tricked by a Fairy moodlet.

Play Trick—Skivvies (level 6): This trick instantly strips the target Sim down to their sleepwear or underwear. The target may get the Embarrassed moodlet. But if they possess the Coward, Diva, Neurotic, Never Nude, Perfectionist, Shy, Snob, or Unlucky trait, they always receive the Embarrassed moodlet.

Meet the Supernaturals

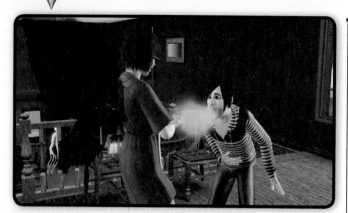

Play Trick—Gold and Toads (level 7): This trick causes the target to vomit up not their last meal, but a special gift. There is a good chance it will be a toad, which negatively affects their Hygiene need. However, there is a chance they will instead up-chuck Fairy Gold, which can be sold for Simoleons!

FAIRY GOLD

Wait a second—what's Fairy Gold? Fairy Gold is a special coin that fairies give out when they pull the Gold and Toads trick. This glittering prize only last for 24 hours, so collect it as soon as you see it or receive it from a fairy. Then feel free to sell the Fairy Gold to the shop for lots of Simoleons. The going rate for Fairy Gold changes, so you may get a different prices from day to day.

Booby Trap Mailbox (Level 8): The fairy hides some bees inside the mailbox. When a Sim opens the mailbox, the small swarm pops out and startles them, also resulting in the Bee Attack moodlet. There is a very small chance the target will get stung, too. That's not very funny...

Booby Trap LLAMA (level 9): Pranking the LLAMA means that the Sim who uses the device for insta-travel gets sent to a location other than the one intended. The destination is random! If setting the trap backfires, the fairy gets the Nauseous moodlet.

Play Trick—Inner Beauty (level 10): The Inner Beauty trick is only a trick on the surface. The target Sim will turn hideous and be shy around other Sims for as long as the trick lasts. If the target looks in a mirror, they get the Strange Reflection moodlet. Totally awful, no? Not exactly. During the day this affect lasts, the target Sim builds Charisma faster, improving their personality. If you're the target of this trick, just make sure you don't use a mean social or else the timer will be reset!

BROWNIE BITES

Fairies have a special cheat interaction on The Claaaaw arcade machine. They return to true form and flutter inside the machine, increasing your chance not only of winning a prize, but winning a valuable prize. See the New Object Catalog chapter for a full breakdown on The Claaaaw and all of the prizes you can win!

Enjoying Nature

Naturally, fairies prefer to commune with nature—syncing with the natural world is core to their being. As such, fairies will enjoy using the Talk to Plants social, which helps satisfy the Social need.

The new Bloom interaction on a harvestable plant, though, is a very useful perk for fairies. Unlocked at level 5 of the hidden Fairy Magic skill, the Bloom interaction directs the fairy to sprinkle a little magic Fairy Dust on a harvestable plant. There is a chance that this will cause the harvestable to have an instant growth spurt and provide high quality harvestables. Bloom can sometimes resurrect dead plants into the wilted stage, or "repair" wilted plants so that they may grow harvestables again.

Now, there is a chance that Bloom will backfire. If so, the plant may suddenly sprout weeds around the base. And on the very off-chance Bloom really tanks out, the interaction can instantly kill a plant.

TIP

Fairies get environmental bonuses off plants and harvestables when they are present on a lot. Make sure you have plenty of green stuff around when you're hosting a fairy!

Fairy Houses

Though you have your own lot, fairies can also maintain separate homes called Fairy Houses. Find these in Buy Mode in two forms: Fairy Bungalow and Fairy Castle. These locations also exist out in the wilds, such as next to the fishing holes, and offer respite to the wayward fairy. Fairy Houses are, as you can see, entirely too small to accommodate a fairy in human form. Fairies transform into true fairy form when they interact with these tiny buildings. It's automatic,

so there's no need to go through a separate interaction just to use the Fairy House.

Here are all of the interactions you may perform on a Fairy House:

- **Sleep/Nap/Relax:** These interactions on the Fairy House function the same as a bed or sofa back on a normal lot. The fairy disappears into the Fairy House and gets some much-needed rest. These actions satisfy the Energy need to varying degrees, depending on the length of the rest period. This sleeping is not interrupted by sound like sleeping on your lot, but you can be woken up by a Fairy House party. These interactions also replenish Fairy Magic.

- **Drink Pollen Punch:** Fairies love to quaff their own label of special punch—Pollen Punch. Inside the house, the fairy downs a bottle. This satisfies Hunger and replenishes spent Fairy Magic.

- **WooHoo/Try for Baby:** Fairies have, uh, needs like any other Sim. Two fairies can WooHoo or Try for Baby inside the Fairy House. Obviously, these only work with two fairies—no non-fairy Sims. Plus, you can only use these interactions if no other fairies are in the Fairy House. Post-interaction, the fairies emerge and return to human form. If a baby was conceived, you will hear a chime.

NOTE

When two fairies Try for Baby and succeed, their offspring will always be a fairy.

- **Throw a Fairy House Party:** Fairies are indeed social Sims (for the most part) and enjoy a get-together. You can throw a party inside a Fairy House and invite other fairies to join, just like a regular party. There is no need to really attend to the partygoers' needs, allowing you to concentrate on having fun. During the course of the party, fairies get the Enjoying Music moodlet.

For a non-fairy, there are few interactions on a Fairy House. You can either just look at it or turn the lights on and off. And if the fairies are having a party, non-fairies can at least stand near the house and dance along with the music to have a little fun and get the Enjoying Music moodlet.

New Socials/Interactions

Fairy Conversation Topics

🔹 **Talk about Flowers:** Fairies with Excitable, Flirty, Green Thumb, Hopeless Romantic, Loves the Outdoors, Perfectionist, or Vegetarian traits are more likely to use this friendly, LTR-building social.

🔹 **Complain about Witches:** Fairies with Can't Stand Art, Couch Potato, Coward, Neurotic, No Sense of Humor, Schmoozer, or Snob traits are more likely to whine about witches, a supernatural that fairies naturally distrust.

🔹 **Brag about Playing Pranks:** Fairies love to laugh and giggle with this Fun social. It builds LTR when successful. More likely for fairies with Artistic, Brave, Childish, Daredevil, Evil, Inappropriate, Good Sense of Humor, or Party Animal traits.

🔹 **Tell a Fairy Tale:** Fairies like to tell stories to other Sims. This social satisfies the Fun need and builds LTR. More likely for Sims with Bookworm, Charismatic, Family-Oriented, Friendly, Insane, Technophobe, or Virtuoso traits.

🔹 **Fairy Frolic:** This friendly interaction on another fairy (which is more likely for Artistic, Charismatic, Flirty, Friendly, and Party Animal Sims) inspires both to transform into true fairy form and flutter about with each other. It satisfies Fun and Social, plus it builds LTR.

Sims to Fairies

🔹 **Ask for Fairy Dust:** This social requests the Fairy Dust gift from a fairy.

🔹 **Request Fairy Gift:** Request either a gift of Fairy Dust or Fairy Gold.

🔹 **Imply Mother was a Glowbug:** This curt social is more likely for Evil, Grumpy, Hot-Headed, Inappropriate, Mean, or Snob Sims. It has a negative effect on LTR.

FAIRY DUST

Ask for Fairy Dust? What's Fairy Dust? Fairy Dust is an item you only receive from fairies. It must be requested or given. Fairies can use it directly on other Sims to give them the Flight of Felicity Fairy positive moodlet.

BROWNIE BITES

I mentioned that there weren't many shortcomings to being a fairy, but there are some things to note. Fairies do not receive much enjoyment from the TV, computer, books, or videogames. They provide less Fun. So, if you do choose to try out a fairy, don't count on these objects to satisfy needs or provide a noticeable mood bump.

Fairy Families

Like many of the supernaturals, fairies age much slower than normal human Sims. Fairies age five times slower than human Sims, which is on par with vampires. These extended lifespans are useful for players who want to tell longer narratives.

When you start in Create a Sim, you may only assign the fairy type to child and older Sims. However, through genetics, you may have fairy babies. Two fairies will always produce a fairy baby. If a fairy mates with a non-fairy, there is a 50/50 chance the baby will be born a fairy.

While babies do not try out their true form, toddler fairies will transform to take care of needs like Hunger and Energy. The toddler transforms and checks into a Fairy House, if available, to satisfy those needs. At the child age, fairies can start flying places, using the new I Can Fly self-interaction, which is fun for the actor.

Witches

Witches are masters of arcane, powerful magics. With magic wands, they bend the natural world to their will, engaging in conjuring and spellcasting that will amaze all fortunate enough to witness such displays of mystical prowess. Though all Sims can develop the Alchemy skill and truly harness its magnificent possibilities, witches are best suited to get the most out of such an intense skill.

But Alchemy is not the only trade of a witch. In fact, if a witch wants to indeed draw upon their true magical might, they require use of a special wand. These wands, which are key to developing a hidden skill, allow them to focus their talents and cast charms, spells, curses, and more.

Create a Sim

Unlike fairies or werewolves, witches do not have special Create a Sim options for customizing their physical essences beyond the normal selection. However, there are several pointers to keep in mind when assembling a potential witch's personality, as they can affect the developmental patterns or potential success in the realm of spells.

One of the key activities for witches is engaging in Spellcasting Duels. While you can always use an interaction to start a duel, some traits encourage autonomous duels: Bookworm, Charismatic, Friendly, and Genius. Conversely, the Couch Potato, Coward, Loner, Loser, or Snob traits discourage auto-duels to the point they never happen without your say-so. If you like total control over a Sim and never want to risk activity that might result in harm or poor mood, setting up a witch who will never whip out a wand without direction, investigate these traits.

Possessing the Evil trait allows witches to use the Conjure Poison Apple interaction (which we'll explore soon). Good and Evil traits also affect what wishes your Sims get, and what types of spells they will cast autonomously.

Witch-inspired Clothing

As always, any Sim can dress in any Create a Sim outfit. However, a number of outfits and accessories seem tailor-made for witches, such as pointy hats and glam gowns that would be absolutely perfect for today's discerning witch. Check out these duds when you're assigning your new witch a wardrobe!

Benefits and Behaviors

Witches have a multitude of perks and special behaviors exclusive to their supernatural type, such as the innate ability to wield a magic wand as well as ride brooms. Being a witch is almost like having a special hidden trait, because witches have certain developmental skills that are affected just by being a witch. Witches, for example, benefit from the increased chance of brewing multiple elixirs with a single Alchemy interaction.

Ride in Style!

Witch Sims take a broom like a taxi when traveling solo. However, any Sim can ride a magic broom. Once a broom is purchased from Buy Mode and placed in the Sim's inventory, it can be designated as the primary transport by just left-clicking on the object.On average, they are as fast as other modes of transportation, save for the Lifetime Reward, Magic Vacuum. This speedy appliance gets a witch from point A to point B with real speed and style.

Magic Vacuum!

Magic Brooms provide a lot of fun for witches, especially when used at the Zoomsweeper Broom Arena. Though we detail this arena in the New Object Catalog chapter, let's have a peek at it here. You can purchase one for your lot via Buy Mode, but there is a free-to-use Zoomsweeper in Moonlight Falls next to the elixir shop. Use the Joy Ride interaction to just zip around the arena and have some fun. Stunt Ride is a little more complicated, as you perform tricks that wow potential crowds. You can even Stunt Ride for Tips and earn a little extra coin. Broom riding is a "hidden" skill that improves as you practice it. For more about hidden skills, see the "New Skills" section of the New Simology chapter.

Witch Sims take a broom like a taxi when traveling solo. However, any Sim can ride a magic broom. Once a broom is purchased from Buy Mode and placed in the Sim's inventory, it can be designated as the primary transport by just left-clicking on the object.

TIP

Do you have *Pets*? Witches who have cats and minor pets, like reptiles and birds, in their household enjoy the Animal Familiar moodlet!

Introduction

New Simology

New Careers & Skills

Meet the Supernaturals

New Venues

Tour of Moonlight Falls

New Object Catalog

New Socials & Interactions

Witches may deploy all default socials, but they also have access to a few new socials that are exclusive to them:

- **Brag about Broom Riding:** This friendly social is accepted by almost any target, as it is relatively harmless. However, Sims with Supernatural Skeptic trait will often put up their hands... unless the witch speaking has high Charisma.

- **Enthuse about Magic:** Witches only use this social with non-witch Sims. Like Brag About Broom Riding, most Sims accept it as a friendly social. Look out for Supernatural Skeptics that want nothing to do with your occult enthusiasm, though!

- **Enthuse About Brooms:** Supernatural Fans use this social on witches to build LTR.

- **Complain about Fairies:** Apparently witches are not big on fairies... this social lands well with Can't Stand Art, Grumpy, Mean, Neurotic, No Sense of Humor, Schmoozer, or Snob Sims. It satisfies Social need as well as builds LTR, unless it's rejected.

Conjure Apple

Witches can conjure apples from thin air via their magic. When you perform this self-interaction, your Sim rubs their hands together and then reveals an apple. This apple goes straight into inventory, where it can be eaten to satisfy Hunger. Most conjured apples are average quality, but a higher Spellcasting skill can result in a higher quality apple. There is a chance that the spell will fail and the witch will craft either a terrible-tasting apple... or worse, a poison apple that puts the eater to sleep via the Dark Slumber moodlet. Evil Sims will always have the Conjure Poison Apple self-interaction available, so they can purposefully craft awful apples that put enemies (and even friends) to sleep.

Spellcasting and Magic Wands

Spellcasting is totally separate from Alchemy, even though witches get a natural boost with the Alchemy skill. With their magic wands—and there are several to choose from, from the default wand found in a new witch's inventory to the wealth of options in Buy Mode—they can cast magical spells and compete in duels.

Using magic, though, draws upon the Magic meter spotted just below your Sim's portrait on the menu. When you cast a spell or use magic for things like repairs, magic is drawn from this bar. When the bar is empty, the witch can no longer cast spells. The quality of your wand directly affects the amount of magic a spell uses.

Wand	Cost	Spell Accuracy	Magic Cost Efficiency	Glow Color
Classic	§360	Lowest	Lowest	Yellow
Argent	§540	Low	Low	Cyan
Azure	§540	Low	Low	Blue
Crimson	§540	Low	Low	Red
Ivory	§720	High	Medium	White
Verdant	§720	Medium	High	Green
Crystal	§900	Medium	Highest	Magenta
Elegant	§900	Highest	Medium	Orange
Iridescent	§1,080	High	High	Rainbow

TIP

To refill the Magic meter, take a spin around the Zoomsweeper Broom Arena for fun or guzzle an Essence of Magic elixir. Magic is also replenished over time.

Magic wands double as both a physical object and a hidden skill. The more a Sim wields a wand, the more they develop the hidden Spellcasting skill. Use the basic Play with Magic self-interaction in the beginning to just have fun. During the practice session, the witch waves the wand around in a display of sparks and light. Glyphs, pyrotechnics, sparkles, and more appear in the air. However, over time you'll want to develop the use of the wand by using spells that in turn raise the hidden skill.

That hidden skill level is directly tied into the success rate of a spell with this simple formula: 80 + (Wand Skill Level x 2) - (Spell Level x 2). So, for example, if a witch with level 7 of the wand skill casts the love charm (unlocked at level 4), the likelihood of success is:

80 + 14 (level 7 of skill x 2) - 8 (spell level x 2) = 86% chance of success

Here are the unlocks for the hidden Wand skill, including all of the spells, charms, and curses that can be yours for investing the time and effort into the skill:

Level	
0	Practice Spellcasting, Choose Favorite Wand
1	Good Luck Charm, Conversion Ritual
2	Fire Blast, Ice Blast
3	Spellcasting Duel, Upgrade objects
4	Love Charm, Toadification Curse
5	Haunting Curse
6	Need Charms
7	Need Curses
8	Sunlight Charm, Pestilence Curse
9	Restoration Ritual
10	Reanimation Ritual

Good Luck Charm

◆ **Level:** 1

◆ **Magic type:** White

◆ **Limitation:** Sims with Evil, Mean, Grumpy, Loner, and Unlucky traits never do this autonomously.

The target of this spell gets the Feeling Lucky moodlet. However, should the spell fail, the witch (not the target) is hit with the Feeling Unlucky moodlet.

Conversion Ritual

◆ **Level:** 1

◆ **Magic type:** White

Have too many unneeded collectibles in your inventory? Take a chance with this ritual spell and attempt to transform the item into a more valuable collectible. Though it depletes Energy and Social, the chance of getting a random collectible (with a slight favor to new collectibles from *Supernatural*) is worth it! Of course, there's always a risk the spell will fail and the collectible will be destroyed...

Fire Blast

◆ **Level:** 2

◆ **Magic type:** Elemental

◆ **Limitation:** Sims with Good, Friendly, Frugal, and Neat traits never do this autonomously. Cannot target a Sim who already has Singed or On Fire moodlets.

This spell spits fire at the target. Most of the time, this results in the target being Singed. However, there is a small chance the target will get the far more beneficial On Fire moodlet. Alternately, if the spell fails, the witch is burnt and hit with Singed instead. Either way, casting decays Social and Energy.

TiP
Witches can use Fire Blast to light a fireplace, and when they've finished enjoying the flames, they can use Ice Blast to extinguish the fire!

Ice Blast

- **Level:** 2

- **Magic type:** Elemental

- **Limitation:** Sims with Good, Friendly, Coward, Hot-Headed, Hydrophobic, and Pyromaniac traits never do this autonomously. Cannot target a Sim who already has Frozen Solid or So Cold moodlets.

With a flourish of ice and snow, the witch casts an Ice Blast and hits the target with the Frozen Solid moodlet. (The So Cold moodlet is also possible.) If the witch targets a fire, it is extinguished. Targeting an appliance like a sink or toilet results in breakage. This spell decays Hunger and Bladder.

Love Charm

- **Level:** 4

- **Magic type:** White

- **Limitation:** Sims with Evil, Mean, Grumpy, Hot-Headed, and Unflirty traits never do this autonomously

When this spell is successfully cast, the target gets the Imminent Romance moodlet. This moodlet means that the next Sim the target speaks to will become a Romantic Interest. They get a lot of LTR, a hit of Romantic STC, and enjoy a great kiss! This moodlet lasts for 24 hours. However, if this spell fails, the target will get the Imminent Nemesis moodlet. This will push the LTR really low, give the Steamed STC, and start a fight!

Toadification Curse

- **Level:** 4

- **Magic type:** Black

- **Limitation:** Sims with Good, Friendly, Coward, and Schmoozer traits never do this autonomously.

This spell turns the target into a... ToadSim! Check it out! This results in the Toadification moodlet. (The caster loses Bladder and Energy, too.) However, there is a good chance the spell might backfire and turn the witch into a ToadSim rather than the helpless target.

Haunting Curse

- **Level:** 5

- **Magic type:** Black

Want to saddle a Sim with a ghost that follows them around? Cast the Haunting Curse and, after an explosion of sparks and mist, a ghost materializes from the ether to follow the target. However, this is a very risky spell. If it fails, the witch is killed on the spot and replaced by a Haunted Gnome. So, be careful (and save!) before unleashing this powerful spell.

This spell decays the Hunger and Energy of the caster.

Need Charms

- **Level:** 6

- **Magic type:** White

Use these simple charms on yourself or another Sim and reverse the decay of Hunger, Bladder, and Hygiene.

Need Curses

- **Level:** 7

- **Magic type:** Black

This is the exact opposite of the Need Charms. This spell tanks the specified need, which can really put the target Sim in a tight spot. Of course, the spell can always backfire...

Sunlight Charm

◆ **Level:** 8

◆ **Magic type:** White

◆ **Limitation:** Sims with Evil, Mean, Grumpy, Hot-Headed, and Unflirty traits never do this autonomously.

This spell energizes the target by gifting them with the Bathed in Sunlight moodlet. As you can imagine, this isn't beneficial for vampires. Plus, it triggers transformation back into human form when used on a werewolf. This spell also removes most negative moodlets from the target. If the spell fails, the witch is dinged with the Dazed moodlet.

Pestilence Curse

◆ **Level:** 8

◆ **Magic type:** Black

◆ **Limitation:** Sims with Good, Friendly, Proper, Neat, and Coward traits never do this autonomously. Cannot be used on a Sim already dealing with the Sick and Tired or Pestilence Plague moodlet.

This nasty bit of spellcasting unloads the Sick and Tired/Pestilence Plague moodlets on the target. The witch casting the spell loses Hunger and Energy, but gains Fun. Should the curse fail, the witch gets those sickly moodlets.

Restoration Ritual

◆ **Level:** 9

◆ **Magic type:** White

This fix-it spell has many uses. It can clear out trash, wash dirty objects, put food away, repair broken objects, and remove booby traps. This decays Social, Fun, and Energy—but it does replenish Hygiene. The risk here, though, is that if the spell fails, all nearby objects either break or turn dirty, food spoils, and trash appears everywhere on the lot.

Reanimation Ritual

◆ **Level:** 10

◆ **Magic type:** Black

This spell is cast only on gravestones and urns. After waving the wand and releasing a shower of sparks, the deceased Sim claws its way out of the ground... as a zombie! And not just any zombie, but a Perma-Zombified Sim. Such magics are so powerful that the caster is severely dinged for Hunger, Energy, and Social. But the ability to unleash a zombie into the city may be worth the cost—and the risk of accidentally turning the spell on themselves. If this spell fails, the witch is then Zombified!

NOTE

If non-witch Sims attempt to use a magic wand, the object sparks and sputters before reminding the player that they are most certainly not a witch.

MAGIC UPGRADES

Witches can upgrade objects just as if they had the Handiness skill or the Inventing skill (from *Ambitions*). Upgrading objects (like adding channels to a TV) costs magic, but the benefit of upgrades far outweighs the expenditure, don't you think? Imagine a magical stove that never catches on fire!

Spellcasting Duels!

Another great method of developing the hidden Spellcasting skill and learning new magics is to engage other witches in Spellcasting Duels. This social interaction with another witch, if accepted, lines up both actors. Wands are drawn. Magical sparks fly. And after a few moments, a winner is determined.

Duels serves multiple purposes. First and foremost, duels are just fun and challenging another witch to a duel is a good way to satisfy a tanking Fun need. Duels also address the Social need and develop LTR with the duel partner. However, the challenge to a duel can be rejected by a witch, which decreases LTR. Watch out for challenging Sims with the Couch Potato, Coward, Loner, Loser, or Snob traits. They are more likely to reject the duel challenge as well as never initiate a challenge of their own.

You do not actually pick the spells to cast in a duel. The spells are awesome displays of light and magic. However, you can certainly affect your chances of winning the duel going into the contest. The biggest booster is mood. The higher your mood, the greater your chance of victory. Your hidden Wand skill is also at play here.

Opponents trade magical blasts of ice and sparks. Depending on your performance chances, you will see you witch block spells or reel from direct hits. And you will launch counter-offensives, hurling bolts in hopes that your opponent's formula is weaker than yours. After several rounds, a winner is determined. The witch that "won" the most rounds—blocked more, landed more magic strikes—is declared the victor and gets the Won a Spellcasting Duel moodlet, which is a towering mood booster. Conversely, the loser is saddled with the Lost a Spellcasting Duel negative moodlet. Some duels end in a tie. If this occurs, both witches get the Spelldrawn moodlet, which is slightly positive.

MAGIC HANDS

Witches have the unique Magic Hands Lifetime Reward, which means they no longer require a wand to use magic. They can engage in duels or cast curses with just their wriggling fingers. Magic Hands operates with the same potency as the best magic wand money can buy!

Witch Families

When two witches have a baby, the baby is always going to grow up to be a witch. If a witch mates with a non-witch, the odds of a magical baby drop to 50/50.

Not sure if your baby is a would-be witch? There are telling behaviors! Toddler witches can accidentally make their toys disappear in a puff of smoke while playing. (Thankfully, the toy reappears after a few moments.) When the Sim ages into child, watch them play with the toy boxes. Every once in a while, they will reach into the box and pull out a weird, wonderful new toy.

By the time the witch is a teen, their magic is fully blossoming. In addition to being able to perform some magical interactions (like Conjure Apple), they also sometimes magically complete their homework. Bonus! More time for socializing!

ZOMBIES! (AND MORE!)

Though there are several selectable supernatural types in Create a Sim, you have undoubtedly discovered that there are additional otherworldly or just plain weird transformations taking place in *Supernatural*. Three supernaturals are not selectable in Create a Sim, but through magic you can manifest them in your town: zombies, ToadSims, and Tragic Clowns.

Zombies: During a full moon phases, there is a chance that, every few hours, a zombie Sim will pop out of the ground and start shambling around town. But that's not the only way for these brain-hungry slowpokes to appear in your game. You can also create zombies by using the zombie elixir (see Alchemy skill) or via a zombie bite.

While a Sim is a zombie, they have the Zombification moodlet. Their skin turns an ashen green. Their eyes widen. Arms are automatically outstretched. Really, they go the full Thriller. Zombies have few social options save for all of the Aaaaarrrgggghhh socials off the Sim's menu. There's also at least one Braaaiiins social, which in turn makes the zombie attempt to nosh on the target Sim. When the Braaaiiins social lands, the target is also temporarily turned into a zombie. This is detrimental to LTR, of course, but it sure is fun! If the target manages to reject the social, they get the Terrified moodlet. A failed Braaaiiins social has the Awkward STC, as you can imagine.

Alternately, zombies can also choose to focus their hunger for harvestables with the Graaaiiiins interaction. Plants dug out by zombies often die following the interaction. Because this isn't a cerebral snack, there's also a small chance the zombie will get the Nauseous moodlet.

Toadified!: When, via a spell, a human (non-pregnant) Sim is transformed into a ToadSim, they get the moodlet Toadified! Now, temporarily, they are turned into a hybrid toad creature with a massive toad head. During this time, they can still change clothes, but cannot change any of their facial features or hair. They can, however, engage in a number of toad-exclusive interactions that are as fun as they are funny.

ToadSims can Catch Flies on trash cans, garbage, spoiled food, and the beekeeping box. The ToadSim monitors the flies around the object and then, in a flash, lashes out with its tongue to gobble up a bug. This satisfies the Hunger and Fun needs, although nearby Sims may get the Grossed Out moodlet.

ToadSims can also have a little fun with the whole "frog prince" narrative. ToadSims can Ask for a Kiss. And non-ToadSims can use Kiss the Toad. If the kiss is successfully landed, it turns the ToadSim back into a human Sim. The catch, though, is that two ToadSims cannot undo their curses by kissing each other. That's cheating!

Tragic Clown: When Sims drink (or are slipped) the Origin of the Tragic Clown elixir, they transform into a Tragic Clown. This temporarily turns the Sim into a rather strange-looking clown with exaggerated face paint and hair. It's rather freaky and, in fact, other Sims in the presence of the Tragic Clown are dinged with the It's Just So Tragic moodlet. During the cursed period, the Tragic Clown Sim is likely to use the Tell Joke social/interaction more often. During the duration of the curse, the Tragic Clown also suffers from a tanked mood (-40) that requires a lot of offsetting if there's any hope of generating any Lifetime Happiness points.

Vampires

Vampires. The (un)living embodiment of danger—and dangerous sensuality. Fear and love entwined. And a hunger that symbolizes desire for more than nourishment. Vampirism, though quite cool, should not be taken lightly without knowing all that surrendering to the night entails. It alters the trajectory of a Sim's life. The daytime is inhospitable. Hungers change. Certain moodlets are off-limits. Your sure-fire tricks for keeping a Sim content may not work on a vampire, but that can also be part of the excitement. You're trying something completely new, like the first time you had a playable ghost.

Use this chapter to understand the vampire way of life so you can decide whether or not it suits you. The special abilities are sure to tempt you. But temper that temptation with the new realities of vampirism. But because once you give in to the fangs, nothing is ever the same again... well, unless you are reverted to human form through an elixir or other such magics.

> **NOTE**
>
> Vampires were first introduced to *The Sims 3* in *Late Night*. However, there have been some changes to vampirism in this expansion, such as the removal of the Plasma Fruit and the Vampire Lounges. However, if you already have *Late Night* installed, the Vampire supernatural type plays out largely the same.

Create a Sim

Once in Create a Sim, you can select the vampire option from the supernatural type menu. Clicking on this turns your Sim's skin paler, adds a certain glow to their irises, and adds a special birthmark to their neck. As far as traits go, you may want to check out Night Owl, as it benefits Sims who stay out late—something quite beneficial for a Sim who must avoid the sun. Brooding certainly seems like a good trait for the overall vampire narrative, but Flirty or Friendly could be greater assets when trying to turn other Sims, because this requires good LTRs.

> **NOTE**
>
> You may use the Accessories tab to change your vampire's fangs or neck tattoo.

Vampire-inspired Clothing

Within Create a Sim, you can select from a wealth of outfits that were designed specifically to enhance the vampire narrative. Gothic dress, high collars, deep reds, and the blackest of blacks—there's an entire closet of Dracula-esque duds just waiting for you.

Behavior & Benefits

As you can imagine, there are some significant upsides to becoming a vampire beyond being ultra-cool to sensitive teenagers the world over. Vampires have a set of special talents they can employ to make the most of the night, such as intelligence boosts that speed skill development or the ability to creep inside the mind of an unwitting Sim.

> **TIP**
>
> Vampires also rarely lose physical fights. Even the highest rated martial artists from *World Adventures* will have a real scrap on their hands if they try to tangle with a vampire. Even the seemingly unstoppable Mummy crumbles before the might of a vampire.

Vampires run with speed greater than top athletes. They move so fast that the air around them vibrates.

Enhanced Skill Development

One of the great benefits of being a vampire is that you develop skills almost twice as fast as a normal Sim during the night hours. During daylight, when vampires are typically avoiding the sunshine, their skill development rate is on par with other Sims. Vampires are not better at developing any particular skill—the acceleration rate is the same for Alchemy as it is for Logic.

> **TIP**
>
> Vampire students in school also complete their homework twice as fast as their non-occult peers.

> **BROWNIE BITES**
>
> For the reason of accelerated skill development alone, I understand the desire to turn vampire. Yeah, all the other stuff—such as the ability to the read minds or influence the hearts of other Sims—is very cool. But considering the amount of time required to develop the upper levels of a skill, becoming a vampire isn't just cool, it's a huge time saver. If you're going for a Lifetime Wish that requires you master one or more skills, being a vampire will greatly help you achieve the goal. And though we'll talk about this in a moment, you can be cured of vampirism so you no longer must deal with the nuances of being a blood-sucker once you have completed your skill goal or Lifetime Wish.

Dark Romance

Another fun benefit of being vampire is that you can affect the romantic thoughts of other Sims. It is extremely difficult for Sims to resist the natural charms of a nightwalker. But vampires can place the seed of romantic interest in another Sim by using the vampire-exclusive Think About Me interaction on other Sims. This forces the target Sim to start imagining the vampire, noted by thought bubbles containing the vamp's portrait over their head. Hearts and bats swirl around them, too.

During the course of this effect, the relationship between the vampire and the target improves, making it a perfect time to hopefully move a relationship to the next level. This is also a good interaction to smooth the path to turning a non-player-controlled Sim into a vampire.

> **TIP**
>
> Romantic socials from a vampire are successful more than 90 percent of the time!

Mind Reading

Whereas normal Sims have to, you know, talk to each other in order to learn their likes, dislikes, and personality quirks, vampires have an unfair advantage. Vamps can read minds. This interaction works on any target Sim. You do not enter into a conversation, so there's no need to worry about picking the right social to go with a mind reading.

Introduction | New Simology | New Careers & Skills | **Meet the Supernaturals** | New Venues | Tour of Moonlight Falls | New Object Catalog

All you need to do is select what kind of information you want to pluck from the target's brain—traits, favorites, astrological sign, relationships, and career. Mind reading is not immediate; it takes a few moments. However, it never fails. So as soon as the interaction is complete, you have the desired details about the target Sim, all at your fingertips in the Relationship panel.

Now, just reading a mind does not improve a relationship. You must use socials to do that. But the intel gathered by a brain scan is useful for picking appropriate socials. For example, if you determine that the target has no sense of humor, you know not to bother with jokes and silly faces.

CAUTION

You cannot repeat this interaction over and over. There is a cooldown period between Read Mind sessions, during which the interaction is not available. Keep checking back to see when you can use it again.

AGELESS

Vampires age differently than normal Sims. They can certainly die—and we'll look at how in the Complicating Matters section, but they age up much slower than other Sims. The young adult and adult sections of the lifespan stretch out longer. However, the elder segment of life lasts the same.

NOTE

Remember that you can tweak the age cycles of a Sim in the Options menu, allowing you to adjust the length of age sequences.

MOOD PERKS

At night, vampires get the Vampiric Vigor moodlet, which indicates their heightened abilities. In addition to not feeling Sore or Fatigued, vampires also never experience the Afraid of the Dark or It's Dark moodlets. Read Mind and Think About Me are also only available at night when the Vampiric Vigor moodlet is active.

New Socials

Vampires in *Supernatural* have some additional socials not found in the *Late Night* version of vampirism. Conversations can be enhanced with Warn Away (more common with Commitment Issues, Coward, Family-Oriented, Good, Insane, Loner, or Unflirty traits), Confess to Being a Vampire (more common to Sims with Brave, Family-Oriented, Good, Hopeless Romantic, or Genius), Deny Being a Vampire (more common with Childish, Coward, Evil, Loser, Neurotic, or Perfectionist traits), and Intimidate (more common for Grumpy, Hot-Headed, and Mean Sims). This last social, Intimidate, can land with a very negative STC and harshly affect LTR, but not always! In certain relationships with Sims, such as those with the Supernatural Fan trait, the LTR effect can be positive. Either way, the vampire at least gets a Fun boost.

Other Sims also have new socials they can offer to Vampires: Threaten to Exploit Weakness, Accuse of Being a Vampire, and Imply Mother was a Chupacabra. All of these are negatives. If a Sim is a Supernatural Skeptic, you can see how these negative socials are handy for sinking relationships and furthering an anti-supernatural narrative.

NOTE

Further details on these socials (and all new socials in *Supernatural*) are located in the "New Socials" section of the New Simology chapter.

LIFETIME REWARD: IMMORTAL

◊ Cost: 30,000

◊ Description: Become the greatest of vampires by tolerating sunlight and never die of old age.

If you want to develop the ultimate vampire narrative, you need to score the Immortal Lifetime Reward. When a vampire is Immortal, they can withstand the otherwise withering heat and light of the sun. While daywalking, their skin sparkles. In addition, this reward halts aging and noticeably reduces the Thirst need, which often results in better moods.

Complicating Matters

It may sound like vampires have it easy, thanks to their increased intelligence and strength after the sun slips below the horizon. But even nightwalkers sometimes get the blues. Before seeking out the turning process, make sure you know exactly what you are giving up and what hazards vampires must be mindful of lest they falter.

CAUTION

Vampires lose all interest in food other than plasma. The moodlets you would normally get from eating great dishes like Angel Food Cake completely evaporate.

Daylight

Vampires are obviously at their best during the night (regardless of the lunar phase), but they can be active during the waking hours, too. However, walking around outside is not exactly good for the vampire. If the vampire remains outside during the daytime for more than a few moments, they receive the Heating Up moodlet. If you do not get back inside soon, that moodlet turns into Too Much Sun, which is a big mood killer.

CAUTION

During the day, vampires develop skill at normal speed. Neither do they enjoy the extra success rate for romantic socials.

If a vampire spends too much time out during the day (when they really should be catching some beauty rest), they eventually lose more than skill-developing speed. When close to exhaustion, vampires cannot Read Minds or use the Hunt ability to seek out the most delicious Sims to feed upon. If they are out too long, they eventually pass out.

TIP

Vampires can also quaff the Vampiric Sunscreen elixir to temporarily ward off the nasty effects of the sun.

Garlic

There are a few things in this world that vampires do not like. Wooden stakes are a biggie, but fortunately those are nowhere to be found. However, the old standby garlic is present and problematic for vampires. If a vampire eats garlic, they pass out and remain out cold for several hours.

But what about other Sims? Because eating foods with garlic gives Sims the Garlic Breath moodlet, vampires must be mindful of who they speak to or whom they feed upon. If a vampire drinks from a Sim with garlic breath, they also pass out. Passing out can also occur a vamp kisses a Sim with garlic breath, but it's more likely they will only become Nauseous.

Survival Instincts

We all know what vampires need to survive—blood. Making sure you have a steady supply of the red stuff to sate a vampire's thirst is critical to enjoying all of the benefits of playing as a child of the night.

The Need to Feed

When a Sim is turned into a vampire, they lose the Hunger need. It is replaced, though, by Thirst. Thirst and Hunger are the exact same, although Thirst cannot be sated by eating regular food or harvestables. Thirst can only be fulfilled by drinking blood.

There are several ways to satisfy the thirst for blood. The obvious is to feed on another Sim. But the easiest is to guzzle a Plasma Orange Juice. Plasma Orange Juice is found in the fridge as a Quick Snack, but it can also be snatched from the grocery store and stored in the fridge, just like regular ingredients or leftovers.

Wait, snatched? Yes, vampires actually do not buy Plasma Orange Juice. Instead, they steal it from grocery stores with the Raid interaction on the shop. The vampire Sim disappears inside and starts grabbing juice boxes (you'll see the count go up in your inventory if you monitor the tab during the interaction). There is no negative from raiding, but it does take time to complete the interaction.

However, as expected, vampires derive the greatest degree of satisfaction from dipping their fangs into a fresh vein. The Drink interaction on a target Sim initiates the bloody snack attack. Now, you cannot just grab hold of strangers and start slurping. You must have a good relationship with a target, regardless of whether or not they are controlled by you or are autonomous.

If you attempt the interaction on a Sim that is not keen on your vampire, they will resist and reject the advance. If the target has a good relationship with your vampire or is romantically interested in your vampire (and here's where interactions like Think About Me help), they will allow themselves to be fed upon.

If the Sims are friends, they offer their wrist. If romance is involved, the vampire moves to the neck for the main course. Either way, this action not only feeds the vampire (and imbues the Sated moodlet), but gives a slight relationship boost to both parties.

TURNING SIMS

When you are a vampire, you may turn other Sims. You can turn Sims that you actively control in your household as long as the Sims are on good terms. However, if you attempt to use the Offer to Turn interaction on a Sim you do not control, you must run a relationship check. You cannot bite just any stranger. You at least need a positive relationship.

If you are zeroing in on the Turn the Town Lifetime Wish, then you need to make sure you're a smooth operator. Developing the Charisma skill is extremely useful, because it will lead to better social interactions and, in turn, stronger relationships. (Bonus: Because you're a vampire, you develop skills faster—just make sure you study at night! And why not use a Magic Mirror to further the skill acceleration?) The Never Dull Lifetime Reward is also useful, because it means none of your socials land with a Dull STC. The Attractive Lifetime Reward, too, is beneficial because it means other Sims cannot resist your charms.

There is a secondary means of turning a Sim into a vampire: a elixir. The Bottled Vampire's Bite is an elixir that Alchemist can whip up at level 7 using Vampirefish, Red Valerian, and Bloodstone Powder. This elixir can be given willingly or mixed into a drink and left out for a non-vampire to use. (It only works on child-aged Sims and above.) Keep an eye on the elixir shop, too, because it may also become purchasable during a daily special.

If a vampire fails to feed enough, they can perish. So, when the Madly Thirsty moodlet appears, stop everything and do whatever you must to get this vampire some hemoglobin, stat. Should the timer below the moodlet zero out, the Grim Reaper appears to take what's rightfully his. The vampire disintegrates into a pile of ashes... but even the

undead can come back as ghosts. Playable vampire ghosts are really cool, because they have the benefits of both vampirism and of ghosts. And if you're in this to tell a really good narrative, a ghost vampire is quite the star.

The Hunt

Not all plasma is the same. Vampires get greater pleasure and extra Thirst satisfaction if they drink from a superior source. But to identify a source of good plasma, vampires must go on the Hunt. To start the Hunt interaction, just click on the currently occupied lot and select it from the available list. Now, the vampire will begin eyeing everybody on the lot.

As Sims around the vampire are "scanned" for plasma quality, they appear with a thermal overlay. After a few moments, the vampire gathers the necessary info to determine which Sim (or Sims) on the lot has particularly delicious plasma. Those Sims will be noted in the Relationship tab of the Status panel and will be marked with an icon in Map View. Your vampire definitely wants to keep track of these special Sims; when he or she drinks from them, the vamp earns the positive Sanguine Snack moodlet. This is more powerful than the Sated moodlet.

Vampire Families

Vampires cannot turn younger Sims—that just wouldn't be right to steal life away from children and teenagers before they are able to make such a momentous decision on their own. Besides, feeding on a little kid? That's just creepy-wrong. Yet there can be vampire children. You may designate a vampire child in Create a Sim. But if you want a vampire baby…

A vampire may become romantically involved with either another vampire or a normal Sim. After successfully Trying for Baby, two vampires produce a child with the hidden Vampire trait. When that child becomes a young adult, they automatically become a full vampire without the growing pains other Sims experience during the turning process.

If a vampire and normal Sim create a baby, there is only a 50 percent chance it carries that hidden Vampire trait.

Though younger vampires do not Drink, Hunt, or Read Minds like fully developed vampires, they still exhibit a few of the physical vampire traits just to let you know what's coming. Look for pale skin or reflective eyes.

A CURE?

So, there is a way to undo vampirism (or any supernatural condition) and return a Sim to human form. Alchemists can brew an elixir called Potent Cure Elixir. At level 7, Alchemists can create this elixir from Wolfsbane, Glow Orbs, and Ruby Powder. Like the Bottled Vampire's Bite, this elixir can be given to a vampire for them to swallow or it can be sneaked into a glass and given to the unsuspecting. Either way, one taste and nightwalking becomes a thing of the past. As soon as the cure is consumed, the vampire returns to normal status and no longer has Thirst. They have the Hunger need again and crave regular food. Life is back to normal... or as normal as it's going to get in Moonlight Falls. Vampires can also forsake their powers and chase an Opportunity chain to return to human form.

Ghosts

Though vampires and werewolves are synonymous with the supernatural these days, there is one otherworldly being that has been linked to the supernatural across the centuries: ghosts. In *The Sims 3 Supernatural*, you can now opt to jump right in as a playable ghost rather than attempt to purposefully off a Sim and go through the effort of bringing them back via an Opportunity at the science facility or whatnot.

Playable ghosts in *Supernatural* do not have extra properties—they operate here in the same fashion as they did in the base game and all expansions. The prime difference is that you have the means of choosing their death from Create a Sim, which determines their spectral glow. There are additional objects that ghost Sims can haunt now, too, such as the beekeeping box and Moondial.

Otherwise, treat a playable ghost as you would any other Sim. Get out there. Find a job. Develop a skill. Design a house. Marry. Have a family. All of the trappings (well, trimmings) of a normal life are available to ghosts. They just have to worry about scaring the pants off some weak-kneed Sims, which can lead to bummer social situations.

Create a Sim: Death Types

Once you have decided to become a playable ghost, you can designate your demise. As you know from *The Sims 3* base game, how a Sim "dies" affects the appearance of their ghost. Click the Ghost Basics tab on the Basics menu to pull up a list of gravestones. Click on each gravestone to sneak a peek at the changing colors that result from different deaths. While the determination of death does not affect how your playable ghost operates in the world, it's certainly cool to be able to select your spectral hue.

Old Age

When Sims shuffle off the digital coil due to old age, they come back as ghostly white phantoms.

Drowning

Drowning victims appear as cool blue ghosts, ready to take one last lap around the pool.

Starvation

Sims that were not adequately fed—well, not fed at all—perish and then return as little purple spirits.

Electrocution

Being shocked to death may result in a ghastly death, but your spectral form looks fabulous. Check out those coursing currents!

Burn to Death

Immolation is a decidedly unpleasant way to go, but when a fire-ravaged Sim comes back to life as a playable ghost, they sport an exciting orange hue.

Mummy's Curse

Sims that were shattered by the Mummy's Curse in *World Adventures* returned to the realm of the living in this gray, opaque form.

Meteor

Really, you couldn't step out of the path of a falling space rock? Well, as a reward for such pokey plodding, you're resurrected as a shade with orange highlights.

Watery Grave

Trapped in water deaths result in the same ghostly blue hue as a Drowned ghost.

Human Statue

Being turned to stone is a terrible way to go, but at least you re-enter the mortal realm as a near-translucent spirit.

Transmuted

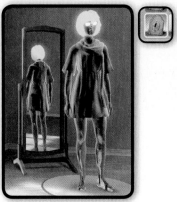

There's a slight chance that using the new Philosopher's Stone Lifetime Reward will backfire and turn the user to gold. That's an instant death. And this gilded ghost is the result.

Haunting Curse

Should a Sim be victim to a Haunting Curse, they come back as this groovy green spectre.

Jelly Bean Death

There is a chance—remote as it is—that nibbling on a jelly bean from the Magic Jelly Bean Bush results in an immediate demise. Such a sweet death leads then to this sweet spectral hue, a glowing purple aura that looks positively dashing.

New Haunts

As a playable ghost, you may haunt objects to have a little fun with other, livelier Sims. There are a handful of new objects introduced in *Supernatural* that ghosts may shake and levitate, thus frightening nearby Sims and possibly hitting them with the Terrified moodlet. The new objects ghost may autonomously haunt are:

- Beekeeping Box
- Fairy House
- Moondial
- Rocking Chair
- Rocking Rider
- Wardrobe

TIP

If you haunt the beekeeping box, you can actually shake it so hard that angry bees erupt from the lid. Nearby Sims risk getting stung and dinged with the Bee Sting negative moodlet.

TIP

We know what you're thinking—can playable ghosts WooHoo? The answer is: yes, if the ghost is of a young adult or adult Sim. You can raise the amorous LTR with a ghost to the point where you can have WooHoo and even Try for Baby. If the interaction conceives a child, there is a chance it will be a ghost baby. You can even do cross-supernatural babies this way, such as vampire ghosts and werewolf ghosts!

MEET BONEHILDA

Look, sometimes houses get messy or kids need watching while a grown-up Sim attends to work or important activities. Hiring a nanny or maid to swing by the lot every day can add up. Why not funnel that cash into hiring Bonehilda, your very own live-in (dead-in?) skeletal maid/babysitter? Employing Bonehilda is as easy as dropping into Buy Mode and selecting Bonehilda Living Quarters for §3,999. Yes, that's steep. But consider all of the benefits that come with owning your very own supernatural help.

Here are some things you should know about Bonehilda before making the investment:

Bonehilda is, in essence, an actual Sim that exists on your lot, even though she is not playable. She cannot be married, though, nor does she age or die.

You cannot engage Bonehilda in relationships. There is no LTR with Bonehilda.

Bonehilda has five traits: Brave, Neat, Workaholic, Athletic, and Perfectionist.

By nature, Bonehilda is somewhat robotic. She will not react to most activities around her, save for a fire breaking out on the lot or the arrival of a Burglar. In those situations, Bonehilda leaps into action to put out the flames or shoo away the Burglar.

When you install Bonehilda Living Quarters on your lot, the maid does not immediately jump into service. She remains in her coffin, no matter how messy the house gets. You must activate Bonehilda with the Awaken interaction if you wish for her to start cleaning or minding children. As soon as Bonehilda emerges, she starts her tasks. The priority is addressing the needs of toddlers and children on the lot, such as feeding. If you have *Pets* installed, Bonehilda will also look after your animals. If there are no pets or kids to watch, Bonehilda will then start a maid route, moving around the lot and tidying up after messy Sims.

If there is no more work for Bonehilda to do, you can Dismiss her, at which point she slips back into her coffin and enters a state of rest. However, if you leave her out with nothing to do, she engages in several idle activities.

If there is a bar in the room, Bonehilda will prepare a quick drink. But when she tries to gulp it down, it passes right through her skeletal frame and results in a puddle on the floor. If there is a mirror nearby, she will admire herself. And if there is a stereo in the room, Bonehilda will turn it on and then start dancing.

Now, you can Chat with Bonehilda, just like any of the other NPC service Sims. Though this does not generate LTR, it does satisfy the actor's Social need. Sims with the Cowardly trait, though, should avoid her because they'll freak out at the sight of a skeleton maid and get the Scared moodlet. In addition, if a maid NPC is in the same room as Bonehilda, they get seriously spooked and flee

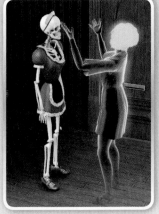

the lot. (At least they don't charge for whatever work they've done so far!)

Sounds cool, right? It is! So start saving those Simoleons so you can get your very own Bonehilda today!

GENIES

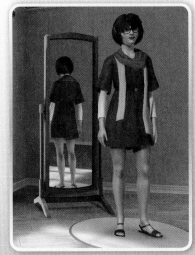

Genies were a sweet part of the *Showtime* expansion. If you found a Dusty Old Lamp. You could free this being of fire and wind. Once out of the lamp, the genie granted three wishes from a list of 10 or so, including resurrecting a deceased Sim, depositing a large sum of Simoleons into your account, and guaranteed fertility. You could even wish to free the Genie and have it join your household.

Well, genies are back in *The Sims 3 Supernatural*. If you have *Showtime* installed, you may select a Genie from the supernatural type in Create a Sim. Selecting the Genie turns your Sim's skin blue and dresses them up in some rather theatrical duds. Now, you are not required to keep these automatic cosmetic options. Feel free to change the skin tone or the outfits.

There are no extra benefits to being a Genie if you select the type from Create a Sim. The Genie is just another supernatural option for assembling a cool household or a mystical narrative.

95

New Venues

• • • •

The introduction of new supernatural types, new careers, and new skills necessitates the arrival some new venues for Moonlight Falls—or any of the existing cities, should you decide to start a supernatural life in, say, Sunset Valley. Though we have a full tour of Moonlight Falls in the next chapter, use this section to dig deep into the newly crafted venues for *The Sims 3 Supernatural*.

Supernatural Real Estate

Should you want to try your hand at the new Fortune Teller career, sell your elixirs on the open market, or carouse with other supernaturals in Moonlight Falls, chances are good you'll make more than one stop at any of these new venues.

Gypsy Wagon

Address: 81 N. Falls Avenue

Venue Type: Career

Operating Hours: Career hours, various

This charming little Vardo is homebase for the all-new Fortune Teller career, a new way for Sims (supernatural or not) to make some Simoleons. The Fortune Teller career was fully explained in the New Careers chapter, but there are other activities available here, such as the ability to have a fortune told.

Primary Use

As mentioned, the primary function of the Gypsy Wagon is the workplace of a Fortune Teller, a new career track here in *Supernatural*. This venue is considered a "rabbit hole," like a stadium or military base. When your Sim reports to work, you set the tone of the work day, but other than that, the Sim is largely unavailable.

To start the Fortune Teller career, you can just click on the Gypsy Wagon and choose the new career. Your Sim is then routed right to the venue and the first day of the career begins. Alternately, you can answer a job ad online or via the newspaper. And if you play around with Opportunities, there is an Opportunity connected to the Orb of Answers object that can lead to the Fortune Teller career track.

Additional Activities

Sims who opt for other careers can still use the Gypsy Wagon. If you click on the Gypsy Wagon, you see a new Have Fortune Told interaction. This initiates a cool little "adventure" once your Sim enters the Gypsy Wagon, not unlike popping into the mausoleum. When your Sim is inside, getting a reading, several small text notes appear on-screen. These offer asides related to the unfolding of the fortune.

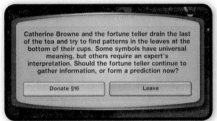

However, at some point you will be asked questions about the fortune process that involve—wait for it—Simoleons. Having your fortune told can actually get quite expensive, depending on how long you want the process to go. You are not required to keep paying the Fortune Teller, but you do get benefits for staying in the Gypsy Wagon, slapping Simoleons on the table.

When you eventually do exit the wagon, whether it's by no longer paying or by reaching the end of the reading, you receive one of four mood boosts. Here they are, in ascending order: Complete Nonsense, Taking Precautions, It May Come True, and Total Believer.

ACCESS YOUR  BONUS EGUIDE NOW!

Your guide comes with FREE access to *The Sims™ 3 Supernatural* eGuide and Interactive Neighborhood Map. Login with the voucher code below:

- Access the Moonlight Shores interactive map and find every collectable.
- Zoom in and out and toggle map markers on and off to reveal only the information you want to see.
- Access the leading *The Sims™ 3 Supernatural* strategy anywhere you have an internet connection.
- Enlarge screenshots, search tables, bookmark pages and so much more.

1. Go to www.primagames.com. Select "Redeem Code" located at the top of the page.

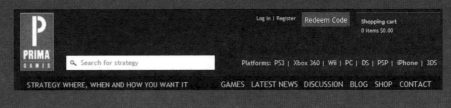

2. Enter the voucher code in the text field and click the "Submit" button.

3. You will be redirected to your content now.

VOUCHER CODE

g3fv-v82q-csp2-zuk9

 Follow us on Twitter

 Like us on Facebook

Your eGuide offer expires 9/4/2013

Introduction · New Simology · New Careers & Skills · Meet the Supernaturals · New Venues · Tour of Moonlight Falls · New Object Catalog

TIP

Total Believer is a +40 moodlet that lasts for five hours. It's quite the handsome mood reward that could very well help you bank a lot of Lifetime Happiness points!

NOTE

Additional factors add even more boost to the resulting moodlet. These traits—Supernatural Fan, Childish, Daredevil, Coward, Easily Impressed, Neurotic and Hopeless Romantic—add time to the moodlet.

CAUTION

On the flip side, having any of these traits—Genius, Bookworm, Proper, Mean Spirited and Perceptive—subtracts time from the post-reading mood boost.

In addition to Having Fortune Told, there is another more... libidinous interaction for the Gypsy Wagon: WooHoo/Try for Baby. If you are in a romantic relationship with another Sim, you may click on the Gypsy Wagon and designate it as an impromptu love hotel. Now, you can either select WooHoo or go ahead and Try for Baby—your choice. However, either selection satisfies Fun and Social needs, and boosts LTR.

CAUTION

Be mindful of how potentially inappropriate it is to WooHoo at somebody's career venue! If neither of the Sims has any meaningful activity at the Gypsy Wagon, such as being a Fortune Teller, Sims consider on-site WooHoo to be very inappropriate. LTR hit in the making, you know.

Aleister's Elixirs and Sundries

Address: 336 Knott Street

Venue Type: Commerce

Operating Hours: —

Witches and Alchemists will get the most out of this venue, although it's certainly open for business to all Sims in Moonlight Falls. Here, Alchemists can trade their goods at the counter, witches can try out magic brooms, and much more.

Primary Uses

The Elixir Shop Consignment Register will get the most use from witches and Alchemists. At the counter, these Sims can put goods up for consignment as a means of making Simoleons either on the side or as a full-time career. To do so, you simply approach the register and access the Buy menu. Then, chose the Consignment tab and off-load items in your inventory. Now, not everything will sell. However, there is typically an active market for specific items and you will receive hints and tips about what's hot and what's not. Fulfill the needs of the town and you will be rewarded. Plus, the faster goods sell, the more you receive for them.

You can buy items from the shop, too. And this is something that all Sims will benefit from, as even though you may not craft your own elixirs, you may find a good use for them. For example, let's say you're desperate for a baby. The Potion of Procreation will practically guarantee that the next WooHoo results in a little bundle of joy.

Additional Activities

In addition to the consignment register, there are multiple objects inside Aleister's Elixirs and Sundries that are incredibly useful. Like the communal exercise equipment at the town gym, the objects in here are free to use and will help you save money when first starting out:

◆ **Alchemy Station:** If you're researching Alchemy to help build up the Alchemy skill, this station is quite useful. Here, study up and develop that skill without dropping a single Simoleon. In addition, you can also use this station to craft new elixirs.

◆ **Gem-U-Cut Machine:** When you just cannot wait for the mail, step up to the Gem-U-Cut Machine here in the shop and transform raw materials into cut gems. Plus, you get to keep the dust left over from the cutting process, and that's useful stuff.

◆ **LLAMA:** Need to zip around town and are short on time? Step inside the LLAMA and you're off in a flash!

Sims who want to practice up Broom Riding can check out the Zoomsweeper Broom Arena just outside. This track lets you go out for joy rides and stunt rides, both of which develop the hidden Broom Riding skill, as well as satisfy needs, such as Fun. For a full breakdown of this arena, be sure to check out the New Object Catalog chapter.

Varg's Tavern

Address: 2303 Waning Way

Venue Type: Bar

Operating Hours: 10 AM to 3 AM

Varg's Tavern is a bar-like venue designed to attract werewolves, although human Sims may sidle up to the counter and order a cool one, too. Vampires, fairies, witches, and other supernaturals—on the other hand—are likely to keep their distance. However, if you are currently playing as any supernatural, you have complete control over going into Varg's Tavern. Just don't expect to find any of your own kind there...

> ### NOTE
> If you have *Late Night*, then you have a good idea of how Varg's Tavern works. It's not exclusive like a *Late Night* haunt, but it does have some of its features.

Primary Use

Varg's Tavern is exactly that—a tavern. But it's designed to cater to werewolves. So, if you are on the hunt for werewolves, either to mingle with your own or perhaps to find the means of turning into a werewolf yourself, Varg's Tavern is the place to be. As mentioned, this is primarily a

haunt for werewolves and humans, but if you are a vampire or fairy (or any other supernatural), you are well within your rights to frequent this establishment.

When you first enter the two-story tavern, you'll spot a bar off to the left. Sims often gather around this area, so if you're here to meet Sims or satisfy Social needs, you can often find somebody to chat up near the bar.

> **TIP**
>
> If you have *Late Night* installed, you can make drinks from that expansion as well as order bar food.

> **NOTE**
>
> If you have *Late Night* installed, these socials are possible: Buy a Round, Pick Up, and Bar Brawl. If you don't have *Late Night*, Bar Brawl is replaced by the more traditional Fight social.

Other social opportunities abound in this establishment, such as near the games in the corner, the music/dance area, and the upstairs bar. The upstairs is a little smaller and thus, a little more intimate. If you are stepping out on a romantic partner or canoodling with somebody else's significant other, this might not be a bad hideaway for your activities.

> **TIP**
>
> Peak werewolf activity at Varg's Tavern occurs during new moon and full moon.

Additional Activities

Other activities inside Varg's Tavern encourage social behavior. Make good use of these objects, especially in the beginning of your adventure in Moonlight Falls, as frequently communal objects saves serious Simoleons.

- **Smack-a-Gnome!:** The Smack-a-Gnome! arcade game in the corner of Varg's Tavern is a hoot. Step up to the machine and bring the hammer down on itty-bitty supernatural heads. Often the heads are related to your supernatural type (for example, werewolves love to bop vampires), but you can choose which heads to smack down. This object satisfies Fun, and if other Sims gather to watch, Social needs are also attended to.

- **Foosball:** Near the Smack-a-Gnome! game, you'll spot a foosball table. Like the arcade game, this table satisfies both Fun and Social needs, whether you opt to play or watch. Just remember that playing with other Sims speeds LTR as opposed to just watching.

- **Moondial:** Upstairs, you'll spot a Moondial. If you want to verify the lunar cycle or read a Lunar Horoscope, use this object. Just be mindful that not every horoscope is positive and you risk getting a bummer of a reading that can lower your mood.

- **Magic Mirror:** All of the interactions available on a Magic Mirror are listed in the New Object Catalog chapter, but if you just need somebody to talk to and not worry about the ebb and flow of LTR, chat up this object. You can talk about the day, gossip, and more. Plus, you can speedily develop the Charisma skill here!

- **LLAMA:** Need to zoom around Moonlight Falls? The LLAMA just outside the tavern is perfect for getting you from one spot to the next. So, if you spot a special werewolf at Varg's and you want to make sure you meet her before she bails, don't fret—LLAMA will get you there in a jiff!

Arboretum

Address: 2303 Waning Way

Venue Type: Fairy/Gardening

Operating Hours: 10 AM to 3 AM

The Arboretum is a "rabbit hole"-type venue located at Fay Rae on Wood Street. Fairies get the most use out of the Arboretum, but Sims with green thumbs and Gardening skills can also report here to enter Gardening competitions to win Simoleons.

Primary Uses

Fairy Sims around town are naturally attracted to the Arboretum, and if you click on the venue itself, you'll soon see why. There are a host of interactions that are centered around the fairy lifestyle, even though they can be enjoyed by non-fairy Sims:

⚬ **Search for Fairies:** Any Sim can use this interaction. When Sims step inside to Search for Fairies, they go on a little adventure (not unlike the mausoleum) and eventually make a choice that directs the narrative of the adventure. There are five potential outcomes. The Sim may end up "finding" a fairy who lives in town and get an LTR boost with them. If the Sim finds Fairy Dust, a small pouch of Fairy Dust goes into their inventory. The third possibility is just finding some random seeds. The fourth possibility is to receive the Become a Fairy Opportunity. Finally, well, there's always a chance of walking out empty-handed.

⚬ **Play Fairy Games:** This interaction is exclusive to fairies and child Sims (of any type). When selected, fairies and children enter the Arboretum for a few hours and play games. You'll hear the sounds of mirth and merriment from within while your Sim has Fun and satisfies the Social need. When they emerge, they have the positive Played Fairy Games moodlet.

⚬ **Talk to Baby's Breath:** Any Sim older than teenager can choose this interaction (except SimBots or Mummies). While inside the Arboretum, Sims commune with the flowers. Magic in the air positive moodlet, which increases the chances of a successful Try for Baby interaction. It's not a bad way to spend a few hours...

Additional Activities

There is a Tour interaction on the Arboretum that is similar to touring the police station or military base. Your Sim goes on the tour either alone or with another Sim (+LTR) and if they don't like supernatural stuff or plants, well, they get bored.

Several times a week, Gardening Competitions are held at the Arboretum. Just mouse over to catch the starting time of the next competition. If your Sim(s) have developed the Gardening skill and have a harvestable in their inventory, they may enter the competition. At the start of the competition, the highest quality harvestable from inventory is entered. Then, the Gardening skill level is assessed. These both figure into a final score. There are eight places in each competition and depending on where you place, you get Simoleons as a prize. Naturally, the better you place, the more you win.

> **TIP**
> First place winners get a trophy to place on their lot!

> **TIP**
> Children without Gardening skills can enter the competitions, too. In fact, there's even a random chance they will win, despite not having developed the skill.

Vault of Antiquity

Address: 108 Wood Street

Venue Type: Research

Operating Hours: All day

Just behind the library, you'll spot the Vault of Antiquity, the records hall for Moonlight Falls, as well as a special place to research the supernatural, which unlocks a series of short adventures that may possibly result in rewards for astute (and lucky) Sims.

Primary Activities

Sims who want to get a jump start on the Alchemy skill can just enroll at the Vault of Antiquity. For a small tuition fee, enjoy a brain download that will have you well on your way to devising elixir recipes and other skill benefits.

Perhaps the most involved activity at the vault is Research the Supernatural. This is an interactive adventure that unfolds once your supernatural Sim slips through the Gothic doors. Depending on the supernatural type, the adventure will pull from specific skills (both visible and hidden) to determine supernatural topics:

- **Vampire:** Logic and Charisma
- **Werewolf:** Athletics and Fishing
- **Witch:** Alchemy and Collection
- **Fairy:** Gardening and Dancing
- **Ghost:** Painting and Cooking

Once the adventure starts, you have multiple choices that determine the course of the event. Depending on which choice you make, a specific skill is "checked." If the skill is decently high, you will move on. If you fail a question due to a low skill (or no skill!), your Sim will be ejected from the vault. (Supernatural Fan Sims even risk having that trait converted to Supernatural Skeptic!) If all choices are successfully passed, the Sim exits the vault and receives a reward, such as a supernatural book, Scary Beary, and more. Sims may also receive the Historian moodlet for completing a vault adventure. Here are charts for the different adventures, broken down by supernatural type, so you can see how the different skills are checked and what rewards await!

GHOST VAULT REWARDS

Scenario	Choice 1	Scenario	Choice 2	Book Reward	Toy Reward	Moodlet Reward	Elixir Reward
Hours of research finally yield some interesting results that could change the way people think about Ghost Studies! Sim has discovered a lost series of illustrated spectral cook books, which are translucent and float a few inches above the table. He/she could examine the illustrations in depth, or he/she could try to decipher the recipes within. What should Sim do?	Decipher the Recipes (Cooking skill check)	Something in one of these books has to explain why Ghosts would hold banquets. They use only ghostly ingredients, but they never appear to actually eat the food. Why? Maybe there are more clues in the books' illustrations. Maybe comparing the recipes, figuring out what the Ghosts liked to prepare, will help shed some light on the subject. What should Sim do?	Compare Recipes (Cooking skill check)	How to Cook for Forty Ghosts	Haunted Magic Gnome	Wow, A Ghost!	"Zombification, Clone Drone, Zombified, Perma Zombie, and Melancholy"
	Examine the Illustrations (Painting skill check)		Compare the Illustrations (Painting skill check)				

VAMPIRE VAULT REWARDS

Scenario	Choice 1	Scenario	Choice 2	Book Reward	Toy Reward	Moodlet Reward	Elixir Reward
Sim has the opportunity to answer two long-standing questions about vampires. Why are they always such snappy dressers, and why do they like the dark so much? Which should Sim research?	Snazzy Clothes? (Charisma skill check)	Sim is getting closer to an answer. What should he/she research now?	Snappy Dressers (Charisma skill check)	This Bites: A Guide to Raising Your Teenage Vampire	Vampire Scary Beary	Wow, a Vampire!	Bottled Vampire's Bite
	Why Darkness? (Logic skill check)		Why Darkness? (Logic skill check)				

WEREWOLF VAULT REWARDS

Scenario	Choice 1	Scenario	Choice 2	Book Reward	Toy Reward	Moodlet Reward	Elixir Reward
Werewolves are natural survivors. Sim can't help but wonder if he/she could survive in the wilderness as some Werewolves do. What survival ability should he/she test?	Physical Stamina (Athletic skill check)	Sim is doing well so far. What should he/she test next?	Food Gathering (Fishing skill check)	GrrrROWLF!!	Werewolf Scary Beary	Wow, a Werewolf!	Bottled Curse of the Lycan
	Food Gathering (Fishing skill check)		Physical Stamina (Athletic skill check)				

FAIRY VAULT REWARDS

Scenario	Choice 1	Scenario	Choice 2	Book Reward	Toy Reward	Moodlet Reward	Elixir Reward
Because Fairies are so obsessed with other beings' behavior, very little is understood about their private culture. Luckily, Sim has uncovered some ancient tomes detailing two popular Fairy activities: gardening and dancing. Which should he/she study?	Fairy Dances (Dancing hidden skill check)	Sim is close to a breakthrough. Could it be that there is a connection between dancing and gardening for the fairies? Where will he/she find the final clue?	Fairy Gardens (Gardening skill check)	The Roots of Fairy Dance	Fairy Scary Beary	Wow, a Fairy!	Bottled Blessing of the Fae
	Gardening Book (Gardening skill check)		Dancing Book (Dancing hidden skill check)				

WITCH VAULT REWARDS

Scenario	Choice 1	Scenario	Choice 2	Book Reward	Toy Reward	Moodlet Reward	Elixir Reward
Witches tell a legend of a caustic elixir that is so powerful it can eat through anything. Sim might be able to produce one, but should he/she focus on the ingredients or the mixing process?	Mix It Right (Alchemy skill check)	Things are off to a good start. It's time to integrate the final batch of ingredients. Where should Sim place his/her focus now?	Right Ingredients (Collecting hidden skill check)	Which Witch?	Witch Scary Beary	Wow, a Witch!	Bottled Witches' Brew
	Right Ingredients (Collecting hidden skill check)		Mix It Right (Alchemy skill check)				

TIP

Alternately, Supernatural Skeptics can complete this adventure and possibly emerge from the vault with the Supernatural Fan trait. This is very rare, but possible!

Additional Activities

The Vault of Antiquity is all about learning—and what better way to prove your education than by showing off in a Trivia Contest? To enter a Trivia Contest, mouse over the vault and look for the timing of the next event. When it's time, select the interaction and your Sim will enter the contest. Your Sim's chances of winning the contest are determined by a number of factors:

- Number of books read by the Sim
- Number of books written by the Sim
- Writing skill
- Logic skill
- Charisma skill

Depending on where you place in the Trivia Contest, winner or runner-up, you will receive a prize: Simoleons! Winners also may be awarded an expensive book for proving themselves to be such smartypants.

NOTE

Like other touring venues, such as the police station, Sims can tour the vault. It's possible to Make Out or WooHoo at the vault. There's even a chance that vampires touring the facility will exit with their Thirst need completely replenished.

Red Velvet Lounge

Address: 20 N Falls Avenue

Venue Type: Bar

Operating Hours: All day

Werewolves aren't the only supernatural in Moonlight Falls with a venue catered to their interests—vampires have their very own bar: Red Velvet. This slightly sinister lounge is a gathering spot for twilight's parasites, giving them a place to commune with their own in a deeply dim atmosphere that suits their aversion to the sunlight.

Primary Activities

Red Velvet is primarily designed to cater to vampires, though the joint is not off-limits to other humans and supernaturals. (In fact, humans looking to turn have a good chance to meeting a willing vamp partner at the Red Velvet.) There are several bars on-site where you can have a social drink, talk up patrons, and see if anybody on the lot catches your eye. Should you need a little private time, there are few small rooms where you may retire from prying eyes.

Additional Activities

Red Velvet has more to do than drink and dine (on plasma). There are a host of objects you can interact with to have fun, develop skills, and satisfy needs.

- **Magic Mirror:** Everybody needs a friend sometimes, and the Magic Mirror is the perfect partner. Chat, gossip, even develop the Charisma skill.

- **Smack-a-Gnome!:** Want to have a little fun? Step up to the Smack-a-Gnome! machine and start swatting little heads back into their holes. This develops the hidden Arcade skill and satisfies the Social need if an audience gathers 'round.

- **Foosball:** Socialize with patrons of Red Velvet over a game of foosball. This also satisfies the Fun need.

The Toadstool

Address: 163 Horseshoe Bend

Venue Type: Social lot

Operating Hours: 7 AM to 1 AM

The Toadstool is where Sims come to hang out and socialize with fellow Sims and supernaturals. While this might be a more congenial environment for fairies than the Red Velvet or Varg's Tavern, it caters to all Sims, not just fairies. In this quaint, two-story facility, Sims can have a quick drink, play the guitar, or try to beat the arcade games. But the main activity to do inside The Toadstool is be with other Sims.

Primary Activities

This is a social venue where solo Sims or groups can come to hang out. There's no shortage of seating, bars for making drinks (including an upstairs bar), and bookshelves for doing a little light reading.

Use the several Spectrum Mood Lamps in the venue to alter not just your mood, but the moods of everyone around the lamp. Assign a color to the lamp so anybody who walks close to it receives the designated moodlet.

> ### NOTE
> There is a restroom downstairs if you need to take care of any business.

Additional Activities

Additional objects and activities inside The Toadstool further encourage socializing and even skill development.

- **Smack-a-Gnome!:** The Smack-a-Gnome! arcade game in the corner of The Toadstool satisfies the Fun need. Smack down supernatural heads with your mallet and, after a few rounds, see if your high score makes you a winner. This helps develop the hidden Arcade game skill, too!

- **Guitar:** Want to develop the Guitar skill or just play a little music? Pick up the guitar in the corner and do a little strumming. Fairies can inspire creativity, so if one is close by, you'll develop the skill faster—especially if they are emitting the Creativity Aura.

- **The Claaaaw:** The arcade claw machine lets you try to lift animals and toys from a pile of cuddly cuteness. If you're really lucky, you may pull a magic gnome from the machine. Fairies can cheat the machine by turning into true fairy form, and slipping inside to increase their chances of pulling out a great prize.

- **LLAMA:** Outside The Toadstool sits a LLAMA, ready to take you wherever you need to go around Moonlight Falls.

Tour of Moonlight Falls

• • •

"With its misty waterfalls, deep forests and fog-shrouded coves, Moonlight Falls casts a spell on all who enter. The town was founded centuries ago by two immigrant families: the Van Goulds—extraordinarily long-lived and sun-averse—and the Wolffs, high-spirited and strangely affected by the full moon. They were soon joined by odd, seemingly magical, forest-dwelling folk.

The town is known for its peculiar potions, made from the plants, gems, and minerals unique to this corner of the world. Some ingredients can only be found at night, but only the truly adventurous stay out after dark... some say it's a whole different world under the moonlight."

—Moonlight Falls Visitors Guide

Welcome to Moonlight Falls, a lovely little town nestled deep in a forest that has long been associated with magic and mystery. How much of Moonlight Falls' magic can be uncovered is entirely up to you, as you delve into different supernatural lifestyles, interact with affected citizens, and explore the charmed (and charming) township.

This town tour pulls back the curtain on every single venue, community lot, and household (both pre-existing and empty lot) available to newcomers. Use this chapter to not only master the lay of the land, but also determine a game plan for exploring as well as collecting. If you dive deep into the all-new Alchemy skill (which is critical to getting the most out of this mystical burgh), a set of maps give you everything necessary to find the best ingredients, minerals, and more.

So, what are you waiting for? Let's unroll some maps, consult the real estate guide, and see why Moonlight Falls has such an envied reputation for being one of the most intriguing places a Sim can call home!

NOTE

This tour includes venues that are installed into Moonlight Falls if you have previous *The Sims 3* expansion packs, such as *Ambitions* and *Night Life*. However, we'll make a note if the venue or lot is directly tied to an expansion.

BROWNIE BITES

Our tour zeroes in on Moonlight Falls, but you can also start a new *Supernatural* life in Sunset Valley, Bridgeport, Twinbrook, or other towns found in previous expansions. The venues associated with *Supernatural*, such as the Gypsy Wagon, are placed in whatever town you choose, much the same way the fire station appears in Moonlight Valley if you have *Ambitions* installed.

NOTE

The all-new venues—Gypsy Wagon, Varg's Tavern, Arboretum, Vault of Antiquity, and Aleister's Elixirs & Sundries—are all detailed in the New Venues chapter.

Career Venues

While many residents of Moonlight Falls take on alternate lifestyles such as vampirism and lycanthropy, there is always a need for career-minded Sims. Many Sims appreciate the set work hours and steady pay offered by these traditional careers. Working day jobs has the added benefit of leaving the evenings free to take in rather intriguing extracurricular activities. Sims can find a wide range of traditional careers by visiting the following establishments or by browsing for jobs in a newspaper or on a computer.

NOTE

The Gypsy Wagon venue, which is where you can explore the Fortune Teller career, is detailed in the "Career" section of the New Simology chapter.

Introduction
New Simology
New Careers & Skills
Meet the Supernaturals
New Venues
Tour of Moonlight Falls
New Object Catalog

Bloom Institute of Wellness

Address: 424 Huckleberry Lane

Function: Hospital/Science Facility

Hospital Interactions

- Join Medical Career
- Get Plastic Surgery
- Plastic Surgery>Cheap Facial Beautification (§950)—*Pets* required
- Plastic Surgery>Cheap Body Modification (§1,100)—*Pets* required
- Plastic Surgery>Expensive Facial Beautification (§2,800)—*Pets* required
- Plastic Surgery>Expensive Body Modification (§3,250)—*Pets* required

Science Facility Interactions

- Join Science Career
- Attend Gardening Class (§400)
- Attend Logic Class (§320)
- Tour Science Lab
- Donate Insects to Science

The Bloom Institute of Wellness is a medical facility that shares space with a science lab. Moonlight Falls' brightest minds gather here to advance research in the fields of science and medicine. Prospective doctors and surgeons can join the Medical career at the hospital. The hospital staff is way too busy healing patients to offer tours or classes. (However, the adjoining science lab offers plenty of activities to Sims coming in off the street.) Young doctors working their way up the Medical career will spend a lot of time at this venue working with patients, issuing vaccinations, and helping out at free clinics.

> **NOTE**
>
> If you have the *Ambitions* expansion pack installed, you can also explore the enhanced Medical career that offers a hands-on approach to treating sick Sims around town.

In addition to joining the Science career at the Bloom Institute of Wellness, Sims can also take tours, attend classes, and donate insects at the science lab. Sims with a green thumb should come here, too. This is where you take the Gardening class that acquaints you with the basics of planting and growing seeds into harvestables. (Alternately, you can also start developing this skill via reading and planting seeds or working with plants.) Sims who want to expand their mental horizons should check out the Logic class, which starts another skill track that can lead to chess victories (as well as enhance the hidden Chess skill) and celestial spotting via the telescope.

> **CAUTION**
>
> Sims can also tour the science lab, but unless they already have at least a slight interest in the sciences, they may be bored by the excursion, which causes a mood decrease.

> **TIP**
>
> The science lab is also more than happy to receive any insects you've found while exploring Moonlight Falls. Who knows, perhaps your insect donation may lead to a major scientific breakthrough!

> **NOTE**
>
> As is the case with many career venues, certain Opportunities will take you to Bloom Institute of Wellness.

PLASTIC SURGERY

Plastic Surgery was introduced with the *Pets* expansion pack. If you have that expansion, and want to change an aspect of your Sim's face or body, you can go to the hospital and have plastic surgery. Once you choose an option, you head to the hospital and have the surgery. If the surgery goes well, you're taken into Create a Sim and allowed to make your choice of changes.

But success is not assured. Sometimes things go horribly wrong and you step back outside looking... different. Your Sim then gets the Embarrassed moodlet. Re-enter the hospital for a fix. Corrective Face Surgery, a new interaction on the hospital, costs §2,050. This selection puts all features back to where they were prior to the procedure.

BROWNIE BITES

Just like the real world, going under the cosmetic knife is not without risk. Cheap plastic surgeries are more likely to go awry, particularly if your Sim has either the Loser or Unlucky traits, (Conversely, the Lucky trait makes the plastic surgery more likely to succeed.) So, bear this mind should to decide to check into the hospital for some upkeep on your Sim's face or body. And do yourself a big favor: save your game before getting a procedure. It's much easier and cheaper to reload a saved game than paying to repair a botched plastic surgery!

Everglow Academy and Coliseum

Address: 123 Horseshoe Bend

Function: School/Stadium

School Interactions

◆ Attend Painting Class (§400)

◆ Go to School (for teens and children only)

Stadium Interactions

◆ Join Professional Sports Career

◆ Attend Athletic Class (§400)

◆ Attend Concert

◆ Attend Game (§60)

Everglow Academy and Coliseum is the place to be in Moonlight Falls for Sims pursuing the Professional Sports career. As they work their way up the ladder, going from a towel holder to a superstar, they report to this coliseum on a near-daily basis. However, the stadium hosts more than the Athletic career. Sims who want to pursue the Athletic skill can get off to rocking start by taking the Athletic class here.

Professional sporting events also unfold at the stadium, which result in big mood boosts for Sims. Concerts (which are now free!) are another special event at the stadium. Concerts boost mood, especially if the attending Sims like music.

TiP

If the Attend Concert and Attend Game options are grayed out, these events aren't currently available. Mouse over these options to see when an upcoming concert or game is scheduled.

Public School 67 is where children go during the day to fill their brains with the knowledge needed to be productive adults. Getting good grades here can lead to a wonderful adult life full of engagement. Adults, however, don't have much to do here other than attend a painting class and perhaps start art-related skill/craft careers.

Commonwealth Court

Address: 111 Wood Street

Function: City Hall/Military Base/Police Station

Introduction   New Simology   New Careers & Skills   Meet the Supernaturals   New Venues   Tour of Moonlight Falls   New Object Catalog

City Hall Interactions

- Join Political Career
- Attend Charisma Class (§400)
- Tour City Hall

Military Interactions

- Join Military Career
- Attend Handiness Class (§400)
- Tour Command Center

Police Station Interactions

- Join Law Enforcement Career

The Commonwealth Court combines all functions of government into one convenient location. (Whoever thought government could be so efficient? City hall offers Sims the chance to try their hand at the Political career.

But Sims who have set their sights on political office will need to boost their Charisma skill. Fortunately, the city hall offers a Charisma class too, giving all Sims a leg-up in social interactions by building the Charisma skill.

Free tours of the city hall are also available, offering a great way to spend a day off as well as satisfy a Sim's Social needs.

The police station isn't exactly a tourist-friendly place. In fact, the only thing to do at this location are join the Law Enforcement career track (and then report back if you indeed accept the badge), If a Criminal Sim is caught, they are sent to the jail, which is located inside the building.

Rounding out this multi-use facility is the military base. Here, Sims can join the Military career in an attempt to rise up the ranks. The base is also open to civilian Sims eager to take a tour of the command center or improve their Handiness skill. Any Sim sick and tired of waiting for repair technicians to fix appliances that constantly go kaput (and then pay the bill for such services) should come here and enroll in the Handiness class. Your Sim will get started in the art of tinkering, which can be a real money-saver once the skill has been developed.

TIP

Attending classes can be a costly (but quick) way to improve your skills. Check the paper every day to find discounted classes.

Deja View Theater

Address: 1109 Merchant Way

Function: Movie Theater/Criminal Hideout

Movie Theater Interactions

- Join Music Career
- Attend Guitar Class (§400)
- Attend Movie (§30)
- Tour Theater
- Attend Guitar Class (§400)—*Late Night* required
- Attend Piano Class (§400)—*Late Night* required
- Attend Bass Class (§400)—*Late Night* required
- Attend Drums Class (§400)—*Late Night* required

Criminal Hideout Interactions

- ◊ Join Criminal Career
- ◊ Raid Warehouse (Special Agents only)

The movie theater in this complex is the destination for Sims with a penchant for entertainment. Whether it is to launch a Music career that will eventually take you to super-stardom or just a place to start noodling around on the guitar (a useful skill indeed), the theater is definitely a place that music-minded Sims should investigate.

You can also take in a film at the movie theater (as described in the name of the venue) and enjoy a great entertainment boost that lasts for hours. This is a relatively inexpensive way to get a mood boost, which can prove beneficial for performance at work the following day. Movies are shown every day starting at 12 PM, making it a great place to start a date.

You can also tour the theater to blow off a little stress or engage other Sims for Social needs. However, if your Sims have no artsy traits, this tour will only leave them bored, which depresses their overall mood.

Behind the theaters is what, an unassuming warehouse? Nothing sinister going on here, right? Wrong-o, sport. This is where Sims interested in a life of crime report, ready to take their marching orders from the top of the Moonlight Falls crime families. The warehouse is not the only career stop for

criminals, though. Sims in the Law Enforcement career also pay visits to the warehouse while hoping to shine a light on the city's seedy underbelly.

> **TIP**
>
> While criminals always have to be on the lookout for the law, they don't have to worry about other criminals breaking into their homes. Hey, at least there's honor among thieves, yeah?

Van Gould Merchant House & Cafe

Address: 1110 Merchant Way

Function: Culinary/Business & Journalism

Culinary Interactions

- ◊ Join Culinary Career
- ◊ Attend Cooking Class (§400)
- ◊ Attend Mixology Class (§400)—*Late Night* required
- ◊ Eat Here (prices vary)
- ◊ Get Drinks (prices vary)

Business & Journalism Interactions

- ◊ Join Business Career
- ◊ Join Journalism Career
- ◊ Attend Writing Class (§400)

The restaurant at the Van Gould Merchant House is one of two places in Moonlight Falls where Culinary careers can be launched. If your Sim has the gift of cooking, then this is a great place to make a living. But even if you don't saunter through the front doors with a Natural Cook trait on your resume, the Cooking classes here are sure to help develop this skill.

> **TIP**
>
> When you dine here, stay for dessert to get a big mood boost!

Naturally, you can start developing the essential Cooking skill at home by just opening the fridge and starting up a meal, but to speed development, lay down a few extra Simoleons for some professional training. It'll pay off in the long run.

The Van Gould Merchant House part of this complex is the first stop for Sims interested in either the Business or Journalism careers. Titans of industry and star news anchors rub elbows here at this venue, making it a fun melting pot of talent in Moonlight Falls. Many opportunities also bring Sims to this business park.

The venue also hosts the classroom for the Writing skill. If you want to speedily start developing the trait, pay the fee to enroll. Once the skill development process is under way, use a computer at home or at the library to advance the talent and work on what could be some very profitable novels.

BROWNIE BITES

Additional career venues pop up in Moonlight Falls if you have *Ambitions* installed. The Community Fire Department appears on Knott Street, complete with trucks and crafting benches. (Those benches are great for developing the Inventing skill.)

BROWNIE BITES

Directly across from it, you'll spot Barney's Salon and Tattoo, which is where you can develop the Salon active career. Of course, you can still enjoy rewarding careers in *Supernatural* without this expansion, but it does open up additional career tracks, including the rather-appropriate Ghost Hunter active career that makes busting feel oh-so-good.

LLAMA SYSTEM

The magical town of Moonlight Falls has a very special method of transportation that not every Sim is aware of... yet. This is the Lightning Leap Atomic Molecular Arranger (LLAMA), a network of telephone booths that can zip Sims from one place to the next in a blink of an eye. It's an excellent way to get from point A to point B without using up too much time, although you are limited only to the LLAMA booths in the network. There are occasions when it may be faster to go on foot or by vehicle instead of by LLAMA.

LLAMA is not on the town map—it's much more intimate than that. You must manually utilize the system. Sims do not automatically take it when directed around town. Instead, click on the LLAMA to select a destination. (By the way, you can rename the LLAMA system, if you like.) LLAMA stations from the menu are:

- Bell's Barbell House
- Everglow Academy & Coliseum
- Moonlight Falls Historical Society & Museum
- Eerie Park
- Mellow Manor
- Moonlight Point
- Library of Lore & Vault of Antiquity
- Hallowed Grounds Cemetery
- Minimally Modern
- Varg's Tavern
- La Shove Beach
- Aleister's Elixirs and Sundries
- Stone Troll Fishing Hole
- Fae Ray Arboretum

111

LLAMA SYSTEM (CONTINUED)

That's quite the network, yes? And best of all, using LLAMA is completely free. No charge, Simoleon or magic. Just hop in, pick a destination, and enjoy the speedy ride through the ether.

Plus, you can buy a LLAMA in Buy Mode and place it right in your house. Now you have access to a lot of Moonlight Falls, right from your very own lot!

Shopping and Commerce

Moonlight Falls may have a quaint economic ecosystem compared to Sunset Valley or Bridgeport, but it too requires places to spend hard-earned Simoleons to remain vibrant and functional. In addition to the restaurant in the previous section, there are more places to trade money for goods and services. Spending Simoleons at these locations not only helps with skills and needs, but also with inspiring moodlets that boost overall mood and keep those Lifetime Happiness points rolling in on a regular basis.

Aleister's Elixirs and Sundries/ Zoomsweeper Broom Arena

Address: 336 Knott Street

Function: Consignment Store/Elixir Shop

Interactions

◆ Visit Consignment Store

◆ Purchase Goods

◆ Joy Ride—Test Track

◆ Stunt Ride—Test Track

This elixir shop is a key venue for entrepreneurial Alchemists in need not only of a place to purchase ingredients for elixirs, but also to sell their completed goods. If you are looking for ingredients you are in current need of but unable to immediately find in the wild, come here with a full wallet—and a little bit of patience. The consignment shop's inventory changes on a daily basis. They will only have one of a specific ingredient in at any given time, but stock changes so you have a good chance of catching something necessary on a different day... or even hour!

Now, if you are looking to make some Simoleons by selling your elixirs, then load them up at the counter. (Though the shop is a 24-hour joint, there must be a cashier present at the counter for any transaction to occur.) While in the shopping window, select the Consign tab. Now put your wares on the market. If and when they sell, you receive payment in the mail, so check your mailbox! And if something doesn't move, it will be returned to you, also via the mail.

Important to note: like objects in Buy Mode, your goods depreciate over time. Selling right away results in the highest price—and the highest profits!

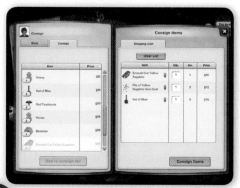

Consignment menu

> **TIP**
>
> For quicker sales, try selling your elixirs during the full moon phase of the lunar cycle.

Inside the consignment shop, you will find more than a counter for doing business. Look for objects to interact with, such as a magic broom and the nearby magic broom arena, called the Zoomsweeper Test Track. Here, witches can take brooms out for a joy ride or stunt ride, which is turn develops the hidden Broom Riding skill. You can also take gems to the gem-cutting station and reduce them to needed forms, including gemdust.

> **TIP**
>
> Is your Sim a self-employed Alchemist? Then be on the lookout for Opportunities that involve the consignment shop, such as special requests for specific elixirs. If you meet the Opportunity's requirement, you receive bonus career experience!

> **TIP**
>
> Witches get an extra 10 percent discount here!

Sam's Market and Diner

Address: 344 Knott Street

Function: Diner/Grocery Store

Diner Interactions

- Join Culinary Career
- Attend Cooking Class (§400)
- Attend Mixology Class (§400)—*Late Night* required.
- Eat Here (prices vary)
- Get Drinks (prices vary)

Grocery Store Interactions

- Shop for Groceries
- Get Part-Time Job
- Attend Fishing Class (§400)
- Sell Fruits & Vegetables
- Sell Fish

Moonlight Falls doesn't exactly have a very formal dining option—it doesn't necessarily fit in with the small town vibe going on 'round these parts. But don't think the simple pleasures of a down-home meal at this low-key cafe won't give your Sims a great mood boost. Eating out or having drinks in general make Sims happy.

Need to get some produce or meat for recipes or to use as bait when fishing? Then make a stop at Sam's. Here, Sims can choose from a variety of produce, fish, meats, and other impulse buys like bubble bath. If you find the price of fish too high, consider catching your own. But first, you'll need to boost your Fishing skill. Conveniently, Sam's offers Fishing classes.

Commerce goes both ways at the grocery store, though. Sims who grow harvestables can sell these here for profit. And Sims who like to put a hook in the water can also sell their haul to the shopkeeper for Simoleons.

Item	Price
Produce	
Apple	§6
Banana	§11
Bell Pepper	§18
Garlic	§23
Grapes	§6
Lettuce	§5
Onion	§11
Potato	§11
Tomato	§5
Fish	
Alley Catfish	§6
Anchovy	§5
Goldfish	§6
Lobster	§25
Rainbow Trout	§9
Salmon	§14
Sea Bat Starfish	§8
Swordfish	§17
Tuna	§11

Item	Price
Meat and Cheese	
Cheese	§8
Egg	§11
Links	§8
Patty	§24
Roast	§30
Steak	§30
Tofu	§11
Home	
Birthday Inferno Birthday Cake	§30
Ducksworth of Bathington	§40
Mood-Lite Candle	§65
World's Brew Bubble Bath	§100

Mind-Body Connection Bookstore and Spa

Address: 348 Knott Street

Function: Bookstore/Day Spa

Bookstore Interactions

◈ Shop for Books

◈ Get Part-Time Job

Day Spa Interactions

◈ Get Part-Time Job as a Spa Specialist

◈ Get Part-Time Job as a Receptionist

◈ Get Tattoo (§300)

◈ Get Massage: Quick Shiatsu Massage (§50)

◈ Get Massage: Relaxing Swedish Massage (§250)

◈ Get Massage: Deep Tissue (§500)

◈ Get Facial: Mini-Facial (§50)

◈ Get Facial: Mud Facial (§200)

◈ Get Facial: Seaweed Facial (§500)

◈ Body Treatments: Steam Bath (§250)

◈ Body Treatments: Salt Scrub (§750)

◈ Body Treatments: Volcanic Clay Bath (§1,500)

◈ Salon: Manicure (§25)

◈ Salon: Pedicure (§50)

◈ Salon: Manicure/Pedicure/Soak (§100)

◈ Packages: Great Escape (§1,000)

◈ Packages: Relaxing Rendezvous (§3,000)

◈ Packages: Soothing Salvation (§7,500)

Need some time to unwind after a stressful day on the job? Or perhaps you just want to curl up at home with a good book? In either case, the Mind-Body Connection Bookstore & Spa has everything you're looking for. Bookstore customers can browse through a wide selection of novels, recipes, and sheet music as well as child development, skill building, and fishing books. You can also sell back any books you've already read, ideal for unloading extra pages of inventory for cold hard cash.

Sims like to be pampered and no place powders 'em up better than the day spa. At this day spa, Sims can come in for a variety of personal treatments, from massage to manicures. Prices for these services range from §50 to §7,500, but you get what you pay for.

TIP
The more expensive the service, the longer the effects last after the Sim leaves. Moodlets from the day spa include benefits like Smooth Skin and Completely At Ease. These moodlets can last for days, too, giving you real bang for your buck.

The day spa offers two different part-time jobs. Sims can grab a few hours a day behind the receptionist's desk or slather healing mud on the well-to-do as a spa specialist. The pay isn't spectacular, but the hours are perfect for Sims with other pursuits.

TIP
Want to buy a Lifetime Reward but are short on Lifetime Happiness points? You can essentially buy them by sending Sims to the day spa and getting treatments that pop their moods into the "bubble" for an extended time.

Title	Genre	Price
One Wolf, Two Wolves. Where Wolf? There Wolf!	Childrens	§25
Ballard's Ballads	Poetry	§60
More Bawdy Tales	Trashy	§65
Haute Knights	Trashy	§65

Title	Genre	Price
Plan 8 from Lunar Lakes	SciFi	§70
Baron Graff Van Gould	Biography	§75
Catch a Magic Fish, Cook a Magic Meal	Nonfiction	§90
Under Siege and Ogre Powered	Fantasy	§95
True Fairy Tales	Childrens	§100
The Wight Wail	Drama	§100
The Sandwich Horror	Horror	§100
Why Do Vampires Suck?	Nonfiction	§100
White Mountain Haikus	Poetry	§100
The Horrors of Horoscopes	Nonfiction	§100
Unfortunate Fortune Telling	Nonfiction	§100
Divine Divinity	Nonfiction	§100
Passing Palms	Nonfiction	§100
Fabrication of Metaphysics	Nonfiction	§100
Tricky Tarots	Nonfiction	§100
Minnie Mystic's Mystical Motifs	Nonfiction	§100
Psychic's Guide to the Elements	Nonfiction	§100
Turning Bad Fortunes Good	Nonfiction	§100
Logical Fallacies You Can Really Believe	Nonfiction	§105
Germ Warfare	Nonfiction	§115
The Secret History of Lost Lemuria	Historical	§120
The Silence of the Llamas	Horror	§120
Seances and Sixth Sense Abilities	Romance	§120
Breaking Wind	Humor	§125
Hotel Diavolo: Hell's Bellhops	Horror	§130
Things That Go Bump In The Night	Nonfiction	§130
Loafing, Whining, and Thou	Poetry	§130
Spellslinger: Have Wand, Will Travel	Fiction	§135
Accumulating Orgone With The Wind	Nonfiction	§135
Predictions of The Future	Nonfiction	§140
Loel and Lola	Horror	§150
Compendium of Curses	Nonfiction	§150
The Epic of the Tattered Trousers	Poetry	§150
Inappropriate Manor	Mystery	§155
How To Win at Videogames Without Really Trying	Nonfiction	§180
How To Cook for Forty Ghosts	Nonfiction	§500
Which Witch?	Nonfiction	§555
GrrrROWLF!!	Nonfiction	§666
The Roots of Fairy Dance	Nonfiction	§777
This Bites: A Guide To Raising Your Teenage Vampire	Nonfiction	§2300

Recipe Level	Recipe	Value
1	Chili Con Carne	§25
1	Vegetarian Chili	§25
2	Mushroom Omelette	§50
3	Hot and Sour Soup	§100
5	Firecracker Shrimp	§300
5	Firecracker Tofu	§300
6	Aloo Masala Curry	§450
7	Porcini Risotto	§580
9	Potato and Truffle Torte	§650
10	Ceviche	§750

Title	Skill	Value
Procreation Elixir Recipe	Alchemy	§75
Liquid Job Booster Elixir Recipe	Alchemy	§132
Potent Enlightenment Elixir Recipe	Alchemy	§187
Potent Personality Adjuster Elixir Recipe	Alchemy	§225
Bottled Water of Youth Elixir Recipe	Alchemy	§471
Perma Zombified Elixir Recipe	Alchemy	§607
Origin of The Tragic Clown Elixir Recipe	Alchemy	§800

BROWNIE BITES

Got *Late Night* installed? Then you will see food trucks motoring around the city, offering grub on-the-go. And if you are using the *Pets* expansion, the ice cream truck roams the town, dispensing frosty treats, and you will also see the equestrian center located rather close to downtown Moonlight Falls.

BROWNIE BITES

The *Ambitions* expansion also adds the junkyard and Landgraab Sell 'n Swap to Moonlight Falls, both of which are directly related to the Inventing skill that can also be converted into a skill-based career. Check into these locations to have fun with scrap metal, inventing, and selling crafted goods! The Sell 'n Swap operates in a very similar fashion to the elixir consignment shop.

Community Spots

Like all towns, Moonlight Falls has many community lots that allow Sims to pursue to new activities or activities that require equipment too expensive to have at home at first blush, such as the skill-developing exercise machines at the gym or a computer at the library.

There is another benefit to visiting these community spots, too—meeting Sims. These locations can get pretty busy, giving you ample opportunities to socialize and meet your neighbors. If your Sim thirsts for socialization, be sure to hit up these spots.

Hallowed Grounds Cemetery

Address: 49 S Falls Avenue

Function: Graveyard

Introduction

New Simology

New Careers & Skills

Meet the Supernaturals

New Venues

Tour of Moonlight Falls

New Object Catalog

Interactions

◆ Visit Cemetery

◆ Get Part-Time Job

◆ Tour Mausoleum

◆ Explore Catacombs

◆ Mourn

◆ Fish

Though there is an undead element to Moonlight Falls, the Grim Reaper does indeed come knocking for many of its citizens—and this is where they end up hanging their hat for the final time. Sims who die are buried here and can be mourned by family and friends. But there's more to do here than mourn or engrave epitaphs on tombstones.

Tip

Some Sims wish to see a ghost. (Good thing they're in Moonlight Falls, right?) In such cases, go to the cemetery after midnight, but before sunrise. You're likely to see a handful of restless spirits roaming around the cemetery during these witching hours. You can even carry on a conversation with them, take photos, and more.

Moonlight Falls Historical Society & Museum

Tip

Hallowed Grounds Cemetery has a pond stocked with fish. So when you're finished sobbing, cast away your sorrows by dropping a line in this fishing hole.

One important feature of the cemetery is the mausoleum. This Gothic structure houses more of the dead, as well as the potential for great adventure. Touring the mausoleum can be educational for some Sims. The option to explore the catacombs below the graveyard is a source of excitement for Brave Sims. Sims without the Brave trait risk getting the Horrified moodlet, which is devastating to their overall mood for several hours. While on a tour, your Sim will often encounter a multitude of strange scenarios, which you can influence by answering a series of questions, such as which direction your Sim goes at an intersection.

Address: 1105 Merchant Way

Function: Museum/Art Gallery

Interactions

◆ View

Don't be fooled by the small-town atmosphere in Moonlight Falls. There is a real appreciation for the arts in this city. The Moonlight Falls Historical Society & Museum is a good spot for Sims who love art to admire works from great talents that have come before. The museum charges no admission fee, so Sims can view art and enjoy the mood benefits without dropping a single Simoleon. Just don't send a Sim with Can't Stand Art to this venue!

There may not be a lot to do here outside of viewing art or coming back during specific Opportunities, but Sims who love art will at least find others with similar interests here. Who knows, your Sim may lock eyes with the love of their life when looking up from a fascinating sculpture.

Fae Ray Arboretum

Address: 164 Wood Street

Function: Fairy Activities/Beekeeping

Interactions

- Enter Gardening Competition
- Search for Fairies
- Play Fairy Games
- Tour Arboretum
- Talk to Baby's Breath
- Beekeeping interactions
- Fairy House interactions

Though any citizen can visit the Fae Ray Arboretum, fairies will get special use out of this community lot, for its is laden with fairy-specific objects like the Fairy House.

 ## TiP

Fairies that spend a little time inside the Arboretum will benefit from the Magic in the Air moodlet, which encourages them to seek out a little love.

There are multiple Fairy Houses at this lot. These are places a fairy can sleep, drink Pollen Punch, throw parties, and more. See the "Fairy" section of the Meet the Supernaturals chapter for the complete rundown on everything that makes a Fairy special, including all of the amazing stuff you can do with a Fairy House!

In addition to Fairy Houses, there are several beekeeping boxes on this lot. Here, you can Feed Bees, Smoke Bees, Harvest Honey, and Clean the Box—everything you need to do to be a great beekeeper. For more on Beekeeping, please see the "Skill" section of the New Simology chapter.

Finally, take advantage of the pond on this lot for fishing. Drop a line and see what you can reel in. Remember, fish are needed for food, Simoleons, and ingredients for elixirs.

H Two the O Indoor Pool

Address: 94 Horseshoe Bend

Function: Swimming Pool

Interactions
- Swim
- Shower

Though Moonlight Falls is situated on the shores, Sims need a more hospitable place to get their toes wet. The H Two the O Indoor Pool is an excellent swimming facility, complete with a pool (no entrance fees!) and no shortage of seating. Upstairs, you'll find additional chairs as well as bars where drinks can be prepared. Additionally, the facility offers showers for rinsing off. These showers are handy for taking care of the Hygiene need while out and about. Heading home to bathe can sometimes consume way too much time, you know!

Library of Lore & Vault of Antiquity

Address: 108 Wood Street

Function: Alchemy/Research

Interactions
- Read
- Use Computer
- Attend Alchemy Class (§100)
- Tour Archives
- Research the Supernatural
- Enter Trivia Contest

Pull up a chair at the Library of Lore & Vault of Antiquity. The library portion of the facility is a basic reading room, complete with books for your perusal. Sims who love to read will get a great mood boost by just being here, leafing through the volume of available volumes.

The library also has computers for Sims who don't have one at home (for space or money reasons), and any computer activity you could do from home like chat, play games, and check real estate can be done from a library computer.

However, slip out the back door of the library to discover the Vault of Antiquity half of the equation. The stairs behind the library lead down to a set of underground passages. Here more books await hungry eyes, and Sims who want to further the study of Alchemy can use an Alchemy Station to enhance the skill.

Sweet—a Moondial? Check your fortune, if you dare!

Want to just sit in a class to learn the basics of Alchemy? The Gothic building behind the library is where Sims can report to take the Alchemy class. In just a few hours, Sims download the essence of Alchemy and are well on their way to learning exciting elixir recipes. Sims can also Research the Supernatural on the building, which unfolds not unlike exploring the mausoleum at the graveyard. The higher your skill and the more luck you have, the better the results of the journey. Unprepared Sims stumble into the daylight (or moonlight) with the Terrified moodlet. Finally, this is a good place to enroll in Trivia Contests. Come back at the designated time (mouse over to see when the next contest is being held) and see if your Sim has the chops to hang with the best and brightest. Winning results in positive mood boosts!

BROWNIE BITES

Hey, wanna see a secret spot? Go under the library and inspect the bookcase in the very back. That's no ordinary bookcase—that's a hidden door. Open it to reveal a special chamber complete with a Moondial, bookcase, urn, and a LLAMA. Oooh, Moonlight Falls is full of mystery!

Bell's Barbell House

Address: 2336 Waning Way

Function: Gym

Interactions

◆ Work Out

◆ Shower

All Sims should exercise, not just those pursuing a career in Professional Athletics or developing the Athletic skill. While it's possible to fill your home with all of the exercise equipment offered here, such purchases aren't cheap. Everything here is absolutely free. Plus, it's a great place for Sims with the Athletic trait to gather and socialize. You can really address multiple needs at the gym in a single visit, so don't overlook this lot.

Introduction | New Simology | New Careers & Skills | Meet the Supernaturals | New Venues | Tour of Moonlight Falls | New Object Catalog

> ### TIP
> Use one of the treadmills in front of the TV and click the Work Out interaction. Choose Strength or Cardio and then have a great time! Or, use the nearby audio system to get your dance on.

Aside from the gym's more obvious features, such as treadmills and exercise benches, your can find a computer at the front desk and showers the downstairs restrooms.

> ### TIP
> It's a good idea to shower after each workout session! Nobody likes being around a stinky Sim, not even the stinky Sim!

Parks and Fishing Spots

Though Moonlight Falls is carved into the woods and wilds, the founders of this fine town saw fit to establish several parks for residents to enjoy, including a metro park and a beach hideaway, as well as a series of small unnamed parks. In addition, Moonlight Falls features a number of fishing spots for would-be anglers to get their hooks wet and reel in a valuable catch.

Eerie Park

Address: 110 Wood Street

Interactions
- Play Chess

Eerie Park is one of the main features of downtown Moonlight Falls, if this bucolic burgh actually had much of a downtown. This lush park features a gorgeous central fountain, which is perfect for appreciating and sitting. There are picnic areas, park benches, and restrooms for common use. Sims who love a good game of chess or want to learn how to play can use on-site chess tables to practice the cerebral contest. This is a great way to boost both the Logic skill and the hidden Chess skill. The more you play, the better you get! Plus, playing chess with other Sims satisfies the Social need, and that's good for everybody.

Playful Playground

Address: 112 Wood Street

Interactions
- Fairy House interactions
- Play on Playground (children only)
- Hang Out on Playground (teens/adults only)
- Swing

Let's face it. Kids are restless balls of energy. Playful Playground is the perfect (and safe) location to release that energy in a positive and playful manner.

Children love coming here to swing, slide, and climb on the playground equipment. Social and introspective teens also find plenty to enjoy here, albeit at a lesser degree than their younger siblings and peers. While teens may have outgrown some of the equipment, it doesn't stop them from hanging out here, perhaps in a subconscious existential exercise to grasp onto their fading youth.

WWW.PRIMAGAMES.COM

But this small park isn't just for the young ones. Adults can also have a surprising amount of fun by swinging on the swing set. You're only as old as you feel, so don't be afraid to cut loose and play like children.

BROWNIE BITES

In addition to playground equipment, the Playful Playground also features a Fairy House stopover for fairies to make use of, whether that's throwing parties, guzzling nectar, or darting in for a quick snooze.

La Shove Beach

Address: 16 La Shove Road

Interactions

- Serve Meal
- Fish
- Shower
- Arcade Claw Machine interactions

Welcome to La Shove Beach, a pleasant little getaway right within the borders of Moonlight Falls. This beach spot is a favorite among Sims who love the outdoors and outdoor activities, like fishing. If you need ocean-based fish for any reason, cast a line and reel in some fat ones while wriggling your toes on the white sands.

Farther up from the water's edge, you will find some free-to-use outdoor grills for making meals. These are good for not only feeding yourself, but also other Sims should you decide to hold a party at this lot. If things get a little dirty (not that kind of dirty, mind you), take a quick shower on-site and improve your Hygiene before getting back out there among the other Sims.

Finally, the beach sports a pair of new arcade machines, cool objects that let you test your skill. Try to wrangle a prize from the machine, such as bears and other toys. (See the New Object catalog for more details on The Claaaaw arcade machine.) And if you visit this beach as a fairy, you can attempt to cheat the machine and get something special.

Stone Troll Fishing Hole

Address: End of Big Pine Trail

Interactions

- Fish
- Fairy House interactions

Introduction

New Simology

New Careers & Skills

Meet the Supernaturals

New Venues

Tour of Moonlight Falls

New Object Catalog

Looking for a good fishing spot? Look no farther. Stone Troll Fishing Hole on the outskirts of Moonlight Falls is an excellent place to cast a line and reel in some fish. Anglers develop their fishing skill just by dropping a hook in the water, but the better you are with choosing bait and developing this skill, the better your catch.

> ### TIP
>
> Fairies can also make good use of the Fairy House right here at Stone Troll Fishing Hole!

That Old Fishing Hole

Address: That Old Trail

Interactions

⬧ Fish

⬧ Fairy House interactions

Welcome to That Old Fishing Hole, a quiet little spot along That Old Trail, which runs closer to the center of Moonlight Falls. From the banks of this pond, you can throw out a line and hopefully pull in some good catches, depending on your bait and skill level. If you check out the collecting section toward the end of this chapter, we detail how to get the best fish in Moonlight Falls and quickly develop the Fishing skill.

> ### TIP
>
> Like the Stone Troll Fishing Hole, you will find a Fairy House on-site!

BROWNIE BITES

Do you have *Pets* installed? Then you are likely to see wild horses around Moonlight Falls, in spaces such as those around That Old Fishing Hole. If you have the gift or are a confident trainer, you can interact with the majestic animals.

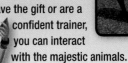

REAL ESTATE

Careers and producing objects are not the only sources of income in your neighborhood. Smart investors can generate a healthy household income through real estate investments. Almost all venues in a town can now be purchased and upgraded. As a result of the investment, the household owning the lot is given a weekly payment. The more you invest in a property via upgrades, the more you make per week.

Real estate in *Supernatural* is built upon the basic investment system from *The Sims 3*. You may invest in a variety of lots and venues. Use the Real Estate filter on the town map to see what exactly is up for grabs.

How It Works

To invest in a venue, choose the Purchase interaction on the establishment from the town map. The base price of the venue is displayed, which must be paid to acquire the venue. There is no payment plan for investing in real estate. Once a venue has been purchased and the deed awarded, you may name the venue anything you wish.

Use a computer (in the game) to monitor your investments. The Check Real Estate interaction lets you monitor your investments and spot open opportunities to buy additional venues. You may also track venue upgrades here.

You may also use Build Mode to create a venue from the ground up. However, you cannot just erect four walls, drop in a treadmill, call it a gym, and then expect a weekly payment. You must meet a set of requirements. These are your upgrades, which are also essential for maintaining the operation of purchased existing venues. Upgrades allow you to improve an establishment, which in turn pays out more Simoleons. In Buy Mode, you may install new objects at a customizable venue (a venue your Sim enters and is still visible—you cannot upgrade the diner, for example) to raise its overall value.

Property Values	Property Type	Cost	Partnership Cost	Buy Out Cost	Partnership Income	Ownership Income
Aleister's Elixirs and Sundries	Property	§95,159				§10,700
Bell's Barbell House	Property	§126,155				§14,200
Bloom Institute of Wellness	Building	§240,000				§27,000
Deja View Theater	Building	§105,000	§30,000	§75,000	§6,300	§11,800
Eerie Park	Property	§9,2207				§1,0375
Gypsy Wagon	Building	§1,6000	§1,000	§15,000	§960	§1,800
H Two the O Indoor Pool	Property	§88,200				§9,920
Hallowed Ground Cemetery	Property	§4,2692				§4,800
La Shove Beach	Property	§3,8005				§4,275
Mind-Body Connection Bookstore & Spa	Building	§80,000	§20,000	§60,000	§4,800	§9,000
Moonlight Falls Historical Society & Museum	Building	§174,677				§19,650
Sam's Market Diner	Building	§40,000	§13,000	§27,000	§2,400	§4,500
Stone Troll Fishing Hole	Property	§21,806				§2,450
That Old Fishing Hole	Property	§18,582				§2,090
The Toadstool	Property	§78,246				§8,800
Van Gould Merchant House & Café	Building	§170,000	§50,000	§120,000	§10,000	§19,000
Varg's Tavern	Property	§173,547				§19,520
Vault of Antiquity	Building	§22,000				§2,475

Houses, Households, and Lots

The town of Moonlight Falls holds many real estate opportunities for Sims, whether that means moving into an existing home or starting from scratch on an empty lot. The existing homes of Moonlight Falls run the gamut from modest to mansion, and several are already hosting pre-existing Sim families. If you'd like to try out life as one of these current clans, such as the Grimms or Crumplebottoms, a simple click after starting a new game is all it takes.

Should you decide to start a new household with one of the provided homes, you can choose to either move into an empty house or pay a little extra for a furnished abode. You may need to splash a few extra Simoleons to buy objects necessary for specific careers, hobbies, or lifestyles, but you always have the basic necessities, such as a bed, toilet, and fridge.

Of course, with Build Mode, you can erect a dream home either at the beginning of a new adventure or at any point later in the life cycle. When you start a new game, you have a somewhat limited budget, but things change with time and effort. If, as either a pre-existing or new Sim, you generate enough wealth through career or craft, you can choose to upgrade an existing, custom-built house or move into one of Moonlight Falls many pre-crafted homes.

Occupied Homes

Witch's Cover

Address: 434 Huckleberry Lane

Rooms: 5br, 3.5ba

Lot Size: 40x40

Not for the faint of heart, any self-respecting witch will be proud to make this house their accessory. The witch hat styled turret really ties this house together to make no mistake that a witch dwells within. But those less witchy types will still appreciate the intricate craftsmanship throughout with no expenses spared in material choice. Even the garage is luxurious!

Household: Crumplebottom

Household Funds: §5,500

Difficulty: 2

The three Crumplebottom sisters have very little in common with one another, and yet they have never been able to live apart. They feel right at home in Moonlight Falls, which, like their family, is full of drama and magic. Will these three witches ever find balance and serenity, or are they destined always to express their love for each other through a combination of trickery and shouting?

Household	Sim Name	Age	Gender	Supernatural Type	Trait	Career
Crumplebottom	Beatrice Crumplebottom	Adult	Female	Witch	Frugal, Grumpy, Proper, Bookworm, Loner	Unemployed
	Belinda Crumplebottom	Young Adult	Female	Witch	Friendly, Good, Natural Cook, Good Sense of Humor, Easily Impressed	Culinary
	Bianca Crumplebottom	Young Adult	Female	Witch	Great Kisser, Flirty, Childish, Commitment Issues, Night Owl	Fortune Teller

Graceful Getaway

Address: 431 Huckleberry Lane

Rooms: 4br, 3ba

Lot Size: 40x40

Show your friends who's reached success by moving into this classical home. Let there be light with gracefully paned windows that circle the house, especially with the dominating rotundas that draw oohs and ahhs from guests. There's just so much to this house that we couldn't possibly fit it all into this small space. You really have to see it for yourself!

Household: Durwood

Household Funds: §4,000

Difficulty: 4

On the outside, the Durwoods would make others jealous with their nice house, two adorable children, and a father with a great job. However, all is not what it seems between a mother in-law who disapproves of her daughter's husband and two kids who always get what they want. Can the Durwoods learn to live together or will the family spiral out of control?

Household	Sim Name	Age	Gender	Supernatural Type	Trait	Career
Durwood	Doreen Caliente	Adult	Female	Witch	Hydrophobic, Mean Spirited, No Sense of Humor, Snob, Neurotic	Unemployed
	Rick Durwood	Adult	Male	Human	Workaholic, Good Sense of Humor, Genius, Unlucky, Computer Whiz	Science
	Serena Durwood	Adult	Female	Witch	Good, Over-Emotional, Charismatic, Lucky, Hopeless Romantic	Unemployed
	Zack Durwood	Child	Male	Human	Good, Mooch, Couch Potato	School
	Zoe Durwood	Child	Female	Human	Evil, Daredevil, Can't Stand Art	School

The Tree House

Address: 404 Huckleberry Lane

Rooms: 2br, 1ba

Lot Size: 40x40

Tree houses aren't just for kids or fairies anymore! This one has modern amenities such as doors and insulation, and any Sim would be proud to call this quirky place home. Enjoy second floor decks for a view of the cars passing by or step out back and gaze over the peaceful pond. Whatever your age or supernatural status, there's no outgrowing this charming house!

Household: Goodfellow

Household Funds: §4,500

Difficulty: 4

Fairies are typically curious about human Sims, and the Goodfellows are no exception. Led by their sprightly matriarch, Flora, the mischievous Goodfellows have engineered several encounters with humans, from simple pranks to elaborate social experiments! Their crowning achievement is an adoption mix-up resulting in Linda Rodgers' newly adopted baby being a fairy with the Goodfellows taking possession of the human baby instead. Will raising Fawn, their human toddler, bring them more than they bargained for?

Household	Sim Name	Age	Gender	Supernatural Type	Trait	Career
Goodfellow	Flora Goodfellow	Elder	Female	Fairy	Family-Oriented, Inappropriate, Green Thumb, Gatherer, Frugal	Unemployed
	Pip Goodfellow	Adult	Male	Fairy	Schmoozer, Good Sense of Humor, Charismatic, Genius, Bookworm	Bookstore Clerk
	Dahlia Goodfellow	Adult	Female	Fairy	Over Emotional, Green Thumb, Loser, Light Sleeper, Vegetarian	Music
	Fawn Goodfellow	Toddler	Female	Human	Grumpy, Light Sleeper	Unemployed

Outdoorsman's Delight

Address: 160 Wood Street

Rooms: 2br, 2.5ba

Lot Size: 40x40

These two roommates are Best Friends Forever and share a love for living off the land! Branch is a fairy with the greenest thumb of all and Dayvid is a vampire who won't touch meat or drink plasma. Can Branch make a living in nature? And how long can Dayvid repress his nature?

Household: Roommates Vegan

Household Funds: §2,700

Difficulty: 2

This quaint home boasts a wide open kitchen complete with large windows for all the natural light you'll ever want. Enjoy the privacy and cleanliness (or lack thereof) of your own bathroom with not one, but two master bathroom suites! An oversized detached garage gives your car plenty of room to park—or a space to put all your non-automobile-related goods.

Household	Sim Name	Age	Gender	Supernatural Type	Trait	Career
Roommates Vegan	Dayvid Musgrave	Adult	Male	Vampire	Vegetarian, Friendly, Dislikes Children, Athletic, Coward	Sports
	Branch Timbley	Young Adult	Male	Fairy	Loves the Outdoors, Green Thumb, Slob, Lucky, Handy	Unemployed

Great Greek

Address: 142 Wood Street

Rooms: 2br, 1.5ba

Lot Size: 30x40

This contemporary Greek Revival–style home boasts three floors plus a basement tucked away for everything your Sim could possibly want in a house. The glow of the fireplace makes the expansive living room extra inviting, so much that guests may never want to leave! But for one lucky family, they'll be able to enjoy that living room anytime they please!

Household: Rodgers

Household Funds: §5,000

Difficulty: 3

Linda Rodgers has more love in her pinky finger than some Sims have in their entire heart! Thanks to the Moonlight Falls adoption center, Linda's lifelong dream of starting a family has come true. Of course, thanks to a little… intervention by some mischievous fairies, Linda will discover she is getting more with her adoption than she ever dreamed of! What will Linda say when little Sophie grows up to be a beautiful young fairy?

Household	Sim Name	Age	Gender	Supernatural Type	Trait	Career
Rodgers	Linda Rodgers	Young Adult	Female	Human	Good, Gatherer, Natural Cook, Family-Oriented, Friendly	Culinary
	Sophie Rodgers	Toddler	Female	Fairy	Athletic, Friendly	Unemployed

Tour of Moonlight Falls

The Bay View

Address: 347 Knott Street

Rooms: 2br, 1.5ba

Lot Size: 30x30

Not too small and not too big, this Greek Revival–style house is just right, whether you're starting a family or just a single Sim who wants it all. The stylish bay window adorning the front adds a welcome touch of class that is sure to be the envy of your neighbors. Better yet, the flexible floor plan offers your Sim endless possibilities to add that personal touch!

Household: Maldano

Household Funds: §2,500

Difficulty: 1

Marigold only recently realized that she's descended from a family of powerful fairies. She was raised by her late grandmother and recently inherited the family home, where she lives alone. Strange things seem to happen wherever she goes. Is she a magnet for supernatural events or is she just crazy?

Household	Sim Name	Age	Gender	Supernatural Type	Trait	Career
Maldano	Marigold Maldano	Young Adult	Female	Fairy	Flirty, Supernatural Fan, Unlucky, Insane, Frugal	Culinary

Dionysus' Dwelling

Address: 1129 Merchant Way

Rooms: 1br, 1.5ba

Lot Size: 30x30

If entertaining guests is a priority, then this house is ready for your Sim! The downstairs is free of unsightly walls that break up the room, for a truly open feeling from the kitchen to the living room—perfect for packing in the guests. Though the upstairs contains some walls, trust us that they're totally necessary!

Household: Grimm

Household Funds: §2,500

Difficulty: 1

Chauncey Grimm is a single guy with a passion for storytelling... especially tales of the supernatural. While he can't prove it, he believes he must be a descendant of the famous Grimm brothers, the writers of many classic fairy tales. Chauncey has come to Moonlight Falls to carry on his family legacy. But will he just write stories or become the main character in his own supernatural story?

Household	Sim Name	Age	Gender	Supernatural Type	Trait	Career
Grimm	Chauncey Grimm	Young Adult	Male	Human	Computer Whiz, Supernatural Fan, Bookworm, Never Nude, Hydrophobic	Journalism

Introduction | New Simology | New Careers & Skills | Meet the Supernaturals | New Venues | Tour of Moonlight Falls | New Object Catalog

Refined Elegance

Address: 1126 Merchant Way

Rooms: 3br, 2ba

Lot Size: 25x25

This well-built home is large enough to comfortably fit a family of Sims but without the ostentatiousness of a large mansion. Your family will love hanging out in the cozy living room and one lucky Sim will have their own balcony attached to their bedroom. You'll find just the right place for all your belongings in this easy-to-accessorize house!

Household: Roommates Supernatural

Household Funds: §2,300

Difficulty: 2

A vampire, ghost, and werewolf all living under one roof? And, what's more, they're all best friends! These three supernaturals are loving life and are excited to be in their new home in Moonlight Falls. Will their human neighbors be accepting of the three roommates or will they have to depend on each other for friendship?

Household	Sim Name	Age	Gender	Supernatural Type	Trait	Career
Roommates Supernatural	Violet Slymer	Young Adult	Female	Ghost	Kleptomaniac, Couch Potato, Unlucky, Over-Emotional, Never Nude	Unemployed
	Argus Brown	Young Adult	Male	Werewolf	Brooding, Inappropriate, Neat, Heavy Sleeper, Unflirty	Medical
	Dante Morganthe	Young Adult	Male	Vampire	Mean Spirited, Flirty, Ambitious, Commitment Issues, Great Kisser	Unemployed

Quaint Settlement

Address: 120 Wood Street

Rooms: 2br, 2ba

Lot Size: 30x30

Sims who adore dormers on their home won't want to miss this one! Three of them speckle the upper floor to give it a nice flair compared to dormer-less homes. Sims with a lesser affection for dormers will be won over by its open floor plan and cute deck in the back. There's something for everyone here!

Household: Swain

Household Funds: §5,000

Difficulty: 2

New to Moonlight Falls, Chester Swain came in the hopes of providing a better life for his daughter Bailey, who he's raised alone. She's his whole world, and he loves her very much even if he can be a little overprotective. Despite the time they spend together, Chester is somehow unaware of Bailey's fanatical obsession with the supernatural. Can Chester find a way to protect his daughter from her own curiosity?

Household	Sim Name	Age	Gender	Supernatural Type	Trait	Career
Swain	Chester Swain	Adult	Male	Human	Angler, Loves the Outdoors, Gatherer, Brave, Unflirty	Law Enforcement
	Bailey Swain	Teen	Female	Human	Supernatural Fan, Clumsy, Light Sleeper, Brave, Loner	School

Pleasant Place

Address: 1120 Merchant Way

Rooms: 4br, 4ba

Lot Size: 25x30

This massive multi-level manor house is meant for a king and his entire court! The custom-designed roofline with its many peaks and gables add to the impressive facade. Your little prince or princess has their own turret tower from which to rule over their kingdom. Give your royal family the palace they deserve!

Household: Hoppcraft

Household Funds: §25,000

Difficulty: 3

Back where James Hoppcraft was from, people worked hard, respected one another, and didn't turn into howling beasts when the moon was full. And that's the way it should be everywhere. The Hoppcrafts are a traditional family that values traditional family values, period. Can the Hoppcrafts survive in such an outlandish town or will their values get the best of them?

Household	Sim Name	Age	Gender	Supernatural Type	Trait	Career
Hoppcraft	Miriam Hoppcraft	Young Adult	Female	Human	Over Emotional, Light Sleeper, Supernatural Skeptic, Evil, Snob	Politics
	James Hoppcraft	Adult	Male	Human	Perfectionist, Coward, Heavy Sleeper, Supernatural Skeptic, Neat	Science
	Alfred Hoppcraft	Toddler	Male	Fairy	Artistic, Clumsy	Unemployed

Mellow Manor

Address: 320 Knott Street

Rooms: 5br, 3ba

Lot Size: 40x40

Enjoy the size of a mansion without the creepy look in this Victorian style home. Balconies aplenty offer views that must be seen to be believed! And with four floors plus basement, one could scream and never be heard. Take a tour of this home and just try and convince yourself it's not for you.

Household: MacDuff

Household Funds: §3,700

Difficulty: 5

This is one large family with another member on the way! To an outsider, this combined family of witches and humans may seem strange and full of chaos, but the MacDuffs are quick to pull together and support each other in a crisis (like that time Faith's hamster died…). The parents, Joanie and Flint, do their best to manage such a large household, but will the addition of Baby MacDuff be one MacDuff too many?

Household	Sim Name	Age	Gender	Supernatural Type	Trait	Career
MacDuff	Joanie MacDuff	Adult	Female	Human	Natural Cook, Frugal, Neat, Green Thumb, Hopeless Romantic	Journalism
	Flint MacDuff	Adult	Male	Witch	Family-Oriented, Workaholic, Absent Minded, Computer Whiz, Handy	Military
	Faith MacDuff	Teen	Female	Human	Brooding, Loser, Artistic, No Sense of Humor	School
	Joe MacDuff (Twin)	Teen	Male	Human	Good Sense of Humor, Coward, Light Sleeper, Perfectionist	School
	Felicity MacDuff	Child	Female	Witch	Brave, Inappropriate, Hydrophobic	School
	Jules MacDuff (Twin)	Teen	Male	Witch	Good Sense of Humor, Childish, Night Owl, Daredevil	School

Lap of Luxury

Address: 323 Knott Street

Rooms: 4br, 4.5ba

Lot Size: 50x50

The mark of an exquisite house is lots of high pitched roofs with a rotunda or two thrown in, and this house is no exception. Step out back and enjoy the serenity of your own pool. Better yet enjoy some barbecues and invite the neighbors! But the real charm can be found inside where your Sims can live in the lap of luxury with an old time feel.

Household: Ivy

Household Funds: §47,000

Difficulty: 3

Once on the verge of living on the streets, the hippie Ivy family now lives the "trustifarian" lifestyle after Rainflower inherited a fortune from a long-lost great-aunt. No longer bound by the shackles of a budget, this family can have anything they'd like, except they don't know what they want! Will the influx of Simoleons be a curse for the Ivy family?

Household	Sim Name	Age	Gender	Supernatural Type	Trait	Career
Ivy	Rainflower Ivy	Adult	Male	Human	Virtuoso, Unlucky, Absent Minded, Heavy Sleeper, Slob	Music
	Peanut Ivy	Child	Male	Human	Coward, Virtuoso, Couch Potato	School
	Daydream Ivy	Teen	Female	Human	Couch Potato, Hates the Outdoors, Heavy Sleeper, Slob	School
	Annalove Ivy	Young Adult	Female	Human	Vegetarian, Technophobe, Supernatural Skeptic, Neurotic, Gatherer	Unemployed

Country Living

Address: 155 Horseshoe Bend

Rooms: 2br, 2.5ba

Lot Size: 30x30

Welcome to this inviting two-story country colonial large enough for nearly any family. The oversize covered front porch will accommodate more than a few friends with room enough for the dog and kids too. And what could say country more than an all-brick fireplace to complete the picture of Home Sweet Home?

Household: Singh

Household Funds: §11,000

Difficulty: 2

The Singhs met in medical school and quickly found themselves swept up in a fairytale romance… But this is a fairytale with a twist! On their wedding night, Param was surprised when his new bride Navita suddenly turned into werewolf and turned him into one too! Will the Singhs live wolfally ever after? Or will Param be haunted by his carefree days as a bachelor (and a human)?

Household	Sim Name	Age	Gender	Supernatural Type	Trait	Career
Singh	Param Singh	Young Adult	Male	Werewolf	Ambitious, Workaholic, Hopeless Romantic, Great Kisser, Hates the Outdoors	Science
	Navita Singh	Young Adult	Female	Werewolf	Loser, Clumsy, Unflirty, Neat, Never Nude	Medical

Spacious Revival

Address: 2316 Waning Way

Rooms: 4br, 3ba

Lot Size: 40x40

This fantastic find has potential written all over it! Though it's a little dated inside, it won't take much to spruce up this old house. The basement makes for a great place to escape, or get out of the dark and into the light with a dedicated sunroom with adjoining patio. Large families will love the spaciousness this fine home provides but won't feel too overwhelmed with its size.

Household: Wolff

Household Funds: §11,000

Difficulty: 5

The Wolffs are one of the oldest and proudest families in Moonlight Falls. The only other family that's been around as long is the Van Goulds, and these two clans are bitter rivals. Debate rages over the identity of the town's original founders, but the Wolffs will never surrender their claim. Will the Wolffs finally find the respect they feel they deserve or will Ayden Van Gould buy his way into Moonlight Falls history?

Household	Sim Name	Age	Gender	Supernatural Type	Trait	Career
Wolff	Dwayne Wolff	Adult	Male	Werewolf	Can't Stand Art, Lucky, Ambitious, Inappropriate, Handy	Politics
	Erica Wolff	Young Adult	Female	Werewolf	Athletic, Hot-Headed, Family-Oriented, Unflirty, Neat	Sports
	Gator Wolff	Toddler	Male	Werewolf	Exciteable, Slob	School
	Wilhemina (Willie) Wolff	Child	Female	Werewolf	Easily Impressed, Couch Potato, Supernatural Fan (this is dependent on CR)	School
	Waylon Wolff	Teen	Male	Werewolf	Computer Whiz, Hates the Outdoors, Clumsy, Proper	Grocery Store Clerk

Manufactured Magnificence

Address: 29 Lupine Lane

Rooms: 2br, 1ba

Lot Size: 20x20

This is a home that all Manufactured Homes aspire to be. Enjoy the opulence of this double wide style with a giant window to view out into the world. Niceties abound in this home with a separate dining room, two large bedrooms, and even a snazzy bay window! What more could you possibly fit into this home?

Household: Nix

Household Funds: §26,000

Difficulty: 3

The Nix family may be the most "normal" family in Moonlight Falls... which makes them one of the most unusual families in Moonlight Falls! Mike and Annie met at a high school dance, dated through college, and then got married when Mike graduated from medical school. Mara was born a year later. Will the Nixes be able to find some friends or are they just too normal for a place like Moonlight Falls?

Household	Sim Name	Age	Gender	Supernatural Type	Trait	Career
Nix	Mike Nix	Young Adult	Male	Human	Angler, Loner, Can't Stand Art, Slob, Lucky	Medical
	Annie Nix	Young Adult	Female	Human	Hot-Headed, Easily Impressed, Childish, Bookworm, Hopeless Romantic	Unemployed
	Mara Nix	Child	Female	Human	Loner, Hydrophobic, Angler	School

Efficient Abode

Address: 13 Lupine Lane

Rooms: 1br, 1ba

Lot Size: 20x20

Why have extra rooms that take up space and cost an arm and a leg? Sims who buy this manufactured beauty know the answer to that question! Get everything you need and nothing more for an efficient abode that'll bode well with your Sim. Kitchen, bedroom, bathroom, and living room—it's all there!

Household: Farmwell

Household Funds: §2,500

Difficulty: 1

Moonlight Falls is a perfect fit for a guy like Gladsten. With all the fishing, the great outdoors, and friendly people, he never wants to leave... and plenty of local ladies are happy about that! Can Gladsten stick around in Moonlight Falls or will he be run out of town by an angry mob of ex-girlfriends?

Household	Sim Name	Age	Gender	Supernatural Type	Trait	Career
Farmwell	Gladsten Farmwell	Adult	Male	Human	Handy, Loves the Outdoors, Athletic, Angler, Commitment Issues	Military

The Humble House

Address: 2 Lupine Lane

Rooms: 1br, 1ba

Lot Size: 20x20

A house for the rest of us, this humble place satisfies the basic needs of a Sim for a roof over their head and a comfortable place to sleep. Great care was taken to ensure minimal walking distance from bed to breakfast for those who wake up with a rumble in their tummy. This centrally located kitchen also means your Sim can grab a snack while watching TV and make it back before the commercials end!

Household: Pappy

Household Funds: §1,700

Difficulty: 1

Pappy is the patriarch of the Wolff clan and was raised with the dogged belief that the Wolffs were the original settlers of Moonlight Falls... a claim hotly disputed by the Van Gould family. Pappy lives alone on the opposite end of town from all those "undead deadbeats." Will the Wolffs and Van Goulds continue their feud? Or can Pappy be the bigger Wolff and make peace?

Household	Sim Name	Age	Gender	Supernatural Type	Trait	Career
Pappy	Pappy Wolff	Elder	Male	Werewolf	Party Animal, Insane, Angler, Loves the Outdoors, Technophobe	Unemployed

Tour of Moonlight Falls

Minimally modern

Address: 277 Valley View Drive

Rooms: 2br, 2ba

Lot Size: 40x40

Sweeping curves, intricate finishes, and lots of history— there's none of that in this stunning home! Instead, Sims will find pleasantly flat walls, tons of glass, and more concrete than they'll know what do with. A great blend of minimalism wrapped in a modern package make this house a rare find.

Household: Pok

Household Funds: §4,300

Difficulty: 2

David Pok always had a thing for assertive women, but when the beautiful Janet slammed his head down onto the hood of her police cruiser he knew he had found The One. With careful planning, David ensured that Janet would be his arresting officer on his next heist. She read him his rights, he read her a love poem scribbled on a counterfeit bill, and the rest is history. Can Janet turn this love into a life sentence, or will she let David go early due to bad behavior?

Household	Sim Name	Age	Gender	Supernatural Type	Trait	Career
Pok	David Pok	Young Adult	Male	Human	Neurotic, Kleptomaniac, Charismatic, Night Owl, Schmoozer	Criminal
	Janet Pok	Adult	Female	Vampire	Hot-Headed, Workaholic, Daredevil, Ambitious, Dislikes Children	Law Enforcement

Abundant Richness

Address: 249 Valley View Drive

Rooms: 5br, 3.5ba

Lot Size: 40x40

Step into this Neo-Classical home and experience luxuries your Sim didn't realize existed. Ever wanted a sun room or a fashionable three story turret? Now you do! And the well-stocked library will unleash the inner bookworm in every Sim. Don't take our word for it. Once you experience the unique architecture and lavish appointments of this home, anything else just won't cut it.

Household: Goth

Household Funds: §20,000

Difficulty: 3

After having the house to themselves for a while, the Goth Ghosts are now living with a human in their house. Will the Goths be able to get accustomed to living with a human for the first time or will the inquisitive Helen Hall ask too many questions?

Household	Sim Name	Age	Gender	Supernatural Type	Trait	Career
Hall/Goth	Samuel Goth	Elder	Male	Ghost	Grumpy, Ambitious, Technophobe, Perfectionist, Insane	Business
	Olivia Goth	Adult	Female	Ghost	Dislikes Children, Natural Cook, Mooch, Easily Impressed, Can't Stand Art	Unemployed
	Frida Goth	Young Adult	Female	Ghost	Grumpy, Loner, Bookworm, Commitment Issues, Perfectionist	Mausoleum Clerk
	Helen Hall	Adult	Female	Human	Computer Whiz, Hopeless Romantic, Excitable, Daredevil, Hot-Headed	Fortune Teller

Massively Massive Mansion

Address: 230 Valley View Drive

Rooms: 3br, 3ba, 3hb

Lot Size: 64x64

A house this massive has everything your Sim wants and then some! Start your stroll from the indoor pool and pass by a library with a secret on the way to a kitchen larger than some apartments. Upstairs things get even better where each luxurious bedroom has its own equally luxurious bathroom. Once a Sim sets foot in this luxurious home, they may never want to leave!

Household: Van Gould

Household Funds: §56,000

Difficulty: 3

The Van Goulds go back hundreds of years to the very first days of Moonlight Falls. Of course, for a vampire family that's just a single generation! Ayden Van Gould, the current patriarch, claims to have had a hand in the actual founding of the town—a claim which is hotly disputed by his rivals, the Wolff family. Can the Van Gould's secure their place as the Moonlight Falls founders, or will the Wolffs rise up and claw it away from them?

Household	Sim Name	Age	Gender	Supernatural Type	Trait	Career
Van Gould	Ayden Van Gould	Adult	Male	Vampire	Absent Minded, Proper, No Sense of Humor, Snob, Never Nude	Business
	Emelie Van Gould	Teen	Female	Vampire	Excitable, Artistic, Party Animal, Night Owl	School
	Tristan Van Gould	Teen	Male	Vampire	Virtuouso, Brave, Vegetarian, Brooding	School

Petite Mansion

Address: 212 Valley View Drive

Rooms: 4br, 4.5ba

Lot Size: 40x40

This elegant home has all the class and style of the large mansion on the hill, but without the colossal size and price tag to go with it. Each of its three stories feature top notch craftsmanship that you won't find in newer homes. And with a spacious floor plan, you may need a run to the furniture store after moving in!

Household: Roommates Wanna Be

Household Funds: §3,000

Difficulty: 3

These roomies met at a supernatural conference because of their shared love of all things mystical. Although none of them possess any un-humanly powers, you wouldn't know it by how they dress and act. They love being around all the interesting characters of Moonlight Falls but how will the town's "real" supernaturals react to their masquerading?

Household	Sim Name	Age	Gender	Supernatural Type	Trait	Career
Roommates Wanna Bes	Malcolm Harris	Young Adult	Male	Human	Genius, Hates the Outdoors, Easily Impressed, No Sense of Humor, Supernatural Fan	Unemployed
	Alice Fitzgerald	Young Adult	Female	Human	Mean Spirited, Perfectionist, Brooding, Kleptomaniac, Loner	Criminal
	Haley Sumari	Young Adult	Female	Human	Technophobe, Mooch, Flirty, Artistic, Schmoozer	Spa Specialist
	Deedee Wynn	Young Adult	Female	Human	Childish, Friendly, Natural Cook, Excitable, Schmoozer	Receptionist

Empty Homes

If you would like to direct your own destiny with Sims you create, but want to dive right in without using Build Mode, stroll through Moonlight Falls and inspect these pre-made homes. Each house has two prices. The first price is for an unfurnished house—no objects within. For a few extra Simoleons, you can buy a furnished house that includes at least the basic amenities. Some of the more expensive furnished houses, however, feature luxury objects.

The Craftsman's Mansion

Address: 204 Lakeside Drive

Rooms: 2br, 1ba

Lot Size: 20x20

Cost (Unfurnished): §13,327

Cost (Furnished): §19,064

This elegant one level home proves that simple is best. The lovely box bay window in the living area as both the natural light and added space. The covert entry and extended roof line offer protection and comfort day and night.

Affordable Elegance

Address: 327 Knott Street

Rooms: 2br, 1ba

Lot Size: 19x30

Cost (Unfurnished): §12,853

Cost (Furnished): §16,028

Not every Sim can afford an expensive Victorian home, so for those on a budget here's the find of a lifetime. An award-winning layout leaves no wasted space with a stylish Victorian inspired design on the front augmented with a sharp front porch. All the class without the cost, that's what you'll get in this stunning house.

Cozy Retreat

Address: 20 Lupine Lane

Rooms: 1br, 1ba

Lot Size: 19x19

Cost (Unfurnished): §12,097

Cost (Furnished): §15,467

This charming low-maintenance manufactured home offers a deep, covered entry large enough for a party. The window frame roof provides plenty of shade and keeps the inside of your home a nice, even temperature. A truly comfortable home for a truly comfortable price.

Stately Starter

Address: 31 Lupine Lane

Rooms: 1br, 1ba

Lot Size: 20x20

Cost (Unfurnished): §12,363

Cost (Furnished): §15,403

This modest comfortable home provides everything you need in your first home. Its sensible layout offers an intimate setting, while still providing plenty of space to move around in. Infinite design possibilities are yours with a surprisingly flexible floor plan.

Comfortable Classic

Address: 37 S Falls Avenue

Rooms: 2br, 1ba

Lot Size: 20x20

Cost (Unfurnished): §13,916

Cost (Furnished): §15,901

Built for a Sim on a budget with a discerning eye, this cozy home has everything you need. It has an extra generous size room that can double as a bedroom, office, or whatever. And no more having to eat out all the time thanks to a kitchen that'll get the job done with ease. Should your Sim outgrow this house, no worries. There's plenty of room for expansion!

Empty Lots

There are a host of empty lots you may purchase with your starting household funds (or accrued wealth later in a game). You this quick-glance guide to see which are within your budget and the size of each empty lot.

Address: 278 Valley View Drive

Lot Size: 40x40

Cost: §3,200

Address: 2327 Waning Way

Lot Size: 39x39

Cost: §3,200

Address: 126 Wood Street

Lot Size: 49x49

Cost: §5,000

Address: 261 Valley View Drive

Lot Size: 50x49

Cost: §5,000

Address: 1138 Merchant Way

Lot Size: 39x39

Cost: §3,200

Address: 89 Horseshoe Bend

Lot Size: 39x39

Cost: §3,200

Address: 29 S Falls Avenue

Lot Size: 64x63

Cost: §8,192

Collectibles

Moonlight Falls is a collector's paradise. Hidden in copses of trees, behind glassy waters, and in shaded glens, wondrous treasures await discovery. These items will help you complete objectives and create elixir with the all-new Alchemy skill, beautify your lot and home, and even make a few extra Simoleons on the side.

Supernatural introduces new fish, metals, gems and more for observant citizens to find in almost every corner of town. You just need to know where to look, and that's what we're here for.

So, what are you waiting for? Collect butterflies and beetles to sell to the science facility (or keep for yourself). Refine precious gems and metals into brilliant treasures or potent elixirs. Reel in some curious fish. Space rocks have crashed to the ground around Moonlight Falls, too.

While the maps in this section pinpoint the spawn locations of all collectibles, randomness factors into collecting. Though we have provided the locations of collectibles, there is a chance they will not be there on the specific day you check. Maybe the next day. Maybe the next week. And if multiple collectibles in a category are listed for a spot, perhaps only one of that group will be present on any given day. But don't give up hope. Keep checking back and you'll find the goodies or ingredients needed for the task at hand!

Fish

Considering Moonlight Falls' natural location, it should be no surprise that fishing is a major pastime of its citizens. There are multiple fishing spots around town, including both lake and ocean, where you can reel in a catch.

If you are pursuing the Alchemy skill and elixir-creation, you will spend some time with a hook in the water. Several elixirs require the new fish introduced in *Supernatural*: Toad, Luminous Salamander, and Fairy Damsel. All three of these new fish are detailed in the tables in this section, including best locations, best bait, and resale value. Upping your Fishing skill is necessary to haul the best fish on to the shore, so don't be hesitant with advancing this skill for fun as well as profit.

> **TIP**
>
> Fishing is a fun way to line your pockets with Simoleons. Sell them to the store to score a payday.

> **TIP**
>
> Sims who Love the Outdoors get a huge mood boost out of fishing, and you can plop a radio next to them to drive that mood even higher. (This works for any Sim, not just those with the Loves the Outdoors trait.) Fishing is a great stress-reliever, too, for any Sims but those who Hate the Outdoors.

There are three new fish introduced to the ecosystem in *Supernatural*. All of these fish appear in every township, not just Moonlight Falls, once *Supernatural* has been installed. The new fish are the common Toad (bait with Agarius Mushroom), the uncommon Luminous Salamander (bait with Mycena Lux-Coeli), and the rare Fairy Damsel (bait with Glow Orb Mushroom).

Introduction

New Simology

New Careers
& Skills

Meet the
Supernaturals

New Venues

Tour of
Moonlight Falls

New Object
Catalog

FISH

Fish	Skill Level Req.	Commonality	Locations Found	Preferred Bait
Supernatural				
Toad	1	Common	Freshwater	Agarius Mushroom
Luminous Salamander	4	Uncommon	Freshwater, saltwater	Mycena Lux-Coeli
Fairy Damsel	8	Rare	Saltwater	Glow Orb Mushroom
The Sims 3				
Minnow	0	Common	Freshwater, Saltwater	Apple
Anchovy	0	Common	Saltwater	Tomato
Goldfish	1	Common	Freshwater	Lettuce
Alley Catfish	1	Uncommon	Freshwater, Saltwater	Cheese
Jellyfish	2	Common	Saltwater	Grapes
Rainbow Trout	2	Common	Freshwater	Egg
Red Herring	3	Common	Freshwater, Saltwater	Hot Dogs
Tuna	3	Common	Saltwater	Onion
Piranha	4	Uncommon	Freshwater	Watermelon
Tragic Clownfish	4	Uncommon	Freshwater, Saltwater	Bell Pepper
Siamese Catfish	5	Common	Freshwater, Saltwater	Minnow
Blowfish	5	Uncommon	Saltwater	Potato
Salmon	6	Common	Saltwater	Lime
Black Goldfish	6	Common	Freshwater	Goldfish
Shark	7	Uncommon	Freshwater, Saltwater	Red Herring
Swordfish	7	Common	Saltwater	Anchovy
Angelfish	8	Uncommon	Freshwater, Saltwater	Alley Catfish
Vampire Fish	8	Rare	Water near Graveyard	Garlic
Robot Fish	9	Rare	Water near Science Facility	Piranha
Lobster	9	Common	Freshwater, Saltwater	Tuna
Deathfish	10	Rare	Water near Graveyard	Angelfish
World Adventures				
Crocodile	4	Uncommon	Egypt	Siamese Catfish
Mummy Fish	8	Rare	Egypt	Pomegranate
Frogs	0	Common	France	Cherimola Blanc Grape
Snails	3	Uncommon	France	Renoit Grape
Crawfish	5	Uncommon	France	Frogs
Doitsu Koi	0	Common	China	Pomelo
Kawarimono Koi	3	Common	China	Plum
Ochiba Koi	5	Uncommon	China	Pomelo
Tancho Koi	7	Uncommon	China	Plum
Dragon Fish	9	Rare	China	Tancho Koi

Fish	Skill Level Req.	Commonality	Locations Found	Preferred Bait
Late Night				
Sea Sludge	0	Common	Freshwater, Saltwater	Hot Dogs
Kissing Gourami	4	Common	Freshwater, Saltwater	Goldfish
Sewer Trilobite	6	Common	Freshwater, Saltwater	Minnow
Showtime				
Orange Starfish	1	Common	Saltwater	Tofu
Purple Starfish	5	Uncommon	Saltwater	Tofu
Silver Starfish	10	Rare	Saltwater	Tofu

Fish Spawned

1. Ocean, Common1 - Anchovy, Jellyfish, Red Herring, Blowfish, Salmon, Swordfish

2. Ocean, Common2 - Anchovy, Jellyfish, Red Herring, Tuna, Tragic Clownfish, Shark, Lobster

3. Ocean Uncommon 1 - Alley Catfish, Red Herring, Tragic Clownfish, Tuna, Siamese Catfish, Shark, Lobster, Starfish Purple, Luminous Salamander

4. Ocean Uncommon 2 - Jellyfish, Red Herring, Blowfish, Angelfish, Swordfish, Luminous Salamander

5. Ocean Rare - Red Herring, Tragic Clownfish, Blowfish, Shark, Angelfish, Starfish Silver, Luminous Salamander, Fairy Damsel

6. Lake Common 1 - Minnow, Goldfish, Rainbow Trout, Red Herring, Siamese Catfish, Black Goldfish, Toad

7. Lake Common 2 - Minnow, Goldfish, Red Herring, Salmon, Angelfish, Lobster, Toad

8. Lake Uncommon 1 - Goldfish, Rainbow Trout, Red Herring, Piranha, Shark, Lobster, Luminous Salamander

9. Lake Uncommon 2 - Alley Catfish, Rainbow Trout, Red Herring, Salmon, Angelfish, Luminous Salamander, Toad

10. Lake Rare - Red Herring, Piranha, Black Goldfish, Shark, Angelfish, Vampirefish, Lobster

11. Robot Fish - Robot Fish

12. Death Fish - Death Fish

Crates

On rare occasions, you will reel in something other than a fish. Litterbugs have discarded belongings in the lakes and ponds, but at least their refuse is another Sim's treasure. When you do manage to reel in a crate, there is a good chance it will contain a valuable item, such as World's Brew Bubble Bath or Death Flower. If you're really lucky, the crate will contain a magic gnome!

CRATES

Crate Item	Percent Chance of Finding
Vial of Bliss	100
Ad Nauseum	100
Invigorating Elixir	100
Jar of Friendship	100
Lean and Mean	100
Large and In Charge	100
Flask of Sleep	75
Flask of Angry Bees	75
Zombification	75
Vial of Enlightenment	75
Vial of Potent Bliss	75
Skill Booster	75
Personality Adjuster	75
Jar of Discord	50
Melancholy Serum	50
Flask of Potent Sleep	50
Procreation Elixir	50

Crate Item	Percent Chance of Finding
Potent Invigorating Elixir	50
Liquid Job Booster	50
Potent Melancholy Serum	35
Jar of Potent Friendship	35
Jar of Potent Discord	35
Vial of Potent Enlightenment	35
Potent Cure Elixir	35
Potent Skill Booster	35
Vampiric Sunscreen	25
Rubber Ducky	20
Birthday Cake	16
Bubble Bath	16
Mood-Lite Candle	16
Opposite Personality	15
Bottled Vampire's Bite	15
Potent Personality Adjuster	15
Age of Instant	15

Crate Item	Percent Chance of Finding
Bottled Curse of the Lycan	15
Fountain of Youth Elixir	15
Bottled Witches' Brew	15
Bottled Blessing of the Fae	15
Guitar	10
Mysterious Mr. Gnome	6
Clone Drone	5
Potent Zombification	5
Origin of the Tragic Clown	5
Midas Touch	5
Wish Enhancing Serum	5
Money Tree Seed	5
Death Flower	3
Flame Fruit	3
Laptop	3

FISHING SKILL

The Fishing skill is good for three things: Keeping food on the table, earning money, and relaxing. Sims with the Angler trait have a head start on other Sims who pick up a rod and reel, but any Sims can take a class to advance the Fishing skill or just plop a bobber in the water and start learning through experience.

Acquire by: Take Fishing Class, Read Fishing Book, Fishing

Development tools: No tools needed

Development Benefits

The Fishing skill begins one of three ways—by reading a book, taking a class, or just going out to a body of water and using the Fish interaction. Once the Fishing skill is under way, the skill increases either by continued reading or continued fishing. Just having a hook under the surface is enough to develop the skill, but this is a slow way to learn. The skill actually gets a bump when you catch a fish. And the bigger the fish, the bigger the skill bump.

When a fish is hoisted out of the water, the Sim holds it up and the weight of the fish is automatically logged in the Skill Journal. If it's a new type of fish, that is also noted.

TIP

Certain traits in addition to Angler affect the Fishing skill. Loves the Outdoors Sims get great moodlets from just being outside and fishing. Hates Outdoors, Easily Bored, or Clumsy dampen the ability to catch fish.

Once the Sim reaches level 3 with the Fishing skill, they can choose the Bait interaction at the water's edge to use a specific type of bait while fishing. Bait is essential if a Sim hopes to catch more than just the basic fish. Gaining levels also unlocks the ability to catch certain fish. However, just unlocking a type of fish does not guarantee actually catching it.

Using any bait slightly increases the chance of catching all fish. It also drastically increases the chance of catching the fish that loves that specific bait type. Higher quality bait tends to catch bigger fish, but only for fish that specifically like that bait. So use Perfect bait to catch the biggest fish. You can also use bait to catch fish that are somewhat higher level than your Sim's Fishing skill. Sims can catch fish up to 3 levels higher than their skill by using the right bait, although it will be harder to catch those fish until the Sim is higher skill.

Skill Challenges

Amateur Ichthyologist: Amateur Ichthyologists have caught at least one of every fish type. Their deep understanding of marine life helps them catch the bigger fish.

Commercial Fisherman: Commercial Fishermen have caught at least 350 fish. They catch more fish in less time than normal Sims.

Plants and Seeds

New plants are harvested during your spooky adventures in Moonlight Falls. Like fish, many of these new plants are essential ingredients for elixirs (remember, the recipes can all be found in the "Alchemy Skill" section of the New Simology chapter) and without them, you will struggle to brew up the best stuff.

There is a wealth of new plants in *Supernatural*, many of which are useful for things beyond selling. These are used in the fine art of Alchemy, for example. Here is a full list of the new plants, including their rarity:

Plant	Rarity
Truffles	Rare
White Caps	Common
Porcinis	Common
Glow Orbs	Rare
Spotlight Mushrooms	Uncommon
Red Toadstools	Common
Mycenas	Uncommon
Ghost Chili Bush	Rare
Mandrake	Common
Red Valerian	Common
Wolfsbane	Common

Seeds for plants also are strewn about Moonlight Falls, which, coupled with a good home garden or the community garden lot, can help you grow necessary (and profitable) plants. Seeds appear at spawn spots scattered throughout town. Each seed is categorized by its rarity. There are four classifications for seeds: common, uncommon, rare, and special. Study the accompanying map and chart find where different seeds spawn.

NOTE

You can also recover seeds introduced from previously installed expansion packs.

Seeds Spawned

1. Common 1 - Grapes, Lettuce, White Caps, Wolfsbane Flower, Apple, Porcini, Red Toadstool, Tomato, Red Valerian Root, Mandrake Root

2. Common 2 - Grapes, Lettuce, White Caps, Wolfsbane Flower, Apple, Porcini, Red Toadstool, Tomato, Red Valerian Root, Mandrake Root

3. Common 3 - Grapes, Lettuce, White Caps, Wolfsbane Flower, Apple, Porcini, Red Toadstool, Tomato, Red Valerian Root, Mandrake Root

4. Common 4 - Grapes, Lettuce, White Caps, Wolfsbane Flower, Apple, Porcini, Red Toadstool, Tomato, Red Valerian Root, Mandrake Root

5. Uncommon 1 - Watermelon, Potato, Spotlight Mushrooms, Mycenas, Onion, Lime

6. Uncommon 2 - Watermelon, Potato, Spotlight Mushrooms, Mycenas, Onion, Lime

7. Uncommon 3 - Watermelon, Potato, Spotlight Mushrooms, Mycenas, Onion, Lime

8. Rare 1 - Glow Orbs, Ghost Chili, Garlic, Truffles, Bell Pepper

9. Rare 2 - Glow Orbs, Ghost Chili, Garlic, Truffles, Bell Pepper

10. Rare 3 - Glow Orbs, Ghost Chili, Garlic, Truffles, Bell Pepper

11. Special 1 - Life Fruit, Flame Fruit

12. Special 2 - ife Fruit, Flame Fruit

13. Special 3 - Life Fruit, Flame Fruit

SEEDS

Seed	Plant Name	Rarity
The Sims 3		
Watermelon Seed	Watermelon Vine	Uncommon
Lime Seed	Lime Tree	Uncommon
Bell Pepper Seed	Bell Pepper Plant	Rare
Garlic Seed	Garlic Plant	Rare
Death Flower Seed	Death Flower Bush	Special
Money Tree Seed	Money Tree	Special
Life Fruit Seed	Life Plant	Special
Flame Plant Seed	Flame Plant	Special
Omni Plant Seed	Omni Plant	Special
Egg Seed	Egg Plant	Special
Cheese Seed	Cheese Plant	Special
Burger Seed	Burger Plant	Special
Steak Seed	Steak Plant	Special
World Adventures		
Grape Seed Char	Grape Vine Char	Common
Grape Seed Mer	Grape Vine Mer	Common
Grape Seed Blanc	Grape Vine Blanc	Uncommon
Grape Seed Blue	Grape Vine Blue	Uncommon
Grape Seed Cab	Grape Vine Cab	Rare
Grape Seed Pin	Grape Vine Pin	Rare
Pomegranate Seed	Pomegranate Tree	Uncommon
Plum Seed	Plum Tree	Uncommon
Pomelo Seed	Pomelo Tree	Rare
Cherry Seed	Cherry Tree	Rare
Ambitions		
Vampire Plant Seed	Vampire Plant	Special
Pets		
Carrot Plant Seed	Carrot Plant	Uncommon
Showtime		
Banana Tree Seed	Banana Tree	Rare

Introduction

New Simology

New Careers & Skills

Meet the Supernaturals

New Venues

Tour of Moonlight Falls

New Object Catalog

GARDENING SKILL

Gardening is a great skill for Green Thumb Sims, Sims who want to cook, and Sims who like the outdoors. This skill tree lets you turn a backyard into a harvestable-growing paradise. But gardening is a lot of work and takes time to master.

Acquire by: Take Gardening Class, Read Gardening Book, Plant Seed, Tend to Plants

Development tools: Gardening Books, Seeds

Development Benefits

Learn the Gardening skill by taking a class or reading a Gardening book. You can also plant a seed and cultivate it to start developing the skill. Once the skill has been acquired, Sims can choose the Plant interaction from seeds and other harvestables in their personal inventories. Once a seed has been planted, Sims can water it. As they continue leveling, they unlock two more critical interactions: Weed and Fertilize.

Here are the unlockable interactions or specials for the development of the Gardening skill:

Weed (Level 2): Once the Weed interaction is unlocked, Sims can yank choking weeds before they damage a harvestable. The higher the skill level, the less time it takes to clear weeds around a plant.

Fertilize (Level 3): Fertilizing is key to growing the best harvestables. The quality of the fertilizer is what affects the potential growth of the harvestable.

Uncommon Seeds (Level 5): Once the Sim reaches this level, they can plant uncommon seeds for plants like the Spotlight Mushroom.

Revive Plant (Level 6): If a Sim has the Green Thumb trait, this interaction is unlocked at level 6. A dying plant can be rescued with a pretty high success rate by using this interaction on it.

Rare Seeds (Level 7): Once the Sim reaches this level, they can plant rare seeds for such desirable harvestables like Ghost Chilis and Truffles.

Special Plants (Levels 8, 9, and 10): At level 8, you get the first of three special gardening opportunities from the chef at the bistro. There is one opportunity per level: 8, 9, and 10. Once all three have been completed, the Sim receives Omni Plant seeds and the ability to plant them.

The better care you give a plant and the higher your Gardening skill level, the better quality fruit a plant produces. Plants range from Horrifying to Perfect, just like prepared recipes from the Cooking skill. Better quality harvestables are worth more when sold.

To raise the best harvestables, you must show no mercy with your plants. Keep growing as many as you can and dispose of the lowest quality ones, so you keep breeding higher quality harvestables. Combine this tactic with raising your skill level to keep growing better harvestables. Using quality harvestables in your cooking and elixirs improves the quality of recipes, which in turn gives out better moodlets.

Skill Challenges

Master Planter: A Master Planter must plant every type of plant available. Once you have mastered the varieties, you can reduce weed growth significantly on future plants.

Botanical Boss: Botanical Bosses must harvest at least 75 Perfect fruits and vegetables. The plants of Botanical Bosses almost never die from neglect.

Master Farmer: Master Farmers have harvested at least 650 fruits and vegetables. The plants of Master Farmers remain watered and fertilized longer, meaning their gardens are more efficient.

Insects

There are two types of insects to collect in *Supernatural*—beetles and butterflies. Collecting these insects gets your Sims out of the house so they can avoid going Stir Crazy and soak up some nature. Insects can be sold to the science facility for Simoleons (the rarer the insect, the more it is worth), kept on your lot in terrariums, or most importantly for *Supernatural*, used in Alchemy practices.

Sims love to have a collection of pretty insects at home, so consider your lot environment before trading these finds in for cash. Having an attractive butterfly or rare beetle in a terrarium could be the difference between an okay room and one that gives your Sim the Nicely Decorated moodlet upon walking into it. And you know how critical it is to build up these moodlets in your quest for Lifetime Rewards.

> ### NOTE
> If you have *Showtime* installed, you can also collect Glow Worms, which unlock special elixirs, like Genie in a Bottle.

Beetles

Watch your step! There's an entire world under your feet. Beetle skitter and scurry about, minding their own business until a curious Sim like you comes along to collect them. There are several types of beetles you can find in Moonlight Falls, all worth different amounts of Simoleons if you take them to the science facility. But keep in mind that the more valuable a beetle is to the science facility, the more of an environmental bonus it will have on your lot.

BEETLE VALUES

Beetle	Rarity	Base Value
Cockroach	Common	§1
Termite*	Common	§5
Ladybug	Common	§10
Spider*	Common	§15
Japanese	Common	§15
Water	Common	§30
Light	Uncommon	§40
Rhino	Uncommon	§90
Stag	Uncommon	§175
Spotted	Rare	§400
Trilobite	Rare	§750
Rainbow	Extraordinarily Rare	§1,400

* = only found if *Late Night* is installed

Beetles Spawned

1. Water - Water Beetle
2. Roaches - Roaches
3. Ladybug - Ladybug
4. Japanese Beetle - Japanese Beetle
5. Lightning Beetle - Lightning Beetle
6. Rhino Beetle - Rhino Beetle

7. Stag Beetle - Stag Beetle
8. Spotted Beetle - Spotted Beetle
9. Trilobite - Trilobite
10. Termite - Termite*
11. Spider - Spider*

* = only found if *Late Night* is installed

Butterflies

Butterflies float and flit around town, filling the air with streaks of color. Like beetles, there are many different butterflies in Moonlight Falls, each with a different value to both the science facility and your home. As tempting as it is to use those pretty little wings to generate elixirs or trade them in for some Simoleons, you may wish to install a handful of butterflies in terrariums around your lot for the beautification factor.

BUTTERFLY VALUES

Butterfly	Rarity	Base Value
Moth	Common	§5
Monarch	Common	§10
Zephyr Metalmark	Common	§25
Red Admiral	Common	§35
Mission Blue	Uncommon	§50
Will O' Wisp Green*	Uncommon	§80
Green Swallowtail	Uncommon	§90
Royal Purple Butterfly	Uncommon	§150
Will O' Wisp Blue*	Rare	§250
Silver-Spotted Skipper	Rare	§325
Zebra Butterfly	Rare	§650
Will O' Wisp Pink*	Rare	§820
Rainbow Butterfly	Extraordinarily Rare	§1,080

* = only found if *Ambitions* is installed

GLOW BUG VALUES

Glow Bug	Rarity	Base Value
Yellow	Common	§10
White	Common	§10
Green	Common	§15
Orange	Common	§20
Blue	Uncommon	§80
Red	Uncommon	§120
Pink	Rare	§300
Purple	Rare	§450

Butterflies Spawned

1 Low 1 - Monarch, Red Admiral, Mission Blue

2 Low 2 - Monarch, Zephyr Metalmark, Green Swallowtail

3 Med 1 - Zephyr Metalmark, Red Admiral, Green Swallowtail, Royal Purple Butterfl y

4 Med 2 - Zephyr Metalmark, Mission Blue, Silver-Spotted Skipper

5 High 1 - Red Admiral, Mission Blue, Green Swallowtail, Royal Purple Butterfl y, Silver-Spotted Skipper, Zebra Butterfl y

6 High 2 - Zephyr Metalmark, Red Admiral, Royal Purple Butterfly, Silver-Spotted Skipper, Zebra Butterfly, Rainbow Butterfly

7 Epic - Moth, Monarch, Zephyr Metalmark, Red Admiral, Mission Blue, Green Swallowtail, Royal Purple Butterfly, Silver-Spotted Skipper, Zebra Butterfly, Rainbow Butterfly

8 Moth - Moths

9 Monarchs - Monarchs

10 Silver - Silver-Spotted Skipper

11 Zebra - Zebra Butterfly

12 Kite - Kite

13 Will-o-the-Wisp - Will-o-the-Wisp*

* = only found if *Late Night* is installed

Introduction

New Simology

New Careers & Skills

Meet the Supernaturals

New Venues

Tour of Moonlight Falls

New Object Catalog

Metals

There are several different kinds of precious metals you can pull off the ground—iron, silver, gold, palladium, and plutonium. However, when you pick them up, they are still in ore form. These metals must be smelted to make them valuable—and pretty. To turn ore into ingots, just send them away via an interaction with your lot's mailbox. When the ingot comes back, the value has improved by up to 75 percent. That's quite a boost for the §40 smelting fee.

Metals Spawned

1. Iron - Iron
2. Silver - Silver
3. Gold - Gold
4. Palladium - Palladium
5. Plutonium - Plutonium
6. Iron/Silver/Gold - Iron, Silver, Gold
7. Tungsten Carbide - Tungsten Carbide*
8. Carbon Steel - Carbon Steel*

* = only found if *Late Night* is installed

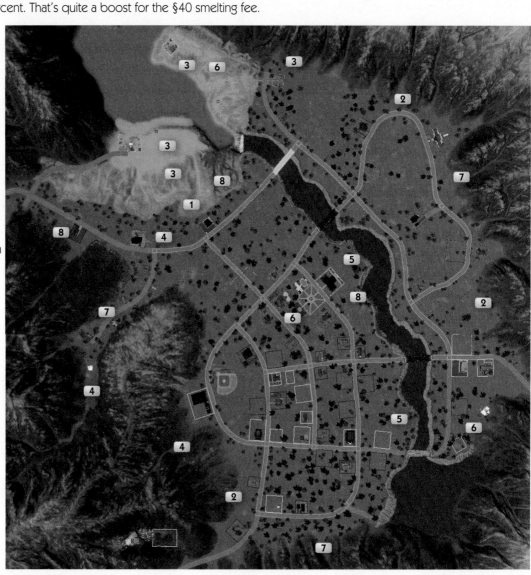

METAL VALUES

Metal Ore	Min. Weight	Max. Weight	Value of Min. Weight	Value of Max. Weight
Iron	1	52	§7	§20
Silver	1	52	§25	§35
Tungsten Carbide*	100	1,095	§35	§70
Gold	1	52	§40	§120
Carbon Steel*	100	1,095	§120	§300
Palladium	80	300	§300	§500

Metal Ore	Min. Weight	Max. Weight	Value of Min. Weight	Value of Max. Weight
Plutonium	0.1	5	§1,000	§1,800
Diamond	1	105	§100	§200

* = only found if *Late Night* is installed

NOTE

There are no new metals, beetles, or butterflies in *Supernatural*.

Gems

While skulking in the shadows of Moonlight Falls, don't just walk by the rocks you see on the ground. Upon closer inspection, your Sim will discover that some of them are actually valuable—well, potentially valuable—gems. However, just picking up a gem isn't the end of the collecting process. Gems require an extra step to maximize their value. You must send them away to be cut into beautiful stones, which increase their value. To have a gem cut, use the interaction on the mailbox or the gem itself. The more cuts you have made, the more become available, and the more money you can earn from the better cuts.

NOTE

Like a lot of things in this world, gem-cutting doesn't come for free. You must pay a fee to have a gem cut, and there are different prices on the cuts. Typically, the more expensive the cut, the more it increases the gem's value.

Gems Spawned

1 Aqua - Aqua

2 Gems Low 5x - Aqua, Emerald, Yellow, Diamond, Bloodstone

3 Gems Low 3x - Smoky, Ruby, Yellow, Tanzanite, Bloodstone

4 Gems Med 1 - Aqua, Smoky, Diamond, Crazy, Bloodstone, Moonstone, Sunstone

5 Gems Med 2 - Emerald, Ruby, Yellow, Tanzanite, Crazy, Bloodstone, Moonstone, Sunstone

6 Gems High - Yellow, Tanzanite, Diamond, Rainbow, Moonstone, Sunstone, Bloodstone

7 Gems Epic - Ruby, Tanzanite, Diamond, Pink, Moonstone, Sunstone, Bloodstone

Supernatural introduces three new gems which are key to many occult parts of this expansion, including Alchemy. The three new gems are:

Bloodstone: This rock has been around for thousands of years and was once used for ancient rituals. Now, it's mainly used for the ritual of rock collecting. It has many uses in ingredients and also makes a fine display piece. The bloodstone is an uncommon gem that will spawn in any township, not just Moonlight Falls.

Sunstone: Some say the sunstone is a moonstone left out in the sun for too long. Others claim it is a piece of a solar flare from the sun. Although the origins of the sunstone are often debated, there's one thing everyone can agree on: it's a sharp looking rock. The sunstone is a rare gem that will spawn in any town or city.

Moonstone: This attractive rock won't actually tell the phase the moon nor does it contain the properties of a real moon that elicits howls from werewolves. It's just a simple rock that shares the name of the big mysterious moon everyone has come to know and love. The moonstone is rare gem, too. It will spawn in any township, but it has a much higher probability of spawning during the full moon and new moon phases of the lunar cycle.

GEMS

Gem	Min. Weight	Max. Weight	Value of Min. Weight	Value of Max. Value
Bloodstone	1	105	§35	§105
Sunstone	1	105	§330	§720
Moonstone	1	105	§375	§855
Blue Topaz	1	105	§9	§21
Smoky Quartz	1	105	§15	§25
Emerald	1	105	§20	§30
Ruby	1	105	§25	§35
Smithsonite*	1	105	§31	§71
Yellow Sapphire	1	105	§35	§60
Tanzanite	1	105	§65	§95
Diamond	1	105	§100	§200
Vampire's Eye*	1	105	§220	§375
Rainbow Gem	1	105	§450	§700
Luminorious Gem	1	105	§150	§350
Pink Diamond	1	105	§1,200	§1,650

* = only found if *Late Night* is installed

GEM CUTS

Gem Cut	Available After # Cuts	Value Multiplier	Cost of Cut
Gemdust	0	0.25	§5
Sun	100	5	§600
Moon	100	5	§600
Emerald	0	1.25	§10
Sculptor's Egg	0	§3	§175
Oval	4	1.5	§20
Pear	8	1.75	§35
Plumbbob	16	2	§50
Marquis	30	2.3	§75
Crystalball	45	2.6	§100
Brilliant	60	3.5	§250
Heart	Collect 10 different types of gem	5	§1,000

TIP

In addition to these new gemstones, there are three new cuts: gemdust, sun, and moon. Gemdust is important for elixir-creation.

NOTE

Woohooium and Flourite Palmstone were introduced in *Ambitions*, but they are only found as part of the sculpting process.

Introduction

New Simology

New Careers & Skills

Meet the Supernaturals

New Venues

Tour of Moonlight Falls

New Object Catalog

GEM LEGEND

Symbol	
Gems Low 5x	Aqua, Emerald, Yellow, Diamond, Bloodstone
Gems Low 3x	Smoky, Ruby, Yellow, Tanzanite, Bloodstone
Gems Med 1	Aqua, Smoky, Diamond, Crazy, Bloodstone, Moonstone, Sunstone
Gems Med 2	Emerald, Ruby, Yellow, Tanzanite, Crazy, Bloodstone, Moonstone, Sunstone

Symbol	
Gems High	Yellow, Tanzanite, Diamond, Rainbow, Moonstone, Sunstone, Bloodstone
Gems Epic	Ruby, Tanzanite, Diamond, Pink, Moonstone, Sunstone, Bloodstone
GemAlchemySpawner	Tanzanite, Smoky, Diamond, Emerald, Bloodstone, Ruby, Yellow, Moonstone, Sunstone, Iron, Silver, Gold

Meteorites

Not every rock you scoop up in Moonlight Falls is of this planet. Some are meteorites that crashed down from space. These rocks can be worth serious Simoleons if you're not afraid of a little risk. There are three sizes—small, large, and huge.

Meteorites can be worth quite a bit of money, but there is a degree of risk when you analyze a meteorite to determine what it is. Sometimes the raw value of a meteorite is greater than its worth once it has been identified. For example, if analysis reveals your meteorite is Ordinary Chondrite, the meteorite is now only worth half of its previous value. After analyzing it, there is no way to reverse the process, so you might be stuck with a less valuable space rock.

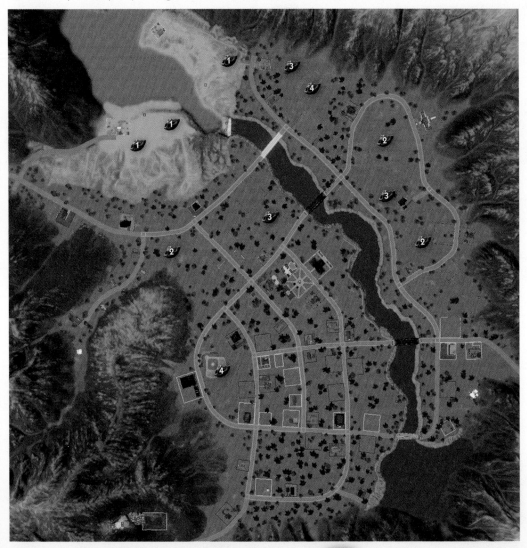

Meteorites Spawned

1 Small - Small Meteorite

2 Medium - Medium Meteorite

3 Small/Medium - Small Meteorite, Medium Meteorite

4 Huge - Huge Meteorite

METEORITE VALUES

Meteorite	Min. Weight	Max. Weight	Value of Min. Weight	Value of Max. Weight
Small	1	65	§10	§30
Large	100	1,050	§50	§200
Huge	50,000	1,001,000	§2,000	§4,500

METEORITE VALUE MULTIPLIERS

Meteorite	Value Multiplier
Ordinary Chondrite	0.5
Howardite	0.7
Acapulcoite	0.7
Eucrite	0.8
Lodranite	0.8
Diogenite	0.9
Ureilite	0.9
Shergottite	1
Angrite	1
Nakhlite	1.1
Chassignite	1.2
Brachinite	1.2
Lunar	1.3
Winonaite	1.3
Aubrite	1.4
Ataxite	1.5
Hexahedrite	1.6
Unusual Bellacite	1.6
Unusual Sporecite	1.7
Kamasite	1.75
Octahedrite	1.8
Unusual Holmberic	1.8
Unusual Custerous Gossticite	1.9
Unusual Rodiekceous	2
Unusual Llamatite	2
Unusual Mazzadrayte	2.1
Unusual Pearsonite	2.1
Unusual Dukeadite	2.2
Rumurutite	3
Pallasite	4
Carbonaceous Chondrite	5
Enstatite Chondrite	6
Mesosiderite	10

CAUTION

Sims find most meteorites on the ground, but there may still be some up in the air, hurtling toward Moonlight Falls. Listen closely. If you hear ominous music creep into the background of everyday Moonlight Falls life, start looking for the hint of a shadow on the ground around your Sim. The second you spot that shadow, make tracks! This is the sign of an incoming meteorite. If you're still inside the meteorite's shadow when it strikes, your Sim will perish.

MAGICAL GNOMES

Supernatural introduces an all-new magic gnome: Haunted Gnome. By now, you should be fairly familiar with these mischievous little fellows. The Haunted Gnome is based on the occult angle in this expansion. There is no sure-fire way to encounter a Haunted Gnome, but there are ways to increase your chances. You can sometimes (okay, rarely) fish a Haunted Gnomes from the The Claaaaw arcade machine. There is also a chance the Haunted Gnome will appear if you fail a Cast Spell>Haunted Ritual.

Should you encounter a Haunted Gnome, get ready for some fun. Once placed on your lot, the Haunted Gnome loves to move around in the middle of the night... typically between the hours of 3 AM and 6 AM. When you wake in the morning, check your Haunted Gnome. He make have moved into a different part of the house. He often makes a silly-scary face.

However, there is a touch of the sinister to the Haunted Gnome. You see, as the name implies, this little gnome is, well, haunted. An NPC ghost sometimes (but not always) haunts the gnome and will show up on your lot for a few hours before disappearing. There is a chance the ghost will possess the gnome and make it float around—but the gnome does stay within its footprint on the lot. Also, if a Sim with the Coward trait gets too close to a Haunted Gnome or the ghost that haunts it, they will become afraid and take a mood hit.

Finally, there is a positive to having a magic gnome on your lot and inside your household. You immediately generate an environmental bump, which can result in mood increases for nearby Sims.

BROWNIE BITES

That wraps up the Tour of Moonlight Falls. You're now armed with the information needed to go out and find great collectibles, enhance careers and skills, or invest in a new home or real estate proposition.

BROWNIE BITES

Moonlight Falls has a much different feel from several of the other cities introduced in previous expansions. It's woodsy, it's spooky, and it feels like a place where folks come to walk on the wild side. It's worth taking the time to explore every nook and cranny and see everything Moonlight Falls has to offer at different points in the lunar cycle.

New Object Catalog

• • •

When you first set foot in Moonlight Falls and start a new life, there's a strong chance that you'll not exactly be rolling in the Simoleons. But don't let that daunt you. In fact, use that as inspiration to get out there, develop skills, and pursue careers that enrich your Sim. And we're not talking just about spiritual and mental enrichment. We're talking about material wealth, too! That's how you can acquire many of the exciting new goodies found in *Supernatural*'s object catalog for your very own lot.

Supernatural introduces a lot of new objects and decorations, from spooky trees for the back yard to strange toys for tots. New furniture takes on a decidedly Gothic bent, as you'll see when you peruse the catalog at the end of this chapter as well as in Buy Mode. In addition to creepy-cool decor, there are many new objects you can interact with to increase skills (both normal and hidden), satisfy core needs, and entertain the different supernaturals. For example, you'll note that multiple objects in this ctalog have interactions exclusive to fairies, which can shrink down and really get inside items like the arcade claw machine or a new train set.

In this chapter, we highlight the topline objects you can interact with new to *Supernatural*. Interactions are explained, as well as the potential results of these interactions. After all, how fair is it to set you loose on a beekeeping box without telling you how to spot angry bees that are likely to sting you? Some of these objects pull double-duty, existing not just here, but in previous chapters where they direct relate to new gamplay concepts and mechanics. For example, the Alchemy Station, so critical for developing the Alchemy skill is also detailed in the "Alchemy" section of the New Careers and Skills chapter.

DEPRECIATION

As soon as you buy an object and then exit Buy Mode, the object loses value. The immediate value hit is significant, but not devastating: 15 percent. With each additional day, the object loses more value: 10 percent per day. The value of an object finally bottoms out at 40 percent of its original value. So, if you bought the SimmerChar Dual-State Stove for §400, the object would lose §60 on the first day. The next day, it would lose another §40. If you sold the object back after two weeks of use, you would get §160 back.

However, not everything in this world goes down in value upon purchase. Some art actually increases in value.

BILLS

Every Monday and Thursday, the postal worker drops off a stack of bills in your mailbox. You have to pay approximately §6 for every §1,000 of stuff you own. For example, if you spent §14,500 on building and objects, your bills will come out to around §85. So keep this in mind when shopping.

To pay your bills, click on the mailbox or computer and choose the Pay Bills interaction or choose the Auto Bill Pay option. You cannot ignore bills and hope they go away. You must pick up bills and attend to them in a timely manner.

If you do not pay your bills within three days—the normal bill cycle—you can count on a visit from the Repo Man on day four. The Repo Man will enter your house without warning and take objects without mercy until he has reached the number of Simoleons you currently owe. Once you enter day four of bills, you cannot quickly pay them and shoo away the Repo Man. It's too late by that time.

Introduction

New Simology

New Careers & Skills

Meet the Supernaturals

New Venues

Tour of Moonlight Falls

New Object Catalog

New Objects & Interactions

If you have played *The Sims* games before, you know that most objects can be used (and abused) by Sims—in fact, that's usually the point of putting an object on your lot. It should serve a function. Some objects have no function beyond boosting a room's environmental score and giving Sims the Decorated or Nicely Decorated moodlets.

Other objects have interactions that provide learning or entertainment or satisfy a need. These objects and their interactions are detailed in this section of the object catalog. To see what interactions are available on an object, just left-click on it. A radial menu appears. Click on an interaction to add it to the action queue in the screen's upper-left corner.

So, while there are many new objects in *Supernatural* in the decoration or furniture categories, we'll drill down on all of the new objects that affect skill development, fun, and those that result in new activities. Many of these objects are referenced elsewhere in this guide, such as the Alchemy Station in the New Careers and Skills chapter (Alchemy skill section) or the Fairy House in the Meet the Supernaturals chapter.

Moondial

Purchase Cost: $180

Benefits:

◈ Lunar-related activities

Description: For thousands of years, Sims have used sundials to tell time with astonishing accuracy. Get ready for the next big leap: the Moondial! Now for the first time, it's possible to get a glimpse into the cryptic cycle of the moon. The sharp-looking Moondial isn't just for lunatics to count down to the next full moon. It'll dress up any drab corner of the house in the snap.

Because the lunar cycle plays such a pivotal role in events that transpire in Moonlight Falls, the Moondial ends up being an intriguing and important object. By clicking on this object, you can either choose to check the current phase of the moon (although this is featured right on your HUD, near your Sim portrait) or check your lunar horoscope. Only teens, young adult, adult, and elders can use this interaction.

When you choose to check your lunar horoscope, your Sim peers into the ball and awaits revelation. Horoscopes are not guaranteed positives, though. There are six possible results, and at any given point in a day, you have a chance of seeing one of two randomly selected outcomes. The possible outcomes directly affect your mood:

◈ **Possibility of Romance:** Increase your chance of finding love or landing successful romantic socials.

◈ **Possibility of New Friendship:** Increase the likelihood of making new friends, accelerating LTR, and landing successful friendly socials. If you have a wish that involves making friends or socializing, you may want to gaze into the Moondial in hopes of getting this fortune.

◈ **Possibility of Prosperity:** Boost your money-making chances in the world!

◈ **Possibility of Great Success:** This boosts your chance of landing successful interactions with objects, opportunities, and more.

◈ **Possibility of Betrayal:** Watch out, this negative horoscope results in a mood hit. Your Sim fears betrayal for a 24-hour period.

◈ **Possibility of Misfortune:** Things could go wrong on this day, should you receive this unfortunate horoscope. Be cautious with risk, lest you end up on the short end of the stick.

These horoscope results last for an entire day—the 24-hour period starts from the moment you ask the Moondial for your horoscope. The positive horoscopes gives you a +10 mood boost. The negative horoscopes result in a -10 mood hit. A moodlet with the name of the horoscope result appears in your mood box.

Tip

To be sure, the odds of getting a positive horoscope are in your favor. Of the six, four horoscopes are positive. But these are chosen randomly, though, so there may very well be a day when the two selected horoscopes are negative. Hopefully that's the day you decide to skip the Moondial, right?

Mrs. Stingley's Beekeeping Box

Purchase Cost: $275

Benefits:

◈ Beekeeping

Description: Step up to Mrs. Stingley's Beekeeping Box and get ready to dive into the exciting world of beekeeping! Sure you can get the honey at the store, but fending off a swarm is the only way for true honey aficionados. Can you tame the delicate dance of the bees and convince the hive to part with its treasures? Give it a go! (Not for sale to bears.)

Beekeeping is an all-new hobby in *Supernatural*. As such, Sims need a new object for this hobby. With this special beekeeping box, Sims can raise a colony of honey bees and produce copious amounts of delicious sweet stuff—provided you put in a little effort. Should you not take good care of the bees, well, they let you know. They sting you!

Though the beekeeping box is detailed in the "Beekeeping" section of New Careers and Skills chapter (in the "Skills" section, as Beekeeping is a "hidden" skill), let's go over the basics here:

◈ The beekeeping box must be placed outside on a lot.

◈ The box produces honey, which can be used in Cooking.

◈ The happier the bees, the better quality.

◈ Any time you interact with the beekeeping box, you risk getting stung. However, happy bees rarely sting!

To make bees happy, you must regularly choose the Feed and Clean interactions on the beekeeping box. Depending on the bees' current state, you risk getting stung or attacked when attempting to clean. But regular cleaning results in a lower chance of being attacked, so you can see how once you get over

the hurdle, beekeeping can be smooth sailing. You must also feed bees regularly. Like cleaning, you risk a bee sting. Both of these activities raise the mood of the bees, but like your Sims' moods, over time the mood of the bees decays unless you attend to them.

Honey is produced every few hours. When honey is ready, you can click on the box and choose the Harvest interaction to claim it. The quality of the honey and how that's determined is detailed in New Simology, but here's the breakdown:

◈ **Happy Bees:** Perfect, Outstanding, Excellent, Great

◈ **Content Bees:** Normal, Nice, Very Nice

◈ **Angry Bees:** Bad, Horrifying, Putrid

To harvest the honey, it's often a good idea to use the Smoke Out interaction to calm the bees. This seems like a win-win, but there are costs to regularly using Smoke Out before harvesting. This interaction reduces both hunger and mood, which can over time lower the quality of the honey or wax. So, keep an eye on the beekeeping box, gauge mood, and then make the best call to avoid getting stung!

TIP

Look for the motion of the bees outside the box to determine mood. If you see some buzzing bees just circling the box, they are happy. If you spot just a few bees buzzing peacefully around the box, the are currently content. If you see a swarm buzzing around the box and hear an aggressive buzzing sound, the bees are angry. And angry bees are likely to sting you 75 percent of the time!

Introduction

New Simology

New Careers & Skills

Meet the Supernaturals

New Venues

Tour of Moonlight Falls

New Object Catalog

Magic Wand

Purchase Cost: Varied

Benefits:

◆ Portable

Description (from Magic Wand: Classic): This is the one that started it all. Carved out of wood from an enchanted forest, this magic wand is light, yet durable—a fine tool for a novice spellcaster. Other ones may be fancier, more accurate, safer, or more powerful, but the classic gets the job done and they don't come any cheaper!

Magic Wands—and there are plenty of them—are critical tools for witches. Wands allow witches (and witches only!) to cast spells, such as charms that affect love, disease, and mood. Wands are also used in duels. Success with a magic wand is directly tied to the Spellcasting hidden skill, which is detailed in the "Witch" section of the Meet the Supernaturals chapter. Here, you will learn everything you need to know about developing your Spellcasting skill as well as all of the benefits and parks with each level.

TIP

Want to raise the dead? Then goose that hidden Spellcasting skill to level 10! You can then bring the dead back to life. But watch out for Zombification!

TIP

Using black magic, you can even turn your fellow Sims into toads! But be mindful of the fact that a failed spell can backfire and temporarily turn you into a ToadSim. Ooops!

Smack-a-Gnome!

Purchase Cost: $795

Benefits:

◆ **Fun:** 5

◆ Never Breaks

Description: You stand, mallet at the ready, muscles tightly coiled and ready to spring, waiting for the telltale snap that preceeds the appearance of yet another disgusting monster. One after another they snap up, again and again, terrible little faces mocking you! There is only one recourse. Crush them! CRUSH THEM ALL! Fun for all ages!

Smack-a-Gnome! is an exciting arcade game where Sims can bring the hammer down on itty-bitty heads to rack up high scores. This is a great way to blow off some steam and have a little fun without expending serious Simoleons. There are no physical prizes, such as those you might receive from The Claaaaw machine, though.

The primary interaction here is Play, which fires up the machine. A Sim picks up a mallet and waits for the first round to begin. At first, just a few heads pop up. But over time, the rounds get faster and more intense, with more heads to swat back down. Depending on skill, which we'll address in a moment, Sims may deliver direct hits, miss the little heads, and even wind up with an epic fail: the mallet bounces back, smacking the Sim playing the machine right in the kisser.

BROWNIE BITES

This arcade game is directly tied to the hidden Arcade skill. It's a very easy skill to develop: just play arcade games! The more you play, the better your Sim performs. You'll get higher and higher scores and in turn have more fun playing! Watch your Sim get better in real-time, too! As the Arcade skill rises, they hit more and more heads during turns.

The way heads are spawned on the machine changes, depending on the supernatural nature of the Sim playing. Now, you can choose which types of heads appear when playing with a special interaction, but otherwise, the Play interaction breaks down like this (player = head):

◆ Werewolf = vampire heads

◆ Vampire = werewolf heads

◆ Witch = fairy heads

◆ Fairy = witch heads

◆ Supernatural Fan human = gnome heads

◆ Supernatural Skeptic human = random heads

◆ Human = gnome heads

In addition to playing the game, you can also have fun watching another Sim play Smack-a-Gnome! Different supernaturals have different reactions to the game. If a werewolf is battering vampire heads, any vampires watching will act offended by such nonsense. However, any nearby werewolf will cheer the player.

The Claaaaw

Purchase Cost: $795

Benefits:

◈ **Fun:** 4

◈ Never Breaks

Description: Is there any feeling as satisfying as seeing that metal claw rise up from the pile with a shiny new prize gripped firmly in its talons? Watching as it deposits your winnings into the incredible victory chute? We sure wouldn't know, because it drops our stupid toy at the last second EVERY TIME. We're sure you'll have much better luck, though!

The Claaaaw is an arcade-style prize machine where your Sim attempts to maneuver a claw over a pile of stuffed animals and other prizes. This machine doesn't cost anything thing to use. You just saunter up to The Claaaaw and select the Grab a Prize interaction to start a game. Your Sim then grabs the little joystick and makes a go of picking out a prize. Now, as you can imagine, your success is never 100 percent. There is a chance you will miss entirely and receive nothing. There's also a chance you will grab a prize but accidentally lose it before the claw drops it in the little chute. However, should you succeed, here is how the prizes break down:

◈ Cheaper toys from *The Sims 3* base game: 50 percent

◈ Stuffed Animals/Toys (including new toys from *Supernatural*)/Bags of Simoleons: 35 percent

◈ Scary Bears/Gems: 12.5 percent

◈ Haunted Gnome/Rare Gem: 2.5 percent

Winning a prize, as you might expect, results in a mood bump. And, as noted in the "Smack-a-Gnome!" section, the hidden Arcade skill affects your chances of success. Namely, the more you play, the more you develop this hidden skill. The higher that skill, the better your chance of grabbing a prize. (Although, higher Arcade skill does not translate into better prizes. That is still determined by the above formula.)

Fairy Sims have a special interaction on The Claaaaw: Cheat the System. When selected, Fairy Sims shrink down into true fairy form and zip into the machine via the prize slot. You can then see the fairy rattle around inside the machine, looking for a prime prize. There is a chance that the fairy will drop the prize before escaping the machine, but if they don't, then when the fairy pops back out of the prize chute, they return to human form and claim the goodie, Cheating the System does not affect the chance of getting rare and ultra-rare prizes; it just increases the chance of successfully snagging a prize from the machine.

Aleister's Alchemy Station

Purchase Cost: $850

Benefits:

◊ **Fun:** 1

Description:
Finally, the powers of the universe can be yours for a price that won't have you wishing you could turn lead into gold.

Aleister's Alchemy Station is user friendly, safe-ish, and fully featured. Right out of the box, you'll be brewing elixirs that'll make conventional science want to go take a little lie-down somewhere. Let Al you put the power in your hands with Aleister's Alchemy Station.

The Alchemy Station is the primary object associated with developing the all-new Alchemy skill. Whether you purchase one for your own lot or use those found in community areas, such as beneath the library, this is the means of becoming a master Alchemist. Now, we really dug deep on the Alchemy Station in the "Alchemy" section of New Careers and Skills, but let's recap the basics here.

From the Alchemy Station, Sims can research Alchemy or mix up some elixirs. When you create something with the station, you choose from a menu of available options, uncovered by advancing the Alchemy skill. Here are the available interactions:

◊ **Mix Elixir:** This interaction brings up a menu of available elixirs for you to fashion. Mix up ingredients to fashion a fresh brew.

◊ **Research Alchemy:** This interaction directs your Sim to carefully flip through the pages of a musty old tome, absorbing arcane knowledge and slowly developing the Alchemy skill.

While using the Research Alchemy interaction, there is a slight chance you will automatically discover an Alchemy Recipe. If the researching Sim is a Bookworm or a Supernatural Fan, this interaction generates additional experience as well as has a higher chance of resulting in an insta-learned Recipe.

Gem-U-Cut Machine

Purchase Cost: $975

Benefits:

◊ Gem cutting

Description: Sometimes you find that perfect gem, and other times you find a gem that could really use some sculpting. For those "other" times, might we suggest the fabulous one-of-a-kind Gem-U-Cut Machine? With this contraption, every gem you find can be beautiful! Attractive, easy-to-use, and much faster than the mailbox method, the Gem-U-Cut Machine will have you turning out your own high-quality gems in no time.

Sometimes, it isn't exactly practical to mail away gems. You need that gem cut right away, and so that's what led to the invention of the Gem-U-Cut Machine. But this machine has an extra bonus besides turnaround time. After cutting a gem, you also receive the gem cut generated during the cutting process.

To use the machine, click on it and choose either Cut Gem or Cut All Gems of Same Type. From that selection, you pick which gems in your inventory you wish to cut and then select from the available gem cuts. The machine then kicks into gear and starts rattling about, cutting the gem(s) to your specifications. After a few moments, the finished goods pop out and go right into your inventory.

TIP

Sims with either the Handy or Gatherer trait have a slightly higher chance of cutting a more valuable gem.

NOTE

Teens are the youngest age group that can use this object.

NOTE

Gems cut with this machine count toward the overall number of cuts, which unlocks additional gem cuts, as detailed in the "Collectibles" section of the Tour of Moonlight Falls chapter.

Zoomsweeper Broom Arena

Purchase Cost: $960

Benefits:

◆ Fun

◆ Broom Riding (hidden skill)

Description: Tired of cruising around town and obeying the traffic laws? The folks at Zoomsweeper feel your pain. Get ready for the no-holds-barred world of tricks and stunts that will drop the jaws of your friends and leave them coming back for more! Going the speed limit is never fun. Don't you deserve a Zoomsweeper Broom Arena?

Sims need someplace to practice their magic broom-riding skills, right? Well, that's why you can now order up a Zoomsweeper Broom Arena right from Buy Mode. Sure there's one available next to the Alchemy shop, but sometimes you just want to step out the back door and put in some good brooming time. (Or place one on a community lot close to you.)

There are two interactions with the Zoomsweeper Broom Arena:

Joy Ride: When this interaction is triggered, your Sim hops on their broom, levitates, and starts making laps in the arena. This action continues until the Fun need is maxed, any need goes critical (like bladder), or the Sim completes around five laps. Then the Sim hops off the broom and the interaction ends.

Stunt Ride: This is a little more intense than a Joy Ride. During these laps, your Sim will attempt some stunts, like loops and rolls. However, there is a chance with each stunt, that your Sim will fail. The higher the hidden Broom Riding skill level, the less chance of failure.

Now, while you are zipping about on your broom, there is a chance you will pick up some spectators. When the Broom Riding hidden skill reaches level 5, a new interaction appears: Stunt Ride for Tips. The more stunts you successfully pull off on a Stunt Ride, the more Simoleons your audience will drop in the cup after the show. This is a nice way to pick up a little extra cash while developing the Broom Riding skill.

Lightning Leap Atomic Molecular Arranger (LLAMA)

Purchase Cost: $1,500

Benefits:

◊ Instant travel

Description: It is a common misconception that portals are a recent achievement from the world of science. In fact, magical portals have been in use for thousands of years. And no name is more trusted in the field of instantaneous magical relocation than the LLAMA. Take your LLAMA to work, to the grocery store, or even to your best friend's house. You'll never be late when you're riding a LLAMA.

The magical town of Moonlight Falls has a very special method of transportation: the Lightning Leap Atomic Molecular Arranger (LLAMA), a network of telephone booths that zip Sims from one place to the next in the blink of an eye. It's an excellent way to get from point A to point B without using up too much time, although you are limited only to the LLAMA booths in the network. There are occasions when it may be faster to go on foot or by vehicle instead of LLAMA.

LLAMAs are not on the town map—the network is much more intimate than that. You must manually utilize the system. Sims do not automatically take it when directed around town. Instead, click on the LLAMA to select a destination. You can add new locations to this network, though, through Buy Mode. Place a LLAMA on your lot and effortlessly bounce across the city. And if you start owning community lots and venues, you can install additional LLAMAs to boost the spread of the network. Pretty soon, you may never need to set foot in a cab!

Spectrum Mood Lamp

Purchase Cost: $325

Benefits:

◊ Mood changes

Description: Understand, this is not some gimmicky lamp that will try to predict your mood. No no no. This is a magical lamp that causes people's moods to... shift in certain ways. A full spectrum of colors, a full spectrum of possibilities. Let the mood strike you with the Spectrum Mood Lamp.

Now, this is real-deal mood lighting. The Spectrum Mood Lamp is a sweet little pick-me-up that, when placed near Sims and activated, can affect mood. The light stays on for only 120 minutes at a time before it automatically shuts itself off. When you place a Spectrum Mood Lamp, you can select which mood color to project from this list:

◊ **Blue Mood:** This generates the Feeling Blue moodlet for all Sims in the same room as the lamp. There is also a chance that a puddle of water will appear around the lamp. (Hey, some Sims love being morose, so this color serves a purpose!)

◊ **Red Mood:** This color applies the Feeling Red moodlet to all Sims in the same room. This moodlet generates a small mood bump.

◊ **Green Mood:** Ooh, now this color applies the Feeling Green moodlet (a +5 mood bump) and generates a slight chance of a Sim in the same room being Toadified! If you aren't a witch Sim, this is an opportunity to try out this most excellent bit of magical mischief.

◊ **Purple Mood:** When this color generates the Feeling Purple moodlet, all affected Sims in the room not only get a nice +5 mood bump, but they also have the following negative moodlets instantly removed: Smelly, Grungy, Garlic Breath, Dirty Surroundings, Filthy Surroundings, Vile Surroundings, and Disgusted.

◊ **Pink Mood:** Feeling Pink is another positive mood bump from the Spectrum Mood Lamp, but in addition, there is a good chance that an hour after being in the presence of the lamp, a Sim will act like they are Amorously Flirting, which can be great for nudging a romance along. Use this mood color if you want to start the fire of passionate love. (The neighbors complain about the noises above...)

Now, in addition to these interactions, you can also Extinguish a mood light or just check out the lamp. Zombiefied Sims are automatically drawn to the Spectrum Mood Lamp. Now, attracting a zombie isn't always a positive, so you may want to have a peek around before switching on the lamp. If a fairy is attracted, they transform into their true fairy form and buzz around the lamp. While doing so, there is a high chance they will get zapped by the lamp and end up with the Singed negative moodlet upon returning to human form. So, watch out!

Orb of Answers

Purchase Cost: $195

Benefits:

◈ **Fun:** 5

Description: The answers to all of life's problems lie within you. You can discover them for yourself through quiet reflection or the application of logic. But who has time for all that? Just reach for the Orb of Answers, and leave the life-altering decisions to us. Friends will just try to spare your feelings—you can only trust the Orb of Answers!

Shall we consult the Orb of Answers? That's a question many Sims ask when confronted with a life decision. Sometimes, you just need an inanimate object to push you in one direction, and that's what the Orb of Answers does. Sims can pick up this fun object, shake it, and ask specific questions about life, hobbies, and more. The answers the Orb gives, though, affect the wishes of that Sim. You see, if a Sim asks if they should learn to play a new instrument and the Orb of Answers comes back with a "yes," the Sim is certain to get a wish related to learning the guitar skill (or another instrument skill, provided you have other expansions installed). If the Orb returns a "no," the Sim gets a completely unrelated wish. In the case of learning an instrument, a negative reply from the Orb slots the wish to clean the kitchen sink.

Here are the questions you can ask the Orb, as well as the resulting wishes of a yes or no answer:

Question	"Yes" Answer Wish	"No" Answer Wish
Should I Learn an Instrument?	Wish to Learn Instrument	Wish to Clean Sink
Should I Become a New Supernatural?	Wish to Use Transformation Elixir	Wish to Check Self in Mirror
Will I Find True Love?	Wish to Kiss Any Sim	Wish to Have 3 Simultaneous Lovers
Should I Have Kids?	Wish to Have a Baby	Wish to Buy Car Worth X Simoleons
Should I Join a Career?	Wish to Join X Career	Wish to Watch TV
Will I Become Rich?	Wish to Be Worth X Simoleons	Wish to Have 3 Rich Friends
Should I Learn a New Skill?	Wish To Learn Any Skill	Wish to Buy a TV
Should I Go Out to Eat?	Wish to Eat at the Bistro	Wish to Cook Something
Do I Need to Lose Weight?	Wish to Workout	Wish to Order Pizza
Should I Play Games?	Wish to Play Game on Computer	Wish to Clean Toilet
Should I Play with My Toys?	Wish to Play with a Toy	Wish to Make Bed
Should I Go Play Outside?	Play Catch or Go into Town	Wish to Play Video Games
Should I Do My Homework?	Wish to Do Homework	Wish to Watch TV
Can I Have a Friend?	Wish to Become Friends with a Sim	Wish to Watch TV

Fairy Bungalow/Castle

Purchase Cost: Varied

Benefits:

- ◆ + Hunger
- ◆ + Group Activity
- ◆ + Stress Relief
- ◆ + Energy
- ◆ + Fun

Description (from the Fairy Bungalow): This modest bungalow will provide your fairy family with cozy accommodations when in their true fairy forms. Fully furnished and move-in ready, this home has been thoroughly checked by fairy home inspectors. After all, even tiny specks of light have needs.

Now, in the "Fairy" section of the Supernatural chapter, we offered a complete explanation of the Fairy House and how it fits into the fairy lifestyle in this expansion. Fairy Houses (and there are two different options) offer a multitude of different interactions that just make fairy life... easier. In these little hideaways, fairies can catch some Zs, quaff a drink, relax, and even WooHoo with other fairies. If you came here first, flip back to the "Fairy" section to learn how each interaction works and what their benefits are.

> ### Tip
> Bonus! There are several Fairy Houses all over Moonlight Falls, such as next to the fishing holes and in Playful Playground.

Magic Jelly Bean Bush

Purchase Cost: $575

Benefits:

- ◆ Fun: 2

Description: In a perfect world, all of life's food necessities like cookies and bacon would grow on magical little plants. Unfortunately, the world isn't perfect but at least jelly beans can grow on bushes. To be clear, is not the jelly bean bush that is magic, but rather an ordinary bush which dispenses Magic Jelly Beans.

Everybody loves jelly beans, right? Little lumps of sugar—where can you go wrong? Well, you can when plucking jelly beans from a Magic Jelly Bean Bush because not every sweet treat that comes from this plant is a delicious bite. Some of

these beans result in icky tastes and negative moodlets. But now that we've got that little warning out of the way, we can also promise you that many of the beans you harvest are yummy-yummy and offer mood bumps.

You don't get to choose which jelly bean you eat. When you approach the Magic Jelly Bean Bush, you have but one interaction: Eat Jelly Bean. Sounds easy enough. But after eating the bean, wait a moment to see what happens. Will you get one of these great moodlets?:

- ◆ Adrenaline Rush
- ◆ Buzzed
- ◆ Fascinated
- ◆ Feeling Lucky
- ◆ Minty Breath
- ◆ Oddly Powerful
- ◆ Stuffed
- ◆ Sugar Rush
- ◆ Educated
- ◆ Warmed
- ◆ All Glowy on the Outside

Or will your Sims's mood be dampened by one of these?:

- ◆ Feeling Unlucky
- ◆ Garlic Breath
- ◆ Hungry
- ◆ Very Hungry
- ◆ Itchy
- ◆ Smelly
- ◆ Nauseous
- ◆ Exhausted
- ◆ Terrified!
- ◆ Disappointed
- ◆ Embarrassed
- ◆ Has to Pee
- ◆ Berry Blue

And that's not all that can happen when you munch on these magic beans. Your Sim can be afflicted by some pretty nasty stuff, such as:

- ◆ The Sim actually catches on fire, and gets the negative On Fire moodlet.
- ◆ The Sim is electrocuted and is hit with the Singed negative moodlet.
- ◆ The jelly bean is too hot and the Sim is tagged with Too Spicy!
- ◆ There is an extremely (emphasis on extremely) rare chance that a jelly bean results in instant death. Oh no! When the Sim becomes a ghost from a bad bean, they appear purple.

> ### Note
> Child Sims will never nosh on a instant kill jelly bean. Never.

Magic Mirror

Purchase Cost: $865

Benefits:

◈ **Fun:** 3

◈ **Charisma:** 2

◈ **Social:** 2

Description: Ever wish you had a friend who was always there, happy to talk or just listen... AND you could hang them on the wall? With this incredible looking-glass you can share gossip, chit-chat, or just ask each other how your days were. And while you may like to admire yourself in the mirror, it's even better when the mirror is admiring you! You may never need another friend with this mirror in your house!

Well, now, we cannot have a fairytale, supernatural world here without a Magic Mirror. This mystical surface is more than just gazing glass, it's a potential confidante for any Sim. Once placed on a lot, a Sim can approach the mirror and engage in a multitude of interactions and conversation starters. The Magic Mirror will respond to the best of its ability, help develop the Charisma skill, and even offer a Magical Make-over—and all while putting on a rather entertaining show with the mask in the glass!

Here are the interactions and what they accomplish:

◈ **Chat:** This interaction satisfies Social and Fun needs, while building Charisma.

◈ **Gossip:** This interaction results in Fun and Social need satisfaction for Sims (with extra fun for Evil and Mean-Spirited Sims), plus the development of the Charisma skill. Here, the Magic Mirror will provide info on other Sims in the the active Sim's Relationship panel. And, if there is a Sim in town more Charismatic than the active Sim, the Magic Mirror will zero in on them for the gossip.

◈ **Ask about Day:** This is a rather pleasant interaction with the Magic Mirror. Resulting in Fun, Social and Charisma-building, this engagement with the Magic Mirror is all about idle chit-chat. No nastiness here!

◈ **Practice Being the Most Charismatic of Them All:** As you would at any mirror, you can practice your Charisma skill at the Magic Mirror. The difference here is that the Magic Mirror offers more experience, which means the Sim develops the Charisma skill faster. You can drag this interaction out in the action queue to practice until Charisma improves, which keeps the Sim there until they pick up a skill point.

◈ **Conspire Against My Enemies:** Whereas this social results in Charisma-building and Social needs for the Sim, Evil or Mean-Spirited Sims get extra fun out of this. There is a slight chance that the Magic Mirror will even offer the Sim a poison apple to use on an enemy. Kinda sinister, no? (Note: you need an actual enemy Sim in the game to use this interaction.)

◈ **Admire Me:** Now, Snob Sims just love this interaction. Ask the Magic Mirror to Admire Me (well, it seems more like a command than a request) and then stand back, allowing the mirror to bask in your glory. If you have a high Charisma level, you receive the new Fairest of Them All moodlet, which is a major mood booster!

◈ **Magical Make-Over:** This interaction results not only in Fun and Social need bumps, but also a new look for the Sim. This special moment is pleasing for the Sim.

Bonehilda Living Quarters

Purchase Cost: $3,999

Benefits:

◈ Bonehilda NPC

Description: This charming cabinet makes perfect living quarters for Bonehilda. It provides a cozy space for your trusty skeletal servant to recharge in between jobs. Who knows what a skeleton has that needs recharging—marrow? Pick one up today and watch your Bonehilda happily rest... in pieces!

We introduced you to Bonehilda in the Supernatural chapter. But surely this mystical maid deserves some special digs to call her own, right? Install this on your lot so Bonehilda has a place to rest between tasks. While Bonehilda will often emerge from the upright casket on her own to perform household duties like nannying and cooking, you can trigger her arrival by selecting Awaken on the casket. You can then chose Dismiss if you want Bonehilda to return to sleep mode.

NOTE

You cannot remove this object if Bonehilda is out of the casket and performing a task. You must wait for her to return.

Scary Bearys

Purchase Cost: $50

Benefits:

◊ **Fun:** 7

◊ Portable

Description (from Scary Bearys: Vampire): Here's a fuzzy little friend that will go straight to your heart like a wooden stake. He may not be able to turn into a mist or a pack of ferocious badgers at will, but he can turn that frown into a smile. And such a snappy dresser. Invite this vampire buddy into your home and let him suck the sadness right out of you!

Supernatural introduces new teddy bears, called Scary Bearys! These toddler toys are based on all of the different occults that appear not just in *Supernatural*, but also previous expansions. (You do not need the expansions installed, though, to collect the bears.) The Mummy Bear is inspired by *World Adventures*, the Genie Bear is inspired by *Showtime*, the Imaginary Friend Bear is inspired by *Generations*, and the SimBot Bear is inspired by *Ambitions*. Can you collect them all?

TIP

Bears are often rewards from the arcade claw machine: The Claaaaw! If you are a fairy Sim, you have a good chance of slipping inside the machine and getting a bear more often than somebody who plays the game without such enhancements.

Very Small Train Set

Purchase Cost: $100

Benefits:

◊ **Fun:** 3

Description: You won't believe the attention to detail put into the latest and greatest locomotive microcosm from Very Small Trains. Modeled after the beautiful Sunset Valley, each set comes preassembled so you are ready for hours of fun out of the box. If you tried to operate a real train people would probably get hurt, so why not buy a Very Small Train?

The Very Small Train Set is a very big deal. This cool toy adds an enormous environmental boost to a room, which can result in some good mood bumps for nearby Sims. But more than this immediate bonus, the Very Small Train Set is such a delight to play with—it satisfies Fun need. Just click on the train set and select View to start having a bit of fun.

But wait, that's not all Sims can do with train set. Well, not fairy Sims, at least. Fairy Sims can transform into true fairy form and Ride Train. In sprite form, the fairy hops aboard the train and has a great time zooming around the track. Watch as the fairy whoops it up! This is a major injection of Fun that lasts until you cancel the interaction, the fairy completes several laps, or a need like Bladder craters and the Sim must attend to basic hygiene.

Take a closer look at the Very Small Train Set. Remind you of any place? Yep, that's Sunset Valley, the original town in *The Sims 3*.

CHANGING PICTURES

Lots of the new pictures you can hang on the walls have special supernatural properties. When a full moon hangs high, the figures in the frames change into Gothic, grotesque forms. Won't you hang a few of these in your house to creep up the place as well as boost the environmental bonus of the room?

Sliding Bookcase Door

Purchase Cost: §1,095

Benefits:

◊ Secret passages

Description: It's finally here! The all-time classic! You don't dare call your home a manor until you've installed at least one Sliding Bookcase Door. Books are considered gateways to knowledge, but now they can be the gateway to so much more. What secrets will YOU you keep behind the bookcase? (Note: For best results, use the Sliding Bookcase Door in the library and not the kitchen or bathroom.)

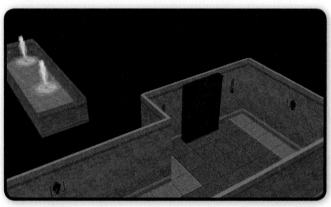

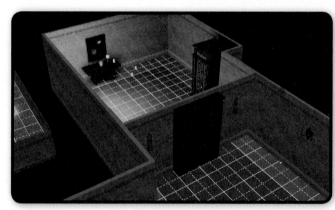

Secret passage are super-cool—and supernatural—right? Installing one of these cool bookcases on your lot adds an air of mystery to the joint. You install this bookcase very similar to a door, but in either Buy Mode or Build Mode. You can set it against a wall to create a secret passage out of a house, or use it to lead off to another series of rooms, such as what you saw downstairs, beneath the library and Vault of Antiquity.

When you attach a Sliding Bookcase Door inside a house or building, and switch off from Build/Buy Mode, the rooms tucked behind it are then "hidden" from view. For a Sim to be able to open the door, they must first use the Inspect interaction on the bookcase. This establishes for the Sim that this is not a normal bookcase. Only then can they use Open, which opens the door and reveals the rooms beyond.

Introduction

New Simology

New Careers & Skills

Meet the Supernaturals

New Venues

Tour of Moonlight Falls

New Object Catalog

Relax-o-Rocker

Purchase Cost: §350

Benefits:

♦ **Environment:** 1

> **CAUTION**
>
> Sims read a slower pace while in the rocker!

Description: It's nice that recliners can go way back, but aren't you tired of chairs that only go halfway? The Relax-o-Rocker with TruSway technology can go back AND forth! Now that's a chair with a full range of motion. Nothing soothes the soul like a gentle sway in a Relax-o-Rocker. You'll lose hours to the comfort and rhythm. It's like sitting—only better.

The new rocking chair has many of the same interactions as a normal living room chair, but with additional benefits. When a Sim chooses the Rock interaction on the chair (which is modified for Sims with Evil, Daredevil, or Diva traits) the Sim sits in the chair and starts swaying. Rocking Sims get the Rocking Out moodlet. Pregnant Sims enjoy reduced stress or removal of the Sore moodlet.

If a Sim has a baby or toddler, they can rock with the infant. If the baby or toddler's Energy is low, the kid will fall asleep in the arms of the older Sim while on the rocker. Rocking with a baby or toddler satisfies Fun and Social, and improves LTR.

Aurora Wardrobe/Ancestral Wardrobe

Purchase Cost: §995/§1,050

Benefits:

◊ Upgradable to Magic Wardrobe

Description (from Aurora Wardrobe): Classic construction and uncompromising quality are the hallmarks of the Aurora Wardrobe. This is no mere cabinet, but a perfect vessel for holding a seemingly endless variety of outfits. Whether you're dressing up for a night on the town or dressing down for a night in with a good book, the Aurora Wardrobe is here to serve you.

This wardrobe is perfectly useful for Sims who desire to change their outfits, put on their uniform (if they are enrolled in a career with a uniform), or drop into Create a Sim to design a new outfit. Sims who are feeling a little frisky can even WooHoo (or Try for Baby) inside of these wardrobes.

However, there is a super-secret interaction you can perform on these wardrobes to upgrade them to magic wardrobes! Witches with a hidden Casting skill at level 3 or above may upgrade the wardrobe so it becomes a magic portal. Now, Sims can step inside the wardrobe and go on short adventures (text-based) where they may come back with strange items or a few extra Simoleons.

Magic Brooms

Purchase Cost: §165-§455

Benefits:

◊ Transportation

Description (from Zoomsweeper Jr.): There is an art, or rather a knack, to flying, and for those who are just starting to learn we offer our dependable line of Zoomsweeper Junior training brooms. Watch young riders push their limits and build confidence with our specially engineered flight simulators. They'll swear they're soaring miles above the ground!

Magic brooms are not exclusive to witches—many other Sims (and different supernatural types) can use these objects to get around town in a flash. Brooms are used just like vehicles, such as bikes or cars, but can be kept in your personal inventory and set as a preferred mode of transport. There are multiple brooms to choose from in Buy Mode, and the more expensive the broom, the faster it moves.

NOTE

Only teens and higher can use magic brooms.

Brooms, as mentioned in the witch section of the Meet the Supernaturals chapter, are attached to a hidden Broom Riding skill. The more you ride a broom or use it at the Zoomsweeper arena, the more you develop this skill.

TIP

To store your magic broom on your lot, you must purchase a Magic Broom Stand for §25.

Giddy-Up Rocker

Purchase Cost: §75

Benefits:

◆ **Fun:** 5

Description: Your little cowboy or cowgirl will be ready to ride into adventure with the Giddy-Up Rocker! They'll feel like they're dashing across the open plains, the frontier wind blowing in their hair—and the best part is, they don't really go anywhere. The Giddy-Up Rocker: keep your kid in one place for a while.

The Giddy-Up Rocker is a wonderful plaything for little children. When children approach the toy, they can choose to either just ride it, or they can pick from a few different fantasy scenarios like Catch the Bandits or Rocking Rodeo. These result in some pretty wild play, which satisfies the child's Fun needs. The Pet interaction satisfies both Fun and Social.

> **NOTE**
>
> Ghost Sims can haunt the Giddy-Up Rocker, so it looks like the toy is riding all on its own!

Brittany's Tiny Garden Planter Bowls

Purchase Cost: §65

Benefits:

◆ Maintain plants/ harvestables indoors

Description: Bring a little of the classic outdoor hobby inside with these enchanting planter bowls from Tiny Garden. All the challenges and rewards of gardening are there in a perfectly manageable space. With Tiny Garden, you can have exactly as much garden as you can handle, and not a bulb more.

Perhaps you don't have room for a garden on your lot. Perhaps you just want the convenience of rolling out of bed and tending to your plants. These objects allow you to maintain harvestables and plants inside your house. All of the gardening interactions—Fertilize, Harvest, Revive, etc.—are available on plants in these bowls.

> **CAUTION**
>
> You cannot use these planters for large plants and trees, such as the advanced growth states of a Omniplant.

> **NOTE**
>
> You can purchase two even less expensive planters in Buy Mode: Clay Tiny Garden Planter Bowl (§30) and Gothic Tiny Garden Planter Bowl (§55).

Bug Lovers Display Case

Purchase Cost: §415

Benefits:

◆ Store insects

Description: Is there anything more satisfying than watching little creatures scurry around and live out their day-to-day lives, completely unaware of the power you could wield over their lives if you wished it? Many people find this very entertaining. That's why we invented this handy display case for all of your insect terrariums. Also features extra storage for all your little odds and ends!

The Bug Lovers Display Case is an all-new object designed to let you display multiple captured insects—beetle or butterfly—on your lot. There is room for four terrariums on the shelving and two storage spots below, which you can access via the Put Away or Open Storage interactions.

Aleister's Antique Alchemy Cabinet

Purchase Cost: §475

Benefits:

◆ Store elixirs, insects, rocks, metals, gems, and more

Description: Want to display all of your fine alchemy creations in a display cabinet as old and distinguished as the art of alchemy itself? The legendary alchemist, Aleister Krummly, drew the original design from this cabinet, and this re-creation is perfect for displaying elixirs, containers, or rare ingredients such as gems, insects, and rocks, It even has extra storage below for any other odds and ends you want to keep handy.

The primary purpose of this object is to store or display certain collectibles such as gems (cut and uncut), tiny meteorites, and metals (both ore and smelted), as well as elixirs. On the object, you will also see interactions such as Put Away for storing up to four items in the cabinet. If you use the cabinet to store 15 or more elixirs, magic dust appears around the shelf. If you store 15 or more gems or ingots, the cabinet sparkles.

New Object Catalog

Object Catalog

The objects in this catalog are listed with prices, important depreciation values, and any effect the object may have on your Sim as well as the environmental rating of a room.

> **CAUTION**
>
> Remember the rules of deprecation when purchasing these objects in Buy Mode. As soon as you click out of Buy Mode, the object you purchased begins depreciating. Each day, the object depreciates 10 percent. The bottom out value is 40 percent of the original price. The value of any object can never drop below 40 percent unless the object is broken or ruined.

image	Name	Price	Daily Depreciation	Total Depreciation	Energy	Stress Relief	Hygiene	Bladder	Hunger	Fun	Charisma	Environment	Speed	Well-Rested	Comfort	Music	Special
	Flawless Sink	460	46	184			4					2					+ Never Breaks
	Throne of Distinction	1,350	135	540				10				2					
	LuxoTub	1,450	145	580	6	5						3					
	Old Looking New Fridge	425	43	170					8			4					
	Antique Stove	550	55	220					5								+ Cooking
	Presumed Classic Microwave	235	24	94													+ Cooking
	By the Book Food Processor	325	33	130													+ Cooking
	**********	-	-														
	Ol' Steamy	1,250	125	500	4												

Introduction

New Simology

New Careers & Skills

Meet the Supernaturals

New Venues

Tour of Moonlight Falls

New Object Catalog

image	Name	Price	Daily Depreciation	Total Depreciation	Energy	Stress Relief	Hygiene	Bladder	Hunger	Fun	Charisma	Environment	Speed	Well-Rested	Comfort	Music	Special
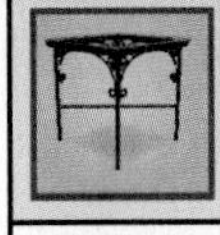	Wickerman's Dining Table	310	31	124								1					
	Twigs-n-Sticks Dining Table	735	74	294								3					
	No Secrets Dining Table	850	85	340								3					
	Twigs-n-Sticks End Table	60	6	24								1					
	Wickerman's End Table	250	25	100								1					
	Handy End Table	260	26	104								2					
	Faithful End Table	350	35	140								2					
	Endless End Table	385	39	154								2					
	Elegance End Table	465	47	186								2					
	Wickerman's Coffee Table	315	32	126								2					
	Appropriate Coffee Table	345	35	138								2					

image	Name	Price	Daily Depreciation	Total Depreciation	Energy	Stress Relief	Hygiene	Bladder	Hunger	Fun	Charisma	Environment	Speed	Well-Rested	Comfort	Music	Special
	Coffee Lovers Table	360	36	144								2					
	Modern Antique Coffee Table	375	38	150								2					
	Adorable Shelf	300	30	120								2					
	Aleister's Alchemy Cabinet	415	42	166													
	Bug Lovers Display Case	415	42	166													
	Aleister's Antique Alchemy Cabinet	475	48	190													
	The Impressor Bar	1,350	135	540						6		3					
	The Darkwood Swallow by EvrSleep	980	98	392	4	3						2		1			
	Twigs-n-Sticks Canopy Bed	1,060	106	424	4	3						2		2			
	Elegant Repose Single by KidStackerz!	1,300	130	520	4	3								1			
	Elegant Repose by KidStackerz!	1,300	130	520	4	3								1			

image	Name	Price	Daily Depreciation	Total Depreciation	Energy	Stress Relief	Hygiene	Bladder	Hunger	Fun	Charisma	Environment	Speed	Well-Rested	Comfort	Music	Special
	Majestic Rest	2,400	240	960	5	3						3		2			
	Altar Bed	2,625	263	1,050	8	3						4		2			
	Earl's Non-Haunted Antique Canopy Bed	3,000	300	1,200	5	3						4		3			
	Twigs-n-Sticks Dining Chair	45	5	18													
	Wickerman's Dining Chair	220	22	88								1			2		
	Corset Chair by Unmentionables	365	37	146								1			2		
	Twigs-n-Sticks Easy Chair	210	21	84								1			2		
	Wickerman's Living Chair	310	31	124								1			2		
	Relax-O-Rocker	350	35	140								1			1		
	Yesteryear Armchair	400	40	160								1			2		
	The Professor Rocking Chair	425	43	170								2			2		

image	Name	Price	Daily Depreciation	Total Depreciation	Energy	Stress Relief	Hygiene	Bladder	Hunger	Fun	Charisma	Environment	Speed	Well-Rested	Comfort	Music	Special
	Sunnytime Antique Rocking Chair	630	63	252								2			1		
	Chair of Madness	725	73	290								2			3		
	Decadent Hug by Unmentionables	815	82	326								2			3		
	The Stately Reader	895	90	358								2			3		
	Yesteryear Sofa	650	65	260								2			1		
	Twigs-n-Sticks Sofa	895	90	358								2			2		
	Wickerman's Loveseat	1,020	102	408								3			2		
	Highback Brackenridge	1,050	105	420								3			2		
	U-Stud Sofa Deluxe	1,165	117	466								3			2		
	The Convince Collection: Loveseat	1,275	128	510								3			2		
	The Emperor's Rest Loveseat	1,350	135	540								3			3		

image	Name	Price	Daily Depreciation	Total Depreciation	Energy	Stress Relief	Hygiene	Bladder	Hunger	Fun	Charisma	Environment	Speed	Well-Rested	Comfort	Music	Special
	Brutal Lounge	1,425	143	570								3			3		
	Solid Backup Chair	630	63	252								1			3		
	The Impressor Bar Stools		-	-								1			1		
	Diatrode Crackler	680	68	272						4						3	+ Athletic, + Group Activity
	Phonograph Life Statement	935	94	374						4						3	+ Athletic, + Group Activity
	Pointer Timepiece Replica	85	9	34													
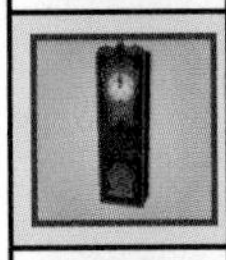	Sim-plicity Wall Clock	130	13	52								3					
	Granddaddy Clock	1,300	130	520													
	Very Small Train Set	100	10	40						3							
	Moondial	180	18	72													
	Mrs. Stingley's Beekeeping Box	275	28	110													

image	Name	Price	Daily Depreciation	Total Depreciation	Energy	Stress Relief	Hygiene	Bladder	Hunger	Fun	Charisma	Environment	Speed	Well-Rested	Comfort	Music	Special
	Magic Wand: Classic	360	36	144													+ Portable
	Antique Chess Table	520	52	208						4							+ Logic
	Magic Wand: Argent	540	54	216													+ Portable
	Magic Wand: Azure	540	54	216													+ Portable
	Magic Wand: Crimson	540	54	216													+ Portable
	Magic Wand: Ivory	720	72	288													+ Portable
	Magic Wand: Verdant	720	72	288													+ Portable
	Smack-A-Gnome!	795	80	318						5							+ Never Breaks
	The Claaaaw	795	80	318						4							+ Never Breaks
	Aleister's Alchemy Station	850	85	340						1							
	Magic Wand: Crystal	900	90	360													+ Portable

image	Name	Price	Daily Depreciation	Total Depreciation	Energy	Stress Relief	Hygiene	Bladder	Hunger	Fun	Charisma	Environment	Speed	Well-Rested	Comfort	Music	Special
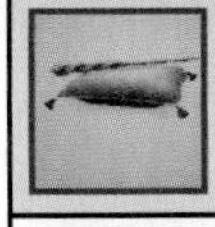	Magic Wand: Elegant	900	90	360													+ Portable
	Zoomsweeper Broom Arena	960	96	384						6							
	Gem-U-Cut Machine	975	98	390													
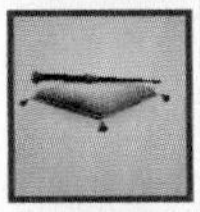	Magic Wand: Iridescent	1,080	108	432													+ Portable
	Lightning Leap Atomic Molecular Arranger	1,500	150	600		1											
	Spectrum Mood Lamp	325	33	130													
	Orb of Answers	195	20	78						5							
	Fairy Bungalow	475	48	190	3	3			1 (one plus sign)	7							+ Group Activity
	Magic Jelly Bean Bush	575	58	230						2							
	Fairy Castle	626	63	250	3	3			1 (plus)	7							+ Group Activity
	Magic Mirror	875	88	350						3	2						

New Object Catalog

image	Name	Price	Daily Depreciation	Total Depreciation	Energy	Stress Relief	Hygiene	Bladder	Hunger	Fun	Charisma	Environment	Speed	Well-Rested	Comfort	Music	Special
	Bonehilda Living Quarters	3,999	400	1,600													
	Sim-plicity Table Lamp	65	7	26													
	Prancing Colt Lamp	70	7	28													
	Fairy Wing Lamp	75	8	30													
	Fancy Antique Lamp	90	9	36								1					
	Corset Lamp by Unmentionables	125	13	50								1					
	FancyTime Table Lightener	150	15	60								1					
	Twigs-n-Sticks Floor Lamp	250	25	100								1					
	Standing Reginald Lamp	440	44	176								1					
	Tri-Lamp by Lum	465	47	186								2					
	Wall Sconce by Unmentionables	95	10	38								1					

image	Name	Price	Daily Depreciation	Total Depreciation	Energy	Stress Relief	Hygiene	Bladder	Hunger	Fun	Charisma	Environment	Speed	Well-Rested	Comfort	Music	Special
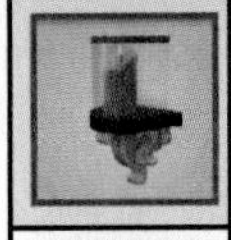	Candlequarium Wall Light	100	10	40								1					
	Dual Candle Shell Sconce	175	18	70								2					
	Tasseled Ceiling Lamp	160	16	64								1					
	Clay Tiny Garden Planter Bowl	30	3	12													
	Gothic Tiny Garden Planter Bowl	55	6	22													
	Brittany's Tiny Garden Planter Bowl	65	7	26													
	Shadow Men	200	20	80								2					
	The Head and The Shoulders	225	23	90								2					
	Portrait of Miranda Glauer	315	32	126								2					
	Photograph of Hiram Samuel Maddox	335	34	134								2					
	Midnight Maddy Portrait	350	35	140								3					

image	Name	Price	Daily Depreciation	Total Depreciation	Energy	Stress Relief	Hygiene	Bladder	Hunger	Fun	Charisma	Environment	Speed	Well-Rested	Comfort	Music	Special
	Cowboy Angel	370	37	148								3					
	Timeless Memories	475	48	190								3					
	The Visitors	760	76	304								4					
	Finding Peace	765	77	306								4					
	Everglow Academy	770	77	308								4					
	Comforts of Home	775	78	310								4					
	Commonwealth Court	775	78	310								4					
	Dark Arcadia	775	78	310								4					
	Binary Betty Portrait	780	78	312								4					
	Pleasing Art	795	80	318								5					
	Enigmatic Tapestry	7,500	750	3,000								10					
	Padded Safety Mirror	325	33	130							3	3					+ Charisma

Introduction

New Simology

New Careers
& Skills

Meet the
Supernaturals

New Venues

Tour of
Moonlight Falls

**New Object
Catalog**

image	Name	Price	Daily Depreciation	Total Depreciation	Energy	Stress Relief	Hygiene	Bladder	Hunger	Fun	Charisma	Environment	Speed	Well-Rested	Comfort	Music	Special
	Pretty Tall Mirror by Glassfinders	785	79	314							3	3					+ Charisma
	Antique Curtains	190	19	76								1					
	Lovely Lovely Drapes	230	23	92								2					
	The Baron's Cascade	290	29	116								2					
	Clive's Fancy Window Hangs	295	30	118								2					
	Frills Upon Frills	315	32	126								2					
	Bunny Rug	120	12	48								2					
	The Natural Synthetic Hide Floor Enhancer	225	23	90								2					
	Floor Helper	525	53	210								3					
	Twigs-n-Sticks Sculpture	545	55	218								3					
	Phun With Phrenology	550	55	220								3					
	Boshentoffer Bust	575	58	230								3					

image	Name	Price	Daily Depreciation	Total Depreciation	Energy	Stress Relief	Hygiene	Bladder	Hunger	Fun	Charisma	Environment	Speed	Well-Rested	Comfort	Music	Special
	Marianne Hatsfordshire Bust	575	58	230								3					
	More Furnished Cabinet	2,275	228	910								9					
	Finders Keepers Hutch	2,690	269	1,076								10					
	Pile o' Books: Small Pile	35	4	14								1					
	Bottled Oddity Nanopede	40	4	16								1					
	Pile o' Books: Medium Pile	40	4	16								1					
	FancyTime Firebox Tools	45	5	18								1					
	Pile o' Books: Large Pile	45	5	18								1					
	Bottled Oddity Bunnies	50	5	20								1					
	Expired Elixirs: Arcane Collection	50	5	20								1					
	Bottled Oddity Alien	55	6	22								1					
	Expired Elixirs: Paranormal Collection	55	6	22								1					

image	Name	Price	Daily Depreciation	Total Depreciation	Energy	Stress Relief	Hygiene	Bladder	Hunger	Fun	Charisma	Environment	Speed	Well-Rested	Comfort	Music	Special
	Expired Elixirs: Mystic's Collection	60	6	24								1					
	Ode de Wand: Trifecta	65	7	26								1					
	Ode de Wand: Classic	70	7	28								1					
	Antique Basin	75	8	30								1					
	Ode de Wand: Imperial	75	8	30								1					
	Walled Wand Collection	75	8	30								1					
	The Classic by Pedestal Warehouse	95	10	38													
	Collector's Plates	150	15	60								2					
	Dark Luxe Pedestal	175	18	70								2					
	The Aristocrat from Pedestal Warehouse	200	20	80								2					
	The Marquee	200	20	80								2					
	Mostly There Mannequin	225	23	90								2					

New Object Catalog

image	Name	Price	Daily Depreciation	Total Depreciation	Energy	Stress Relief	Hygiene	Bladder	Hunger	Fun	Charisma	Environment	Speed	Well-Rested	Comfort	Music	Special
	Ye Olde Sign	235	24	94								2					
	Urn of Mystery	435	44	174								3					
	Nectar Tantalus	625	63	250								3					
	Library Signpost	750	75	300													
	Gymnasium Signpost	775	78	310													
	Pool Sign	800	80	320													
	Permalibro Bookcase	1,020	102	408							3	4					+ Cooking, + Handiness, + Logic
	Children's Chest of Drawers	300	30	120								2					
	Sheppult Dresser by Aleckzandor Fleppe	695	70	278								3					
	U-Stud Armoire	860	86	344								5					
	Twigs-n-Sticks Vanity	865	87	346							4	5					+ Charisma
	Antique Vanity	925	93	370							4	5					+ Charisma

image	Name	Price	Daily Depreciation	Total Depreciation	Energy	Stress Relief	Hygiene	Bladder	Hunger	Fun	Charisma	Environment	Speed	Well-Rested	Comfort	Music	Special
	The Empress Vanity by Vanité	975	98	390						4		5					+ Charisma
	Aurora Wardrobe	995	100	398								6					
	Ancestral Wardrobe	1,050	105	420								6					
	Scary Bearys: Fairy	50	5	20						7							+ Portable
	Scary Bearys: Genie	50	5	20						7							+ Portable
	Scary Bearys: Imaginary Friend	50	5	20						7							+ Portable
	Scary Bearys: Mummy	50	5	20						7							+ Portable
	Scary Bearys: Robo-Bearbot	50	5	20						7							+ Portable
	Scary Bearys: Vampire	50	5	20						7							+ Portable
	Scary Bearys: Werewolf	50	5	20						7							+ Portable
	Scary Bearys: Witch	50	5	20						7							+ Portable
	Giddy-Up Rocker	75	8	30						5							

New Object Catalog

image	Name	Price	Daily Depreciation	Total Depreciation	Energy	Stress Relief	Hygiene	Bladder	Hunger	Fun	Charisma	Environment	Speed	Well-Rested	Comfort	Music	Special
	Cornucopia Toybox	160	16	64						5							
	Victorian Vikki Dollhouse	705	71	282						7							
	Sylvan Motor Carriage	79,000	7,900	31,600									6				
	Magic Broom Stand	35	4	14													
	Zoomsweeper Junior		-	-									1				Child Only
	Zoomsweeper Classic	265	27	106									2				
	Zoomsweeper Neo-Classic	385	39	154									4				
	Zoomsweeper Pegasus	455	46	182									7				
	Centennial Fence	20	2	8													
	Glass Houses Door	300	30	120													
	MaxiGlass French Doors	585	59	234													
	Scrollington's Deluxe Entryway	585	59	234													

Introduction

New Simology

New Careers
& Skills

Meet the
Supernaturals

New Venues

Tour of
Moonlight Falls

New Object
Catalog

image	Name	Price	Daily Depreciation	Total Depreciation	Energy	Stress Relief	Hygiene	Bladder	Hunger	Fun	Charisma	Environment	Speed	Well-Rested	Comfort	Music	Special
	Glass Houses Sliding Door	590	59	236													
	Sliding Bookcase Door	1,095	110	438													
	Priorities Window	155	16	62													
	Painless Windows	185	19	74													
	Priorities Double-Wide Window	195	20	78													
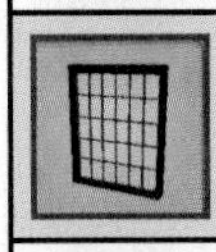	Priorities Mega-Window	205	21	82													
	Priorities Mega-Window Topper	205	21	82													
	Total Transparencies Double Window	205	21	82													
	Victorian Bay Window	295	30	118													
	Autumn Bay Window	350	35	140									3					
	ColuMaster Spiral Column	400	40	160								3					
	FancyTime Olde Time Firebox	2,970	297	1,188						6		6					

image	Name	Price	Daily Depreciation	Total Depreciation	Energy	Stress Relief	Hygiene	Bladder	Hunger	Fun	Charisma	Environment	Speed	Well-Rested	Comfort	Music	Special
	Sweet Heat Home Warmer from Romanco with Cement Chimney	3,800	380	1,520						6		6					
	Pyro-Pit with Beige Brick Chimney	3,950	395	1,580						6		3					
	FancyTime Firebox	4,750	475	1,900						6		7					
	FancyTime Firebox (Extra Fancy Edition)	6,000	600	2,400						6		6					
	Cottonwood Tree	195	20	78								2					
	Faux Ardahkt Tree	210	21	84								2					
	Spruce Tree	210	21	84								2					
	Scotch Pine Tree	235	24	94								3					
	Glauer Tree	475	48	190								4					
	Huckleberry Bush	45	5	18								1					

DOWNLOAD

PRIMA OFFICIAL STRATEGY APP FROM ITUNES® TODAY!

The Sims™ 3 Prima Official Strategy app is free to download and includes hundreds of tips for *The Sims™ 3* and *The Sims™ 3* expansion packs FOR FREE! Additional strategy tools and content are available for purchase.

FREE WITH YOUR DOWNLOAD:

• Want to discover every alchemy recipe in *The Sims™ 3 Supernatural* or learn essential tricks to advance your career? Get hundreds of FREE tips for *The Sims™ 3* and most of your favorite expansion packs just for downloading the app!

ADDITIONAL IN-APP TOOLS:
($0.99 per expansion or $4.99 for all 6)

• Tour your favorite neighborhoods unlike ever before! Using interactive neighborhood maps, you can view screenshots and read revealing details for every empty lot, residence, business, park, collectable, and fishing location!

• Browse a complete catalogue of traits, wishes, needs, moods and opportunities, cheats, as well as how to make the most out of skill development, wish fulfillment and social interaction for each expansion pack using the Advanced Strategy feature!

• Can't get that next promotion or having difficulties managing your sims mood? Make sure you're using the right objects by discovering their hidden benefits using the Object Catalog!

REDEFINE THE WAY YOU PLAY THE SIMS!
IMPORTANT: THIS IS NOT A GAME. (COVERS THE SIMS 3 PC\MAC PRODUCTS ONLY)

PRiMA OFFiCiAL GAME GuiDE

Written by Catherine Browne

Prima Games
An Imprint of Random House, Inc.
3000 Lava Ridge Court, Suite 100
Roseville, CA 95661
www.primagames.com

Catherine Browne

Catherine grew up in a small town, loving the proverbial "great outdoors." While she still enjoys hiking, camping, and just getting out under the big sky, Catherine also appreciates diving into the bustling The Sims™ 3 world. Her mastery of all things The Sims 3 helped her obtain her "Lifetime Wish", writing The Sims 3 guides for you to enjoy. Some of her notable achievements include writing The Sims 3, The Sims 3 World Adventures, The Sims 3 Ambitions, and The Sims 3 Late Night guides.

We want to hear from you! E-mail comments and feedback to

cbrowne@primagames.com

The Prima Games logo is a registered trademark of Random House, Inc., registered in the United States and other countries. Primagames.com is a registered trademark of Random House, Inc., registered in the United States. Prima Games is an imprint of Random House, Inc.

Project Manager: Todd Manning
Design & Layout: Elise Winter
Copyeditor: Asha Johnson

Special Thanks: Josef Frech

Important:
Prima Games has made every effort to determine that the information contained in this book is accurate. However, the publisher makes no warranty, either expressed or implied, as to the accuracy, effectiveness, or completeness of the material in this book; nor does the publisher assume liability for damages, either incidental or consequential, that may result from using the information in this book. The publisher cannot provide any additional information or support regarding gameplay, hints and strategies, or problems with hardware or software. Such questions should be directed to the support numbers provided by the game and/or device manufacturers as set forth in their documentation. Some game tricks require precise timing and may require repeated attempts before the desired result is achieved.

Printed in the United States of America
Standard Edition ISBN: 978-0-307-89530-1
Mini Edition ISBN: 978-0-307-89568-4